ESSENTIAL WORDS FOR THE TOEFL®

Test of English as a Foreign Language

7TH EDITION

Steven J. Matt

Acknowledgment

With love and appreciation, I would like to recognize Stephanie Matthiesen for the special contributions she has made to this 7th edition of *Essential Words for the TOEFL.*

All inquiries should be addressed to:
Barron's Educational Series, Inc.
250 Wireless Boulevard
Hauppauge, New York 11788
www.barronseduc.com

Library of Congress Catalog Card No. 2016959109

ISBN: 978-1-4380-0887-5

PRINTED IN CANADA
9 8 7 6 5 4 3 2

CONTENTS

INTRODUCTION

SUCCESS ON THE TOEFL

What vocabulary is necessary to score high on the TOEFL?
Why is it especially important to have a strong
vocabulary for the current TOEFL?
Why must I improve my vocabulary and how can I succeed?
How can I be a better TOEFL test taker?

Essential Words for the TOEFL answers these questions and provides you with a proven plan for improving your English vocabulary while also preparing you for the TOEFL. The words and practice questions that appear throughout this book will help you to maximize your understanding of words that will likely appear in every section of the TOEFL. Important information about how to maximize your score on the TOEFL is given in addition to vocabulary building hints and exercises. By following the program and mastering the words in this book, you will be ready to earn a higher score on the TOEFL.

This 7th edition of *Essential Words for the TOEFL* has an extensive, revised list of 500 words with improved exercises and updated reading selections. This edition makes *Essential Words* one of the most thoroughly researched books of its kind. It is the product of extensive study of previous TOEFLs and academic materials from which the questions on the TOEFL are produced. The result of this research is this powerful book of words that will lead you to success on the TOEFL.

MAXIMIZING YOUR VOCABULARY POTENTIAL—A DESCRIPTION OF THIS PROGRAM

This book is divided into six chapters. This introduction gives you basic information about their contents and how to use the book. Let's look at the six chapters.

Getting to Know the iBT

Chapter 1 describes the complete iBT test format and contains sample questions from each part. The questions are explained in detail and test-taking strategies are introduced.

Understanding the Internet-Based TOEFL

Chapter 2 describes the importance of building a strong vocabulary in order to score well on the iBT. You will find sample reading passages typical of those found in Section One of the iBT with a detailed analysis of the kinds of words and questions that are found on the TOEFL. In this chapter you will learn important strategies and hints to follow that will increase the probability of maximizing your score on the TOEFL.

Improving Your TOEFL Vocabulary

Chapter 3 gives you a plan for studying vocabulary. You should use the plan when studying the words in this book.

Building Your TOEFL Vocabulary

Chapter 4 provides powerful information that helps you build your TOEFL vocabulary. You will be introduced to "roots, prefixes, and suffixes"; parts of words that provide or add meaning. You will also be introduced to dictionary and thesaurus use, both print and online resources that contribute to any strategy to build your TOEFL vocabulary.

The Essential TOEFL Vocabulary

Barron's TOEFL Vocabulary Building Program is explained in Chapter 5. The carefully selected words that appear on the list are important for all TOEFL test takers. An explanation of the program is given, including how to study the list, how to understand the words, and how to follow the program from beginning to end. Thirty carefully developed vocabulary lessons follow the explanation. Each lesson ends with practice questions like those that appear on both the iBT and the ITP, the paper-based TOEFL.

The iBT Practice Reading Test

Chapter 6 contains a complete practice iBT reading test, typical of those found in Section 3 of the TOEFL. The test gives you practice with reading comprehension and vocabulary questions that closely follow the iBT format. At the conclusion of the practice test, you will be able to assess your iBT knowledge and skills by using the included answer key and conversion tables to convert your number of correct answers to a score on the TOEFL scale. Both the iBT and ITP scales are included. Chapter 6 is followed by an index of the 500 essential words presented in this book, followed by the page number where the word can be found in the text.

A Final Word

This 7th edition of *Essential Words for the TOEFL* is a product of more than 25 years of research and continuous updating. Among the thousands of words that professional TOEFL test makers can use, this edition of *Essential Words for the TOEFL* includes those that are most likely to appear on the Internet-based TOEFL (iBT) and on the Institutional TOEFL (ITP). By mastering the words and applying the strategies presented in this book, you will be well on your way to success on the TOEFL.

Steven Matthiesen

CHAPTER 1

GETTING TO KNOW THE TOEFL

WHAT IS THE TOEFL?

The TOEFL is a comprehensive English language examination that helps colleges and universities in the United States, Canada, and other parts of the world make admission decisions. It is also used by some organizations to certify professionals to practice their vocations both in the United States and abroad.

ABOUT THE iBT (INTERNET-BASED TOEFL)

Many years ago, the TOEFL was administered only in a paper-based format. Examinees marked their answers with a pencil on an answer sheet. The test primarily assessed listening comprehension, grammar, vocabulary, and reading skills. Then, beginning in the late 90s, the Educational Testing Service (the maker of the TOEFL) began offering a computer-based TOEFL known as the iBT. Taking advantage of advances in technology, the iBT has expanded the range of skills tested by adding speaking and writing sections to the test as well as integrating reading, grammar, and vocabulary skills to mimic how we use language every day.

ABOUT THE ITP (INSTITUTIONAL TOEFL PROGRAM)

Some educational institutions use a paper-based TOEFL, known as the ITP TOEFL. The Educational Testing Service makes this form of the TOEFL available to institutions who often use the test to generally assess individuals' English language skills for placement purposes. Institutions also use results to assess the effectiveness of their English language instructional programs. These TOEFLs are typically previously administered paper-based TOEFLs. Generally, colleges and universities do not accept ITP TOEFL scores in place of an iBT score. The two versions of the TOEFL are quite different. A description of both formats follows.

THE iBT

The iBT is a timed test that consists of the four sections listed below.

Section 1	**Reading** 3–4 Passages	**60–80 minutes** 12–14 questions per passage
Section 2	**Listening** 2–3 Conversations 4–6 Lectures	**60–90 minutes** 5 questions per conversation 6 questions per lecture
Section 3	**Speaking** 2 Independent Tasks 4 Integrated Tasks	**20 minutes**
Section 4	**Writing** 1 Integrated Task 1 Independent Task	**50 minutes**

SECTION 1: READING

The iBT reading section is presented in two formats. The short format iBT gives you three passages of approximately 700 words. The long format contains four passages. After each passage, you will answer 12–14 test questions. If you are taking the long format iBT, only three sets of the test questions will be answered. The responses to the questions for the other two passages will be evaluated by ETS for use on future iBTs. You will have 60 minutes to read all of the passages and respond to the questions (80 minutes for the long format). You will be allowed to take notes while you read. You will see some words or phrases highlighted. You may see an explanation or definition of the word or phrase by clicking on it.

The majority of questions in this section are in the multiple-choice format. Make your answer choice for each and proceed to the next question by clicking on **Next**. To return to the previous question, click on **Back**. At any time, you can click on **Review** to see a list of the questions that you have and have not answered. You may return to any question while you are working on this section, but once you have left the reading section, you may not return to it. A clock will appear on the screen to help you manage your time.

In this section, you first read the passage completely. You do so by using the scroll bar to view the entire passage on the screen. The computer will not give you the questions until you have scrolled the entire reading selection. At that point, click on **Next**.

There are different response formats in the reading section. These involve clicking on a word, phrase, or sentence. Vocabulary items are usually tested by asking you to click on another word in the text that means the same thing as a bolded word. Sometimes you will be asked to click on a sentence or group of sentences where the answer to a particular question can be found. Sometimes, you may be asked to insert a sentence into the text. On cohesion items, you will be asked to click on the word or phrase in the bolded part of the passage that the cohesion word refers to. After you click on the word or phrase, it will darken.

Finally, another type of test question ("reading to learn") will require you to complete a summary or fill in a chart by selecting which provided text options to include. The summary questions are worth up to two points each, and the chart questions are worth three to four points, depending on whether five or seven options are presented.

SECTION 2: LISTENING

The listening section of the iBT tests your ability to understand spoken English that is typically found on the campuses of colleges and universities. The listening tasks are those that are typical of social and academic conversations found in these settings.

There are two formats for the listening section. In the short listening section, you will hear two conversations and four lectures. The long format contains three conversations and six lectures. Each conversation and lecture requires you to respond to five or six questions, most of which are multiple choice. The responses to the questions of the extra conversation and lectures do not count. These questions will be evaluated by ETS for use on future iBTs. Since you do not know which passages will count, it is important for you to do your best on all of the test questions. You have 25 minutes on the short format listening section and 30 on the long format section. A clock appears on the screen to help you manage your time. It does not include the time while you are listening to the lectures and conversations.

You will hear each lecture and conversation and each of the questions only one time. You are allowed to take notes as you listen and use them to answer questions. Once a question is answered, you are not allowed to return to it, so be sure to choose your answers carefully.

On the iBT, stimuli will come to you through headphones, not aloud as is the case with the ITP TOEFL. On the iBT, you will both see and hear each question; on the ITP TOEFL, you only hear the question. Following the question, the answer choices appear on the screen; the question stays on the screen until you have made your response. For multiple-choice items, each option is preceded by an oval [○], instead of the letters (A), (B), (C), or (D).

On the iBT, you will be told both the context and the topic of the conversation. The extended conversations typically involve a main presenter who gives the information, and one or two other persons who ask questions of the main presenter. All speakers are pictured on the screen. Each stimulus is normally followed by three or four questions on what was said.

The iBT lectures also include an introduction that tells you who is speaking and the topic. Going back to the minitalk on Chicago, the introduction might be as follows:

"Listen to a tour guide as he tells a group of visitors about the city of Chicago."

In the iBT lectures, the presentations usually simulate a lecture by a professor who is using visuals. The professor and the visuals are depicted on the screen. Using your mouse, you answer each question, after it is asked.

The iBT uses a greater variety of response types. For example, there may be more than one correct answer, and you will be asked to click on the oval next to all correct answers. Whenever there is more than one correct answer, you will be told how many correct answers you should identify. To see an example, read the minitalk about Chicago on page 8. Then answer the following question:

What can be inferred about the weather in Chicago?
(Click on 2 answers)

○ It is influenced by a glacier.
○ Summers are unpleasantly warm.
○ The wind is usually accompanied by cold.
○ It is very dry during the winter months.
○ It is temperate and stable.

In the above example, you would click on the ovals to the left of the second and third statements.

Sometimes, a response format is visual. In that case, you click on the correct visual with your mouse. Sometimes, a response will involve matching. In that case, you must classify each new piece of information you are given into three or four categories, according to classifications or distinctions you learned when reading the stimulus. You do this with your mouse.

SECTION 3: SPEAKING

The speaking section tests your ability to use spoken English in academic settings. This section contains six speaking tasks. Each task requires you to respond to a single question, a talk, conversation, or lecture. The tasks will require you to listen to a lecture or conversation or to read a short passage. You will then respond to a question. You may take notes and use them to help you respond to the questions.

Your speaking proficiency is evaluated on the general fluency and accuracy with which you use the English language.

The speaking section lasts 20 minutes. You are given 45 to 60 seconds to respond to each question. Before responding to questions, you will be given 15 to 20 seconds to think about how you will respond to the question. A clock appears on the screen to help you manage your time.

SECTION 4: WRITING

The writing section tests your ability to perform the writing tasks that are typically required in college courses.

In the iBT, you will respond to two writing prompts. There are two types of writing tasks, an integrated essay task and an independent writing task.

The integrated essay task combines the language skills of reading, listening, and writing.

You will read a short passage, hear a short lecture on the topic, and then write an essay in response to a specific set of directions for the essay. You may take notes and use them to help you write your essay. You will have 20 minutes to plan and write your essay.

The independent writing task asks you to give your opinion on a familiar topic. You will have 30 minutes to plan and write your essay.

A clock appears on the screen to help you manage your time as you complete your essays.

THE ITP (THE PAPER-BASED TOEFL)

The paper-based ITP TOEFL is a timed test that consists of three sections. It is administered in two forms: Level 1 (Intermediate to Advanced) and Level 2 (High Beginning to Intermediate). Throughout the years, the Educational Testing Service has determined which questions from previously administered TOEFLs are appropriate for each of the two TOEFL levels. The Level 1 TOEFL is longer than the Level 2 test, but each form of the test has the same types of questions. Section One tests Listening Comprehension, Section Two, Structure and Written Expression, and Section Three, Reading Comprehension. Here is the format of each section:

ITP TOEFL—LEVEL 1 (Intermediate to Advanced)

Section 1	**Listening Comprehension**	**50 questions** **35 minutes**
Part A	Short Conversations	30 questions
Part B	Extended Conversations	7–8 questions
Part C	Minitalks	12–13 questions
Section 2	**Structure and Written Expression**	**40 questions** **25 minutes**
Part A	Structure	15 questions
Part B	Written Expression	25 questions
Section 3	**Reading Comprehension**	**50 questions** **55 minutes**
	TOTAL	**115 minutes**

ITP TOEFL—LEVEL 2 (High Beginning to Intermediate)

Section 1	**Listening Comprehension**	**30 questions** **22 minutes**
Section 2	**Structure and Written Expression**	**25 questions** **17 minutes**
Section 3	**Reading Comprehension**	**40 questions** **31 minutes**
	TOTAL	**70 minutes**

SECTION 1: LISTENING

This section of the TOEFL tests your ability to understand spoken American English. After you hear taped conversations you will answer questions.

Short Conversations

Part A contains short dialogues between two people followed by a question about what the people said in their conversation. They may have different purposes for speaking to each other. A speaker may give advice, apologize, or ask for information. Generally, key information is found in the second speaker's sentence. You will need to understand the meaning of the conversation and also the context, such as the time or place in which it could occur. The correct choice is the one that directly answers the question.

YOU WILL HEAR:

(Man)	Did you get to go shopping last night?
(Woman)	They'd already locked the doors by the time I got there.
(Man)	What does the woman mean?

YOU WILL SEE:

Ⓐ She arrived in time to shop.
Ⓑ She was too late.
Ⓒ She locked the doors.
Ⓓ She had to buy the door.

The correct choice is **(B)**. Since the doors were locked when she arrived, she could not have gone shopping. Note that the other choices use words heard in the conversation. Choices that contain such words are usually not correct. Part A contains samples of informal American English. Idiomatic expressions and two-word verbs are common in this part.

Extended Conversations

In Part B you will hear extended conversations between two or more people, a student and either a professor or a campus service provider. Usually, there are two conversations, and the language is more formal. After each conversation, there are between three and four spoken questions about its content. Choose your answer from among the four choices that appear in your test booklet.

The extended conversations and minitalks (see below) are generally preceded by an introductory statement that tells you the context for the conversation. Pay particular attention to this information as it prepares you for what follows.

Minitalks

Part C contains short presentations given by a single speaker. There are usually three. The English in this section is generally more academic, typical of English lectures that take place in a university or college setting. There are generally three lectures followed by four to five spoken questions about its content. You may take notes while you listen and refer back to them when you answer the questions. Choose your answer from among the four choices that appear in your test booklet. Look at the example of the minitalk below.

YOU WILL HEAR:

Listen to this talk by a tourist guide.

(Man) Good morning ladies and gentlemen. Welcome to this tour of one of the nation's most important cities, Chicago. Before we begin, I'd like to give you some background information that will make the tour more enjoyable for you. The city was founded in 1837. Its strategic location on Lake Michigan quickly made it the center of commerce for the Midwest section of the country. It currently is the third largest metropolitan area in the United States. The city's site is generally level, built mostly on a glacial plain. The narrow Chicago River extends one mile inland from Lake Michigan, where it splits, dividing the city into North, West, and South sides. Chicago's weather is subject to rapid changes, but generally the climate is cold and windy in the winter, and hot and humid in the summer.

(Woman) What gave Chicago an advantage over other Midwestern cities?

YOU WILL SEE:

Ⓐ Its level site
Ⓑ Its location on Lake Michigan
Ⓒ Its large population
Ⓓ Its location along the Chicago River

According to the minitalk, **(B)** would be the correct choice. Remember that you will not have a written copy of the speaker's presentation or conversation and you will only hear it once. You must concentrate on details, such as names, dates, and the main idea of the selection that you hear. Do not read the choices as you listen to the talk. Listen carefully and try to remember what you hear.

SECTION 2: STRUCTURE AND WRITTEN EXPRESSION

This section contains two types of questions, both designed to test your ability to recognize correct style and grammar in written English. The sentences are academic; ones that you typically find in college-level texts, journals, and encyclopedias. The sentence topics include the social sciences, physical and life sciences, and the humanities.

Structure

The structure questions test your ability to recognize correct structure and word order. These questions consist of a sentence with one or more words missing. You must make the choice that best completes the sentence. Here is an example of this type of question.

YOU WILL SEE:

_______ a short time after the Civil War, Atlanta has become the principal center of transportation, commerce, and finance in the southeastern United States.

Ⓐ While rebuilt
Ⓑ It was rebuilt
Ⓒ Rebuilt
Ⓓ When rebuilt

The correct choice is **(C)**. The other choices make the sentence incorrect or awkward.

Written Expression

The written expression questions test your ability to recognize errors in grammar or expression. These questions consist of complete sentences with four underlined words or phrases. You must identify the underlined part of the sentence that needs to be changed in order to make the sentence correct. An example follows.

YOU WILL SEE:

The Navajo Indians have displayed (A) a marked (B) ability to incorporate aspects of other cultures into (C) a changing, flexibility (D) lifestyle.

The correct choice is **(D)**. *Flexibility*, a noun, appears where an adjective must occur. In addition to inappropriate parts of speech, be sure to check for missing words or extra words that are inappropriate for the context.

SECTION 3: READING COMPREHENSION

Good reading skills and an ample vocabulary are keys to doing well on all sections of the TOEFL. In this section of the TOEFL, these skills are specifically tested. Many TOEFL test takers complain that they do not have enough time to carefully answer all questions in this section. It is very important that you follow the instructions in this book, so that you will use all the allotted time to your advantage.

Reading Comprehension Items

Your ability to read and understand college-level reading material is tested on this part of the TOEFL. You will find five or six reading passages, each followed by nine to eleven questions. You must work quickly and efficiently. Here is a sample passage.

YOU WILL SEE:

A lens has one or more curved surfaces that refract, or bend, light rays passing through it to form an image on a surface beyond the lens. Examples of such surfaces are the retina of the eye or a movie screen. The distance from
(5) the lens to the focal plane is known as focal length. In cameras, telescopes, and similar devices, the lens is turned on a screw-thread mounting to adjust the focal length. This action allows focusing of images of objects at various distances. In the human eye, focal length is
(10) adjusted by muscles that alter the lens curvature. Light rays of different colors are bent by varying degrees as they pass through a curved surface. This causes a distortion of the image, known as chromatic aberration. In cameras, sharp images are obtained by arranging two

(15) or more lenses so that the aberration of one cancels out the aberration of another. Such an arrangement of lenses is called an achromatic lens.

YOU WILL SEE:

According to the passage, what is focal length?

Ⓐ A curved surface that refracts light
Ⓑ The distance from the focal plane to the lens
Ⓒ Adjustment by the muscles that alters lens curvature
Ⓓ The degree that light rays of different colors are bent by the lens

This is a factual question. The information needed to answer this question is directly stated in the text. Choice **(B)** is the correct answer. Some questions will ask you to draw conclusions based on material in the passage; others will ask about the main idea of a selection. Some may even ask what information does not appear in the passage.

Vocabulary Items

The vocabulary questions in this section test your English vocabulary. There are between 12 and 17 questions focusing on specific words from the reading passage. Each word is taken from a specific line in the text; the line is referred to in the question. You must choose the word that has the same meaning from among the four choices given. Here's an example from the previous text.

YOU WILL SEE:

The word "distortion" in lines 12 and 13 is closest in meaning to

Ⓐ classification
Ⓑ deformation
Ⓒ reaction
Ⓓ reflection

The word that is the closest in meaning to the tested word, **distortion**, is choice **(B)**. Additional hints for vocabulary questions can be found in Chapter 2.

Cohesion Items

Another type of question that is used to test reading comprehension is called cohesion. Cohesion occurs when elements of a passage are linked to other elements. Cohesion allows the author to refer to previously mentioned information, and it allows the reader to keep previously mentioned information in mind while continuing to read the passage. To understand cohesion when it is used, one must understand the passage. Thus, TOEFL uses cohesion to test reading comprehension. Cohesion items typically test object pronouns (it, they, them) and demonstrative pronouns (this, these, those). Here is an example of a question that involves cohesion.

YOU WILL SEE:

The word "This" in line 12 refers to

Ⓐ surface
Ⓑ adjusting
Ⓒ light
Ⓓ bending

The word that "this" refers to is **bending**, option **(D)**. A typical version of the TOEFL will contain about five such items, or an average of one per passage.

During your experience taking the TOEFL, you will see process verbs. These words give you important clues as to the type of response that the question or task requires, so it is necessary for you to have a good understanding of them. Among the process verbs commonly seen on the TOEFL are:

Process Verb	**Definition**
claim	to express an unproven opinion
clarify	to explain in more detail
contradict	to express an opposite belief
define	to identify the meaning of a concept
demonstrate	to show or explain a process or idea
describe	to list the characteristics of an idea or object
discuss	to give information or ideas
infer	to form a new idea or opinion from stated facts
prove	to show by factual explanation
rebut	to prove that something is false by factual explanation
refute	to defend by explaining why something is not true
show	to give information supporting an idea
state	to express or give information
stress	to give special attention to an idea
support	to provide information that confirms an idea or opinion

SOME HELPFUL HINTS FOR BOTH FORMATS OF THE TOEFL

You can get most of the answers to your questions about the TOEFL at *www.ets.org/toefl*.

Information on testing centers, practice questions, and general descriptions of the TOEFL can be found at the official TOEFL website.

On all parts of the TOEFL, be sure to answer all questions. On the iBT, you are penalized for not answering questions. On multiple-choice test items, if you must guess, choose (B) or (C), since they are slightly more likely than (A) or (D) to be the correct response.

On the iBT, some questions will have more than one answer, particularly if the question deals with factual information presented as a series in the passage or text. A box under a question may tell you to "Click on two answers." You may also have to manipulate data with the mouse. For example, you may be given a series of events to place in a specific order. You will click on the sentences and drag them to the appropriate slots that appear on the test item screen.

Because the iBT requires a greater variety of response formats, always read the directions for each test item carefully. Ask yourself, "What do I need to do here?"

Manage your time wisely! Both the ITP TOEFL and iBT are timed. The amount of time available is stated at the beginning of each section. If you are taking the ITP TOEFL, be sure to wear a watch (deactivate any sounds your watch may make before entering the test session) and be aware of the time you have remaining. No watches are allowed in the room for the iBT. Whether you are taking the iBT or the ITP TOEFL, you should become familiar with the directions and the examples for each section before you take the tests.

Remember, when time has expired on a section, you may not return to it. Work quickly and accurately. If it seems obvious to you that you will not have enough time to finish a section of the TOEFL, GUESS (B) or (C).

In the reading section of the iBT, you may skip questions, or go back and change answers. However, do not waste time doing this unless you are fairly certain that you have made a mistake! You cannot return to questions in a previous part once you have clicked on **Continue** after the last question in that part. Change your answer only if you find a better answer.

Prepare yourself for the test. Being well prepared will give you the confidence you need to achieve the very best result for you. In addition to this book, *Barron's TOEFL iBT (Internet Based Test)* provides you with practical hints designed to help you maximize your TOEFL score, a CD-ROM that simulates the experience of taking the iBT, and academic skills hints, including tips on note taking, paraphrasing, summarizing, and synthesizing.

CHAPTER 2

UNDERSTANDING THE TOEFL READING SECTION

Developing a good English vocabulary is the most important way to prepare for the vocabulary you will see and hear on the TOEFL. It is also a good way to prepare for the test generally. In addition to developing a good English vocabulary, it is very important to know the kind of vocabulary you will see on the TOEFL and to understand how it is tested.

The reading section of the iBT contains approximately three to five passages with 12–14 questions for each passage. In the ITP, there are four to five reading passages and up to 50 questions. It is important for you to remember that your general vocabulary is tested in all sections of the TOEFL. However, it is in this section of the TOEFL where your knowledge of specific vocabulary items is tested.

Passages from which vocabulary questions are drawn are written in a formal, academic style, typical of most college- or university-level texts and journals. The topics of these passages are those a first-year college student in North America would be likely to encounter. The topics come from such areas as the Natural Sciences, Business, Liberal Arts, and the Social Sciences. Some passages contain references to North American places and personalities. Others will refer to historical events and may include dates. It is important for you to understand that your knowledge of these North American places and personalities is never tested on the TOEFL. You do not have to be familiar with the content of the passages to be successful on this section of the TOEFL.

SAMPLE QUESTIONS

The following passage and the questions that follow are used to illustrate and discuss the types of reading comprehension questions and tasks that you will find on the TOEFL. First, as a warm-up, you will read a sample passage for the ITP and work through the test questions. Then you will read a sample iBT passage and work through those questions.

Through a somewhat controversial process, Hawaii was the last territory to become a state. In 1842, the United States recognized the Kingdom of Hawaii as an independent country. In subsequent years, Americans and other foreign groups moved to the islands. They began to influence local politics. In 1887, Hawaiian King Kalakaua gave the United States exclusive rights to use Pearl Harbor as a naval base in exchange for certain trading privileges. [A ■] After the King died, his sister, Queen Liliuokalani, followed him to the throne. In 1894, a bloodless revolution led by American businessmen removed her from office. She was replaced by Stanford B. Dole. With the support of the Americans running the local government, Hawaii became a U.S. territory in 1900. [B ■] In 1959, the U.S. Congress approved legislation permitting Hawaii to convert to statehood. [C ■] Shortly afterward, Hawaiians voted almost 17 to 1 in favor of statehood. [D ■]

1. What does the passage mainly discuss?

Ⓐ Democracy in Hawaii
Ⓑ The history of Hawaiian monarchs
Ⓒ The evolution of Hawaii's political status
Ⓓ American military control in Hawaii

On the ITP TOEFL, you would darken the oval containing the letter **(C)** on your answer sheet.

2. The word "controversial" is closest in meaning to

Ⓐ adversarial
Ⓑ remarkable
Ⓒ gratifying
Ⓓ debatable

This type of vocabulary item is typically used on the ITP TOEFL. The correct response is **(D)**.

3. The word "They" in the passage refers to

Ⓐ the United States
Ⓑ Americans and other foreign groups
Ⓒ in subsequent years
Ⓓ the islands

This is an antecedent question. The item tests whether you understand what **they** refers to. The correct answer is **(B)**.

4. Look at the phrase "in exchange for" in the passage. In saying that the United States got exclusive access to Pearl Harbor "in exchange for certain trading privileges," the author means the United States:
   - Ⓐ traded access to its markets for a naval base in Hawaii.
   - Ⓑ offered to rent the land it needed for a base in Hawaii.
   - Ⓒ absorbed Hawaii by granting it membership in the union.
   - Ⓓ was excluded by the Hawaiian king from Hawaiian markets.

This is a whole phrase item. It tests whether you can separately understand the words in a group and then assemble them to arrive at an understanding of their meaning as a group. One clue to the meaning of this phrase is the word **exchange**. Since you are already familiar with exchanging money or exchanging addresses, you can probably guess that this has something to do with a two-way transfer—in this case, the right to use some land in Hawaii for access to U.S. markets. Once you have pieced together the larger context, it is easier to see that the correct response is **(A)**, **traded access to its markets for a naval base in Hawaii**.

5. According to the passage, which of the following is true about King Kalakaua?
   - Ⓐ He was replaced by Stanford B. Dole.
   - Ⓑ He made a trade agreement with the United States.
   - Ⓒ He welcomed foreign groups into the island.
   - Ⓓ He supported bloodless revolution.

This is an example of a fact question. The response to the question is directly stated in the passage. You would darken circle **(B)**, since he was the leader of Hawaii who gave the United States exclusive military rights in exchange for a trade agreement.

6. Why does the author mention Americans and foreign groups in the passage?
   Ⓐ They exerted a powerful influence in local politics.
   Ⓑ They promoted trade between Hawaii and other countries.
   Ⓒ They approved legislation giving Hawaii its statehood.
   Ⓓ They supported Queen Liliuokalani's plan to remain an independent nation.

This item requires you to identify the author's purpose for mentioning a specific fact in the passage. You would darken circle **(A)**, since the foreign groups that arrived in Hawaii did, indeed, exert great political power in local Hawaiian politics.

7. Find the phrase "in favor of" in the passage. In saying that "Hawaiians voted 17 to 1 in favor of statehood," the author means that they:
   Ⓐ supported independence.
   Ⓑ voted against statehood.
   Ⓒ wanted to join the union.
   Ⓓ became a favorite resort.

Here, you would darken circle **(C)**, **wanted to join the union**. In the passage, the word **favor** is a good clue to the meaning of the whole phrase, as is the adjoining phrase **voted almost 17 to 1**. This phrase strongly suggests that a vote has been taken and that the Hawaiians supported statehood by the margin given. Therefore, **in favor of** must indicate a positive vote, or formal support for a particular proposition or candidate.

Examine the task below. In this type of task, you must insert the sentences into the appropriate place in the passages. Your choices are marked with a box [■].

8. Look at the four squares [■] that show where the following sentence could be inserted into the passage

   In so doing, it became the fiftieth state.

   Where could the sentence best be added? [A], [B], [C], or [D]

The correct placement for this sentence is [**D ■**].

9. An introduction for a short summary of the passage appears below. Complete the summary by choosing three of the six choices that best summarize the information in the passage. Some sentences do not belong in the summary because they are not included in the passage or are minor points from the passage.

The story of Hawaii's path to statehood is a subject of controversy.

-
-
-

Ⓐ Hawaii's climate played a major role in its acceptance of statehood. Its agricultural products were sought by many nations around the world.
Ⓑ After the death of Hawaiian King Kalakaua, and the ousting of Queen Liliuokalani, foreign interests became intensely involved in the political matters of the island.
Ⓒ Largely due to American influence in local politics, the United States recognized Hawaii as an independent nation just before achieving statehood.
Ⓓ An American businessman seized the opportunity that weak leadership presented and led a peaceful movement to remove Queen Liliuokalani from her position of power.
Ⓔ Due to the political power that the Americans had in local government, a very close relationship formed with the United States that permitted the suggestion of statehood for the island nation.
Ⓕ Because of the agreements that were made between Hawaii and the United States, Pearl Harbor was able to play an important role in World War II.

The best sentences to be added to the summary are **(B)**, **(D)**, and **(E)**. You would darken those three circles.

iBT Reading Comprehension Sample

Single causation rarely accounts for complex historical events. Instead, most noteworthy historical events are caused by a plethora of conditions and events. For example, many scholars believe that the Great Depression in the United States can be attributed to sev-
(5) eral national and worldwide conditions.

First, though it may not have been a direct cause of the Great Depression, the Mississippi Valley in America experienced a severe drought around the time of the Great Depression. The area affected included 100,000,000 acres in parts of Texas, Oklahoma, New
(10) Mexico, Colorado, and Kansas. Along with the drought, farmers had not rotated crops or used cover crops to prevent erosion. Thus, when they plowed the topsoil, the natural grasses that would normally trap moisture and keep the soil in place were displaced. As a result, the region experienced severe dust storms and agricultural damage.
(15) [A ■] In fact, the term "Dust Bowl" is often used to refer to this period of severe dust storms when the soil dried and blew away in dark clouds. [B ■] With the land useless, many farmers could not pay their taxes and debts. They had little choice but to sell their farms and travel to other states to find work, even if it meant migrating
(20) from farm to farm to pick fruit for low wages. [C ■] Their plight was captured by the American writer John Steinbeck, in books such as *The Grapes of Wrath* and *Of Mice and Men.* [D ■]

Second, the stock market crash of 1929 resulted in stockholders losing more than $40 billion. On "Black Tuesday," October 29,
(25) 1929, share prices of the New York Stock Exchange plummeted. As stock prices fell, more and more investors decided to leave the stock market, resulting in about 16 million shares traded on Black Tuesday. Although some prominent investors, such as members of the Rockefeller family, bought large quantities of stock to demonstrate
(30) their confidence in the market, their efforts could not prevent the crash. While it is true that the stock market began to recover in the days and weeks after the crash, it did not recover enough to prevent America from entering the Great Depression. The Great Crash sparked a twelve-year economic slump that affected Western indus-
(35) trialized countries.

Third, over 9,000 banks failed during the 1930s. Unlike today, bank deposits were not insured, meaning that many people lost their savings. Banks also became more hesitant to loan money. Fourth,

Americans stopped purchasing items and, as a result, production
(40) fell. In turn, because production was reduced, employers reduced their workforces. Unemployment rose to over 25 percent in 1933. As people lost their jobs, they became unable to pay for items they bought on installment plans, and so their goods were repossessed, which resulted in an increase in businesses' inventories.

(45) Fifth and finally, the U.S. government passed the Smoot-Hawley Tariff Act, or the Tariff Act of 1930. The act was sponsored by U.S. Senator Reed Smoot, a Republican from Utah and chairman of the Senate Finance Committee, and Representative Willis C. Hawley, a Republican from Oregon and chairman of the House Ways and
(50) Means Committee. The act, which raised U.S. tariffs on over 20,000 imported goods, had as its main purpose the protection of American jobs from global competition. The act was not without its opponents, however. For example, in May 1930, 1,028 economists signed a petition asking President Hoover to veto the legislation. Henry Ford
(55) and J.P. Morgan chief executive Thomas Lamont also met with the president to request that he veto the act. President Hoover opposed the bill but nevertheless signed it into law. Foreign governments also opposed the act. While the bill was moving through Congress, foreign governments had threatened retaliation by raising the tariff
(60) rates on American goods imported into their countries. After the bill was signed into law, foreign governments lived up to their threats. For example, Canada, the U.S.'s largest trading partner, retaliated by imposing new tariffs on products that accounted for approximately 30 percent of U.S. exports to Canada.

1. What does the passage mainly discuss?
   Ⓐ Policies involving U.S. trade
   Ⓑ Causes of the Great Depression
   Ⓒ Reasons for stock market crashes
   Ⓓ Books written by American authors

You would click the oval next to the second option.

2. The word **plethora** in line 2 is closest in meaning to
   Ⓐ few
   Ⓑ shortage
   Ⓒ complexity
   Ⓓ overabundance

The correct response is **(D)**.

3. According to the passage, all of the following are mentioned as causes of the Great Depression EXCEPT
   Ⓐ bank failure
   Ⓑ higher tariffs
   Ⓒ installment plans
   Ⓓ stock market crash

The correct response is **(C)**.

4. Find the word **it** in line 32. Using your mouse, click on the word or phrase in the passage that **it** refers to.

This is an antecedent question. The item tests whether you understand what the pronoun **it** refers to. Using your mouse, you would highlight the phrase by clicking on **the stock market** in the passage.

5. According to the passage, which of the following is true about President Hoover?
   Ⓐ He refused to meet with Henry Ford.
   Ⓑ He followed the advice of Thomas Lamont.
   Ⓒ He supported the Smoot-Hawley Tariff Act.
   Ⓓ He signed the Smoot-Hawley Tariff Act into law.

This is an example of a fact question. The response to the question is directly stated in the passage. You would click on response **(D)**.

6. Why does the author mention economists in the last paragraph of the passage?
   Ⓐ Because they caused the economic crisis.
   Ⓑ Because they opposed the Smoot-Hawley Tariff Act.
   Ⓒ Because they acted in ways that worsened the economy.
   Ⓓ Because they exerted undue influence on President Hoover.

The correct response is **(B)**.

7. The word **sparked** in line 34 is closest in meaning to
   Ⓐ started
   Ⓑ hastened
   Ⓒ hampered
   Ⓓ anticipated

The correct response is **(A)**.

8. The word **sponsored** in line 46 is closest in meaning to
   Ⓐ backed
   Ⓑ paid for
   Ⓒ attacked
   Ⓓ subsidized

The correct response is **(A)**.

9. The word **veto** in line 54 is closest in meaning to
   Ⓐ bar
   Ⓑ reject
   Ⓒ revise
   Ⓓ consider

The correct response is **(B)**.

10. Find the word **they** in line 12. Using your mouse, click on the word or phrase in the passage that **they** refers to.

This is an antecedent question. The item tests whether you understand what the pronoun **they** refers to. Using your mouse, you would highlight the word by clicking on **farmers** in the passage.

11. Look at the four squares [■] that show where the following sentence would be inserted into the passage:

    The dust clouds sometimes traveled hundreds of miles.

    Where could the sentence best be added? [A], [B], [C], or [D]

    Click on a [■] to insert the sentence into the passage.

You would click on the square of your choice in the passage to place the sentence in the passage. The correct placement for this sentence is **[B ■]**.

12. With which of the following statements would the author of the reading most probably agree?
    Ⓐ The Great Depression had many causes.
    Ⓑ Stock market crashes should be prevented.
    Ⓒ Economists do not always know what is best.
    Ⓓ High tariffs should be used to protect farmers.

The correct response is **(A)**.

13. An introduction for a short summary of the passage appears below. Complete the summary by choosing three of the six choices that best summarize the information in the passage. Some sentences do not belong in the summary because they are not included in the passage or are minor points from the passage.

The Great Depression in the United States was not caused by one event or condition; instead, it was caused by several.

•

•

•

Ⓐ The drought that resulted in the Dust Bowl meant that many farmers could no longer pay their debts. As a result, they had to leave their farms.
Ⓑ The farmers had not rotated their crops or used special crops to prevent erosion.
Ⓒ On Black Tuesday, stockholders sold their shares of stocks and lost more than $40 billion, sparking a long-term economic downturn.
Ⓓ The Rockefeller family bought large quantities of stock.
Ⓔ The Smoot-Hawley Tariff Act led to trade retaliation, hurting U.S. exports.
Ⓕ The Smoot-Hawley Tariff Act was sponsored by two Republicans who were leaders in the Senate and the House of Representatives.

The best sentences to be added to the passage are **(A)**, **(C)**, and **(E)**. Using your mouse, you would click on each of the three answer choices, and then drag and place each next to one of the three dots above the option.

STRATEGY FOR THE iBT AND ITP TOEFL

Each TOEFL vocabulary item refers you to a word (or phrase, such as a two-word verb) in a specific line of the passage. You are then asked to identify a synonym for that word. These choices are marked by the letters: (A), (B), (C), and (D). *You must identify the word among the choices that is closest in meaning to the word in quotation marks.* Words that are very close or identical in meaning are called **synonyms**. Now go back and examine question 2 on page 16 again.

This question is typical of vocabulary items on the ITP TOEFL. The topic is from U.S. history, and the question contains a single word in quotation marks. The correct answer is **(D)**, **debatable**. **Debatable** is a synonym for **controversial**. As in this example, the word you select is the one that best matches the meaning of the word in quotation marks. Note that all four of the choices make sense in the sentence and that they make use of other information given in the passage. Many vocabulary questions are written so that the context of the sentence or the passage seldom helps you to determine the meaning of the word. Therefore, you must know the word in order to make the correct choice.

Because the context may not help you, you should simply look at the underlined word and choose its synonym from among the four choices, then check to see if the synonym makes sense in the sentence in which it appears. It is best for you to use this strategy because it will prevent frustration and save time. You will need this time for the reading comprehension questions. Remember, on the TOEFL, (B) and (C) answers tend to be used slightly more than (A) and (D). So choose (B) or (C) when guessing. Also remember that answer choices that contain the same prefix or suffix, or are pronounced like the underlined word are seldom the correct answers.

Note that choice **(A)**, **adversarial**, sounds and has letters similar to **controversial**. Such words are not usually the correct choice. Such words are often used to distract you. Unless you are sure of the answer, do not choose these words.

Let's see how to use our strategy with a sample item. Look at question 2 on page 16 again, noting the word in quotation marks. Do not reread the line referred to or the paragraph that contains it. Instead, read the four choices and make your selection of the best synonym.

> This is an example of how you should read vocabulary items.
>
> + + + + + + + "controversial" + + + + + + + + + + + + + + +
>
> + + + + + + + + +
>
> Ⓐ adversarial
> Ⓑ remarkable
> Ⓒ gratifying
> Ⓓ debatable

You should pay attention only to the word in quotation marks and the choices that follow. If you know the meaning of the word and recognize the synonym, there is no need to read the context in which it is used. If you do not know the meaning of the word, you must make an educated guess about its synonym. The context will not usually help you to determine the correct choice. All of the choices from the example above fit into the original context.

> Through a somewhat *adversarial* process, Hawaii was the last territory to become a state.
>
> Through a somewhat *remarkable* process, Hawaii was the last territory to become a state.
>
> Through a somewhat *gratifying* process, Hawaii was the last territory to become a state.
>
> Through a somewhat *debatable* process, Hawaii was the last territory to become a state.

These sentences show that the context does not help you to determine the meaning of the word being tested. If you simply cannot decide on the answer, you can refer to the sentence in which it is used. In the case of the phrasal examples above, there may be some clues in the context that can help you tease out the meaning of the phrase, as shown above. It may also help you to remember any previous experience you have had with the word. However, you are often better off ignoring the context if you know the answer, and you should not waste a lot of time analyzing contextual information. If you cannot make sense of any of the clues available in the context, or recall the phrase from another context, simply make a guess and move on.

Essential Words for the TOEFL gives you additional practice in ignoring the context of vocabulary items on the TOEFL through the matching exercises that are found in each lesson. In these exercises, you are given a word followed by four possible synonyms. Your task is to mark the letter of the correct synonym. The following matching exercise uses the example previously introduced.

Controversial

Ⓐ adversarial
Ⓑ remarkable
Ⓒ gratifying
Ⓓ debatable

REMEMBER

- Do not waste time rereading the context in which the word is used. Look only at the word in quotation marks and search for a synonym among the answer choices.
- Analyze words quickly. Spending too much time studying word roots, prefixes, and suffixes can cause you to misuse valuable time.
- Work quickly, but carefully. You should try to spend only 30 seconds on each vocabulary question.
- Words that contain similar sounds and spelling are usually not the correct answer.
- Always answer every question. If you must guess, choose (B) or (C) as your answer. Your score on Section 3 is based solely on the number of correct answers.

Timing and checking your work. Depending on the format of the TOEFL you are taking, you will have between 31 and 55 minutes on the ITP and 60 minutes on the standard iBT to complete this section. If you take the long iBT, you will have 100 minutes to complete this section. Some test takers report that they do not have enough time to complete the reading questions, so you should work quickly. If you follow the strategies in this book, you will have adequate time to complete the reading section of the TOEFL.

Manage your time wisely! If you finish early, use the ***Review*** icon to go back to test items and check your answers. Checking your responses will allow you to identify and correct any errors. Also, because vocabulary items do not require you to reread and comprehend the entire passage, they can be checked more rapidly than reading comprehension items. After you have checked your responses to the vocabulary items, if you still have time, beginning with the first passage, check your answers to the reading comprehension test items.

CHAPTER 3

IMPROVING YOUR TOEFL VOCABULARY

THE IMPORTANCE OF READING . . . A LOT!

One of the best ways to build your vocabulary is to read authentic English language material. You should read material that a college student would read. Examples of such material are newspapers, college textbooks, encyclopedia articles, magazines, and academic books. Any material that has an academic theme will help you to get used to the kinds of words and the style of writing you will find on the TOEFL. Reading articles on a variety of topics of interest to you will help you to develop your vocabulary. Pay attention to new groups of words, expressions, and phrases you encounter in your reading. Take advantage of resources—teachers, native speakers of English—to learn their meanings.

MAKE WORD LISTS

Another good way to learn new words is to make word lists. Many students use a small notebook, word processing program, or the note pad on their tablet or smart phone for this purpose. When you discover a new word, or group of words, add it to a list of words to be learned. On one side of the page, list the new words. To the right of this list, write synonyms for the new words. Study the words by covering the synonyms, looking at the new word, and recalling the synonyms. It is also useful to reverse the process so that you practice both the new words and their synonyms.

LEARN WORDS FROM OLD TOEFLs

Learn words that have been tested on previous TOEFLs. The underlined words on previous TOEFL tests are sometimes tested again, but they frequently appear among the four choices presented as synonyms for new words that are tested. You can find words to put on your word lists on any TOEFL tests that you have. TOEFL tests can be found online and in the TOEFL test kits available from the Educational Testing Service.

LEARN THE WORDS IN THIS BOOK

Include all of the words listed in this book on your lists. These words have been carefully researched and selected, and many will appear on the TOEFL.

You should learn prefixes, suffixes, and word roots. For a list of them, see Chapter 4. Suggestions for studying word roots, suffixes, and prefixes can be found in that chapter.

LEARN TO USE A THESAURUS

Become familiar with a thesaurus. A thesaurus is a word list of synonyms. When you find a word that you don't know, look it up in the thesaurus. Note a synonym for the word on a word list. If you find a synonym, but still don't know the meaning of the word, look it up in a print or online English language dictionary. *If you can't find the word in the thesaurus, it will not be tested on the TOEFL.* The TOEFL tests only those words that have a variety of synonyms. For more information about the use of a thesaurus, see Chapter 4.

VOCABULARY BUILDING STRATEGIES

- Read often. Choose material that is written for college-level readers.
- Make word lists of new words with synonyms and practice them often.
- Learn words that have been tested on previous TOEFLs.
- Learn word roots, prefixes, and suffixes found in Chapter 4.
- Study the list of 500 essential words in Chapter 5 of this book.

CHAPTER 4

BUILDING YOUR TOEFL VOCABULARY

DEVELOPING WORD ATTACK SKILLS

When readers find an unfamiliar word in a sentence, they are sometimes able to determine its meaning by reading the other words in the sentence. The other words give the "context" that allows readers to make an educated guess about the meaning of an unfamiliar word.

Words fit into contexts in two ways. One is purely grammatical: The *form* of the word is grammatically correct for its position in the sentence. For example, you know that the space between "the" and "student" belongs to an adjective, so you know that "brilliant" fits into that space correctly, while "brilliance," which is a noun, does not.

However, we already know that on TOEFL vocabulary questions all of the possible answers fit the grammatical context of the sentence. Therefore, the degree of success you will have on this part of the TOEFL depends upon whether you understand a word's *meaning* as well as its form. That in turn depends upon how well you can understand its parts and how well you can read its context for clues to its meaning. In this chapter, you will learn how to determine the meaning of a word by studying its parts.

Many English words consist of more than one part. Let's examine three important parts you should know in order to improve your vocabulary.

Word Roots

Many words in English contain Latin and Greek roots. These roots convey the basic meaning of the word and they occur repeatedly throughout the language. Knowing these roots will help you to determine the meaning of words with which you are not familiar. On page 33 is a list of common roots and their general meanings.

Learning these roots will help you to recognize the basic meaning of hundreds of English words. Let's look at the word *manufacture*. Manufacture is a combination of two root words, *manu* and *fact*. Using the list on page 33, we can see that *manu* means "hand" and *fact* means "make" or "do." Therefore, we can infer the meaning "make by hand."

Let's look at another example, *biography*. Again, using the list on page 33, we see that *bio* means "life" and *graph* "write." Therefore, we can conclude that the word's meaning relates to the "writing of a life," the written story of a person's life.

How to Study Word Roots

There are several ways to study word roots. One effective way is to make a flash card for each one. On each card write the root and a word containing the root. Also, write the meaning of the root and a synonym for the example word on the back of the card. As you practice with the cards, first identify the meaning of the root, then the word containing the root. Next, give a synonym for that word. As you study the roots, set aside those you have learned and concentrate only on those roots and synonyms that you have not learned. Save all of the cards for review.

Make word lists. When you read English material, make lists of words that contain the roots that you have studied in this section of the book. Identify the root and look up the word in a thesaurus. Write the meaning of the root and a synonym of the word. This method will help you to identify root words and synonyms on the TOEFL.

Root	Meaning	Example
belli	war	rebellion
biblio	book	bibliography
bio	life	biology
cosm	order	microcosm
cycl	circle	cyclone
dic	two	dichotomy
dict	word	dictate
duc	carry, lead	conducive
duct	carry, lead	conduct
fac	do, make	facsimile
fact	do, make	manufacture
fect	do, make	perfect
form	shape	uniform
fort	strong	fortify
geo	earth	geography
gram	write	telegram
graph	write	autograph
homo	same	homophone
log	speech, study of	dialog
logy	speech, study of	analogy
man	hand	manage
manu	hand	manual
mater	mother, home	maternity
matri	mother, home	matriarch
medi	middle	mediocre
miss	send	dismiss
mit	send	submit
multi	many	multiply
nom	name	nominate
nym	name	synonym
pater	father	paternal
pathy	feeling, suffering	sympathy
patri	father	patriarch
ped	foot	pedal
port	carry	transport
scend	climb	ascend
scrib	write	scribble
script	written language	postscript
secut	follow	consecutive
sent	feel	consent
sequ	follow	subsequently
tact	touch	contact
tempor	time	contemporary
tract	pull, draw out	attractive
vene	come, go	convene
vent	come, go	advent
vers	turn	reverse
vert	turn	convert
voc	voice, call	vocal
vok	voice, call	revoke
volu	turn, roll	convoluted
volve	turn, roll	involve

Prefixes

Prefixes are the second important part of words. A prefix is a part of a word that is attached to the beginning of a word root. A prefix adds meaning to the base word. Thus, if you know the meaning of the prefix, you will be better prepared to determine the meaning of the word. Knowing both prefixes and word roots will unlock the meaning of thousands of English words.

There are many prefixes in English. The list below contains some of the most common prefixes found on the TOEFL.

Prefix	Meaning	Example
ante	before	anterior
anti	against, not in favor	anticipate
auto	self	autonomous
bi	two	biased
circum	circle, around	circumvent
co	with, together	coherent
col	with, together	collect
com	with, together	complex
con	with, together	condense
de	down, reverse	decline
dis	no, not	disregard
e	out, from	emit
ex	out, from	expel
im	no, not	improper
in	in	inactive
inter	between, among	interact
ir	no, not	irrelevant
micro	small, tiny	microscopic
mis	wrong, bad, not	mistake
mono	one	monotone
non	not	nonsense
post	after	postpone
pre	before	preconception
prim	first	primary
pro	for, in favor of	promote
re	again	recover
sub	under	submit
sup	under	supposition
trans	across, over	transmit
tri	three	triple
ultra	excessive	ultrasonic
un	no, not	undeniable
uni	one	unique

Let's examine the word *contact*. We can determine from the list of prefixes that *con* means "with." Upon further examination of the word, we see the word root *tact* means "touch." Without knowing the exact meaning of the word, we can guess that the word is related to "touch" and "with." Indeed, *contact* conveys the meaning of communication with another person. Referring to the root words and prefixes in this chapter we can ascertain that *autobiography* means "self, life, and write," or the story of a person's life written by that same person.

You can approach your study of prefixes with the same method you are using to learn word roots. Make a flash card for each of the prefixes. On each card write the prefix and a word containing the prefix. Write the meaning of the prefix and a synonym for the example word on the back of the card. As you practice with the cards, first identify the meaning of the prefix, then the word containing the root. Next, give a synonym for that word. Save all of the cards for review.

Make word lists. When you read English material, make lists of words that contain the prefixes you recognize. Identify the prefix and look up the word in a thesaurus. Write the meaning of the prefix and a synonym for the word. This method will help you to identify words with prefixes and synonyms on the TOEFL.

Suffixes

The final word part is the suffix. A suffix is added to the end of a word. Similar to a prefix, a suffix adds meaning to the root word. However, the meaning is often grammatical, telling us the tense or the function of the word. Suffixes seldom change the actual meaning of the word in the way that prefixes do. Suffixes are attached to verbs, nouns, and adjectives. There are not many questions that test suffixes on this part of the TOEFL, and you may already know many of them from your grammar study. Nevertheless, you should become familiar with all the English suffixes in the lists on pages 36 and 37.

ADJECTIVE SUFFIXES

Suffix	Meaning	Example
able	capable of	affordable
ant	tendency to	dominant
ative	tendency to	innovative
ent	tendency to	persistent
etic	relating to	sympathetic
ful	full of	harmful
ible	capable	discernible
ical	relating to	identical
less	without	harmless
ous	full of	famous
ness	a quality of being	kindness
ry	occupation	ministry
ship	condition or state	citizenship
some	tendency to	bothersome
y	a quality of being	arbitrary

NOUN SUFFIXES

Suffix	Meaning	Example
ary	place	library
ation	process	population
cule	small	minuscule
dom	state of being	wisdom
er	one who does	teacher
ery	occupation	dentistry
hood	state of being	manhood
ist	one who does	geologist
less	without	careless
ly	like, similar to	manly
ment	state of being	contentment
ness	state of being	happiness
ous	full of	enormous
ship	state of being	citizenship

ADVERB SUFFIXES

Suffix	Meaning	Example
ly	the way	predictably
ways	the way	sideways
wise	the way	otherwise

VERB SUFFIXES

Suffix	Meaning	Example
ade	process of	persuade
ate	to make	accentuate
en	to make	broaden
er	process of	shelter
ize	to make	emphasize

MPORTANT VOCABULARY BUILDING TOOLS

The Dictionary

'or students of English as a Second Language, a good English dictionary is essential. It is a source of valuable information, and if it is used correctly, the dictionary will serve as a useful tool to help you toward your goal of English fluency.

There are many types of dictionaries that a student may consider, ncluding collegiate, learner's, unabridged, and bilingual dictionaries.

For more advanced students, collegiate or college dictionaries are preferred. In addition to the standard word entries, collegiate dictionaries often contain separate sections that contain abbreviations, foreign expressions used in English, and biographical listings. Some may also contain geographical listings.

Highly recommended are learner's dictionaries. This type of dictionary is specifically written for students of English as a foreign language. Definitions are written in clear, easy to understand English. These dictionaries often anticipate learner's questions with special explanatory sections. They also use a standard phonetic alphabet to indicate the pronunciation of the entries.

Unabridged dictionaries are the most comprehensive, but not practical for second language learners because of their detail. An unabridged dictionary is an excellent source for determining the historical development of words, examples of sentences that demonstrate proper usage, antonyms, and synonyms.

A bilingual dictionary that contains words in your native language and English should be avoided. Often these dictionaries are incomplete and give only basic native language equivalent words. These words are frequently out of date or inappropriate for the context of the sentence in which you want to use the unknown words. Therefore, entries in bilingual dictionaries can be misleading. In fact, they can actually cause you to make mistakes. It is worthwhile for English language students to switch to a learner's dictionary as soon as possible, or to use it in conjunction with a bilingual dictionary. You will find that your vocabulary will increase faster by using an English language dictionary.

What You Can Learn

A dictionary gives you the information required to choose the best word for your needs. A typical dictionary entry contains the correct spelling of a word, followed by the word written in a phonetic alphabet. In addition, many online learner dictionaries provide the spoken word to serve as a guide to its pronunciation. Following the phonetic spelling of the word, its part of speech is indicated. The meanings of the word are given in a numerical order, sometimes followed by a sentence that shows the proper use of the word. While many modern dictionaries list the meanings of words from the most common and current meaning to the oldest meaning, some list their definitions from the earliest meaning to the latest meaning. Therefore, before you choose a definition, you should read all the meanings of the entry, then choose the one that meets your needs. Some dictionaries provide synonyms, or words with the same general meaning, and antonyms, words that have the opposite meaning. Some dictionaries give the derivation, a historical development of the word that follows a word back through different languages to its origin.

English language dictionaries contain entries listed in alphabetical order, that is, in an A to Z order. Two guide words appear at the top of each page in a dictionary. The word on the left is the first entry of the two pages; the word on the right indicates the last entry on the two pages. You can use these guide words to determine if the word you are looking up is contained among those entries on the two pages.

> **max • i • mum** (măk′sə-məm) *n. pl.* **-mums** or **-ma** (-mə). *Abbr.* max. **1.a.** The greatest possible quantity or degree. **b.** The greatest quantity or degree reached or recorded; the upper limit of variation. **c.** The time or period during which the highest point or degree is attained. **2.** An upper limit permitted by law or other authority. **3.** *Astronomy.* **a.** The moment when a variable star is most brilliant. **b.** The magnitude of the star at such a moment. **4.** *Mathematics.* **a.** The greatest value assumed by a function over a given interval. **b.** The largest number in a set. **—maximum** *adj. Abbr.* **max. 1.** Having or being the greatest quantity or the highest degree that has been or can be attained: *maximum temperature.* **2.** Of, relating to, or making up a maximum: *a maximum number in a series.* [Latin, from neuter of *maximus*, greatest.]

As we see, the word entry is for the word *maximum*. By examining the word entry, we can determine that it contains three syllables; each syllable being separated by the mark •, max•i•mum. The word is followed by a phonetic spelling of the word inside parentheses, (măk′sə-məm). At the bottom of every page of the dictionary, you will find a pronunciation key that will give you the speech sounds of the symbols. Following the pronunciation, you will find a part of speech label. Here are the traditional speech labels found in most dictionaries.

WORD LABELS

abbr.	abbreviation	ph. v.	phrasal verb
adj.	adjective	pl.	plural
adv.	adverb	prep.	preposition
ant.	antonym	pron.	pronoun
conj.	conjunction	sing.	singular
interj.	interjection	syn.	synonym
intr.	intransitive	tr.	transitive
n.	noun	v.	verb

Following the pronunciation entry for the word maximum, an *n.* and the plural forms (identified by the abbreviation *pl.*) *pl. -mums*, or *-ma* appear. According to the labels, these abbreviations mean that the word is a noun and its plural can be formed two ways, by replacing the last syllable mum with *mums* (maximums) or *ma* (maxima). The plural forms are followed by the abbreviation of the word, identified by Abbr. *max.* Each definition of the word is marked by a number.

In many dictionaries, the order of the definitions reflects the frequency of use of each meaning of the word. The definitions that follow the first definition reflect more specialized uses. Your dictionary will explain the order in which the meanings are presented. When the numbered definition has closely related meanings, they are marked with *1.a.*, *b.*, and *c.* as in the example on page 38. Also note that words with specialized definitions in academic disciplines are identified. In the sample entry, there are two specialized uses of the word maximum, one in *Astronomy*, *3.a.* and *b.*, and another in *Mathematics*, *4.a.* and *b.* After all meanings of the noun form are defined, the entry continues with the definition of the adjective form. The last item of the entry gives the derivation, or word origin, inside brackets [ ].

Please note that several styles of usage are normally indicated in a dictionary entry. These styles are typically identified in the following ways:

Nonstandard	—	Words that do not belong to any standard educated speech
Informal	—	Words that are often used in conversation and seldom in formal writing
Slang	—	Usually a highly informal word that is often figurative in use. Its meaning is usually short-lived
Vulgar	—	A word that is taboo or not socially acceptable in most circumstances
Obsolete	—	A word that is no longer in common usage
Archaic	—	A word that was in common usage, but now rarely used
Rare	—	Words that have never been common in the language
British	—	Words that are in common usage in British English
Regional	—	Words that are used in a limited geographical area

The Thesaurus

A *thesaurus* is a collection of words with similar meanings, usually presented in alphabetical order. These words are called *synonyms*. Use of a thesaurus is helpful when you must change a word to another word with a similar meaning. Many thesauruses list whole phrases in addition to single words. For example, one well-known print thesaurus contains more than 330,000 words *and* phrases in over 1,000 categories. Thus, it provides useful information about how words group or combine in the language as well as clues to their meanings and synonyms.

The entries in a thesaurus typically contain the synonyms in most frequent to least frequent occurrence. In a modern print thesaurus, guide words also appear at the tops of pages. Their function is the same as that of the guide words in dictionaries, indicating the first and last words of the pages. All words on the page appear in alphabetical order. Not all words have synonyms, yet almost all words on the TOEFL are words with many synonyms. Therefore, regular use of a thesaurus, either in print, online, or in a word processing program, will build your vocabulary and help you to prepare for the TOEFL.

Most of the same word labels used in dictionaries appear in a thesaurus. Many entries do not specify the difference between adjective and adverb, since the same forms can often appear both as an adjective and as an adverb. The abbreviation *mod.* is used to mark such a word. Let's examine an entry for the word *maximum.*

> **maximum**, *mod.—Syn.* supreme, highest, greatest: see best 1.
> **maximum**, *n.—Syn.* supremacy, height, pinnacle, preeminence, culmination, matchlessness, preponderance, apex, peak, greatest number, highest degree, summit, nonpareil; see also climax. *–Ant.* minimum*, foot, bottom.

There are two entries for this word. The abbreviation *mod.* in the first entry indicates that the word could be used as a modifier of other words. Following this, *syn.* indicates that synonyms for the word follow. At the end of the listing appears the suggestion *see best 1.* This suggestion refers us to the first entry for the word *best* if we wish to see more words with meanings related to *maximum.*

The second entry gives the synonyms for the noun form of the word. The *n.* indicates that the word is used as a noun, and *syn.* indicates that synonyms follow. This entry also refers the reader to the word *climax* for additional words related to *maximum.* At the end of the entry, antonyms, marked with the label *ant.*, are listed.

The dictionary and thesaurus are two powerful learning tools that you should have for reference. They are essential for a good vocabulary building program. In addition, many publishers offer idiom dictionaries and phrase books that can be useful in learning word combinations commonly used in academic settings. Instructional material focusing on idioms and phrases is available online at numerous websites catering to ESL and EFL students. When you study such material, be sure to focus on academic vocabulary, not slang. Slang does not appear on the TOEFL. Often, slang will be indicated as such in a dictionary or thesaurus. Some academic words have phrasal equivalents. A few examples are listed below:

Single Word	**Phrasal Synonym**
adjust	straighten out
endanger	put in jeopardy
clandestine	in disguise
settle	take root
vague	ill-defined

As a general rule, single words are preferable to phrases in formal academic style when both options are available. However, the use of phrases is still correct. Sometimes the words in phrases are so closely associated with each other that they are written with a hyphen, as in *ill-defined* above. Hyphens are also used to link word sequences that might otherwise appear ungrammatical.

CHAPTER 5

THE ESSENTIAL TOEFL VOCABULARY

This chapter contains 30 lessons. Each lesson presents a set of key TOEFL words. Following the entries, there are 10 matching exercises. At the end of each lesson, there are 10 TOEFL-like vocabulary questions that contain most of the words presented in each lesson. All of these TOEFL-like questions provide an excellent vocabulary review as well as solid preparation for not only the reading section of the TOEFL, but also for all sections of the TOEFL.

You should study the lessons in order. For example, after studying lesson 1, go directly to lesson 2. Do not study lessons out of order. The book is designed to provide systematic review of words in previous lessons. By studying the lessons out of order, you will be defeating the review system.

Let's examine a sample entry to see the kinds of information you will learn.

intricate	*adj.* having many parts; finely detailed
adv. intricately *n.* intricacy	*syn.* complex

The *intricate* design of the vase made it a valuable piece for her collection.
I cannot begin to understand all of the *intricacies* of modern automobile motors.

The entry features the word *intricate.* Directly under the word, you will find other forms of the same word. These words have the same general meaning; they represent the different parts of speech of the word. For each of the forms, the part of speech is given. The following abbreviations for parts of speech are used in the word entries:

adj.	→	adjective
adv.	→	adverb
conj.	→	conjunction
v.	→	verb
n.	→	noun
ph. v.	→	phrasal verb
prep. ph.	→	prepositional phrase

In the case of *intricate*, the adjective form, **adj**., is presented as the key word. Other forms of the entry, *intricately* and *intricacy*, are listed below the main entry.

The key word is then defined in clear, easy to understand English. In this example, we see that *intricate* means *something having many parts* or *something that is finely detailed.*

Under the definition you will find a synonym for the key word. The synonym is a word that has the same or a similar meaning and it is marked with the letters *syn.* In the example on page 43, the synonym given for *intricate* is *complex.*

Below the synonym, there are two sentences that show the usage of two different forms of the word. The sentences are rich in context; that is, the words surrounding the key word tend to support and clarify the meaning of the key word. Let's look at the two sentences in the example.

> The *intricate* design of the vase made it a valuable piece for her collection.
>
> I cannot begin to understand all of the *intricacies* of modern automobile engines.

The key word will *usually* appear in the first sentence. The key word sentence is followed by a second sentence illustrating the use of one of the related words, but with a different form of the word. If no related words are given, then the second sentence serves as another illustration of the meaning of the key word.

Some word forms are not included in the entries. These are words that are not in common usage and not likely to appear on the TOEFL.

The word entries provide you with all the information that you need to build a powerful TOEFL vocabulary.

STUDYING THE WORD ENTRIES

To learn vocabulary efficiently, you must have a study plan and follow it carefully. The following plan has been useful to many students who are building their TOEFL vocabulary.

Plan to spend at least an hour studying the words in each lesson of this book. Do not study words that you already know.

Read
First, read the word entries of the lesson carefully, including the definition, different forms, synonym, and example sentences. It is important for you to associate the key word with its meaning and synonym. These are the three most important parts of the word entry.

Reread
Next, read each word entry again. Look up unfamiliar words that appear in the example sentences. This time when you study the entry we suggest that you cover the key word, then look at the meaning and its synonym. Then identify the key word. When you are able to identify the key word, reverse the process by identifying the covered synonym. Finally, cover everything in the entry, except the meaning, and identify the key word and its synonym.

Find the Synonyms
You are now ready for the matching exercise at the end of the word list. Let's look at a typical matching question.

1. intricate

Ⓐ functional
Ⓑ complex
Ⓒ predominant
Ⓓ inordinate

The purpose of the question is to test your knowledge of synonyms, a key skill for the TOEFL. You will see four choices. In this example, you must choose the synonym for the word *intricate*. The correct choice is **(B)**, **complex**. Nearly all the words that appear as answer choices are key words introduced in the same and previous lessons. Check your answers by referring to the Answer Key found at the back of this book.

You are now ready to test your skill on actual TOEFL-like questions. Let's look at the following test question.

The intricate design of the building's facade is typical of buildings of the nineteenth century.

Ⓐ functional
Ⓑ accurate
Ⓒ standard
Ⓓ complex

This test question is typical of the questions on the vocabulary section of the TOEFL. You must choose the word that has the same or similar meaning as the underlined word in the sentence. Most TOEFL questions do not use the word in context-rich sentences. Therefore, as we learned in Chapter 2, you will probably not be able to determine the meaning of the word by reading the sentence. Therefore, look directly to the underlined word and do not read the sentence. Look for its synonym among the four choices. The correct answer is **(D)**, **complex**. Most of the answer choices for the test questions at the end of each lesson are key words introduced in that lesson.

After you have studied the word entries and their synonyms, and completed the practice exercises, make flash cards. On one side of the card, write the key word and its related forms. On the other side of the card, write its synonym. Review these cards several times during the weeks before your TOEFL test session. If you are preparing for a specific TOEFL test date, make a study schedule based on how much time you have before the TOEFL. For example, if you have six weeks before your test date, plan to study five lessons each week

Be sure that you organize your cards. It is suggested that you organize your cards in alphabetical order by **synonyms** or by the **lesson number**. Keep two groups of cards; one group for the words you have learned, the second group for those words you need to learn. Review the second group more often than the first group of words that you already know.

As your vocabulary grows, return to the exercises and test questions in each lesson.

By following this study plan, you will know that you are better prepared for the important day when you take the TOEFL.

ANSWERING PHRASAL QUESTIONS

At least one phrase-type question is provided in each of this book's 30 lessons. Each question contains a short passage that illustrates the use of a vocabulary item in combination with other words that it is often grouped with. For example, *densely* is a word that appears as a single item in one of these lessons, but it is often combined with the word *populated* to form the phrase *densely populated*. Therefore, *densely populated* is treated as a whole phrase in one of the phrasal questions in the book. It is always useful to learn the meanings of single words, but it is also important to learn how these words combine with other words in common word pairs or word groups.

In answering these questions, it is helpful to use what you already know about the words in isolation and to keep a few simple strategies in mind. Let's look more closely at the *densely populated* example.

First, you should read the passage carefully. A lot of what you need to know about the word in combination and the meaning of the whole phrase is already available in the passage itself. In this case, you know that the phrase has something to do with the distribution of people in a particular country: Some live close together in cities, while others live far apart in the countryside. Therefore, you have a sense of what the words mean in combination because you understand the general meaning of the passage that illustrates and defines them.

Understanding the general meaning and the phrase's context is probably enough for you to come up with the right answer to the practice question in this book:

> In stating that the Netherlands is *densely populated*, the author means that its
>
> Ⓐ people are very unevenly distributed.
> Ⓑ population is the largest in Europe.
> Ⓒ population is the largest per square kilometer.
> Ⓓ cities are the largest cities in Europe.

Without going much further, you can probably guess that the best answer here is **(C)** since it comes the closest to saying that the country as a whole contains a lot of people without saying that it contains more than any other country in Europe. However, there are other steps you can take just to be sure.

You can also take a look at the entry for the target word, in this case *densely*. Notice that the word is an adverb. This means that it limits or modifies an adjective and a verb; in this instance, it tells you *how heavily populated* a particular European country is—how many people it contains per square kilometer. Other word combinations or phrases fall into other categories. For example, some contain verbs followed by prepositions (*conforms to*), some contain nouns preceded by prepositions (*on impulse*), and some contain nouns preceded by adjectives (*crushing blow*). In other words, try to use as much information about a word's form or part of speech as you can in arriving at its meaning, and specifically at an understanding of its relationship with the other words around it.

Finally, recall any other instance of the phrase you have heard or seen. For example, you may discover that you have already encountered the phrase in your reading—in developing your awareness of vocabulary through extensive reading—and you may have recorded it on one of your flash cards. These phrases have been chosen because they are commonly used in the language. For that reason, you are likely to come across them in a variety of contexts. Their frequent use is also the reason why understanding these words in combination can give you a deeper and more general understanding of the language as a whole.

Word Combinations in This Book

The table beginning below includes the word combinations and phrases highlighted in the book's 30 vocabulary lessons.

In the first column on the left, you can see grammatical information about each word combination's part of speech. For example, *disapprove of* is described as a verb because it fills that role in an English sentence:

Sheila *disapproves of* students who make a lot of noise.

In the second column, the chapter in which each word combination is found is specified. Finally, an illustrative sentence is given in the third column.

The table will help you learn new phrases and word combinations, as well as general strategies for learning new words in combination wherever you find them.

Word Combinations in This Book

(See the second column for lesson number)

VERBS		**Example**
disapprove of	1	Many communities now disapprove of cell or car phone use.
(see an) advantage in	2	Many people can see an advantage in moving to big cities.
conform to	3	A chameleon changes color to conform to its surroundings.
(be) determined to	4	Many residents are determined to restrict the movement of deer.
work out	5	No one could work out the problem.
carry out	12	The government carried out the plans for the construction of new roads.
(be) reported to	12	They were reported to have powers that protected them from attack.
come across	18	John came across some old coins while cleaning out the basement.
look over	19	The architect looked over the house plans carefully.

VERBS (continued)		Example
take the initiative	20	The center forward takes the initiative and moves the ball forward.
react to	21	The colorant reacts to the presence of acid by turning red.
run into	21	The students ran into some problems during the lab.
account for	22	Scientists seek to account for patterned circles in grain fields.
bring about	22	The industrial revolution brought about many changes in manufacturing processes.
(be) renowned for	23	The orchestra is especially renowned for its violin players.
(be) peculiar to	24	Water storage is peculiar to a class of animals called ruminants.
stem from	24	His good grades stem from his dedication to studying.
(be) open to interpretation	26	Historical facts about the pyramids are open to interpretation.
factor in	26	She had to factor in the cost of shipping when shopping online.

ADJECTIVES + NOUNS		
intriguing question	5	Where human life first arose is still an intriguing question.
crushing blow	8	The airplane's invention was a crushing blow for ballooning.
face-to-face encounters	13	Lack of eye contact is a sign of disrespect in face-to-face encounters.
heightened awareness	16	Heightened awareness has led to worry about greenhouse gases.
gradual decrease	17	A gradual decrease will not stimulate spending or employment.
balanced view	18	TV news rarely gives a balanced view of people, products, and events.
curative powers	28	A substance with curative powers would actually kill bacteria.

ADVERBS + ADJECTIVES		Example
well-suited	5	The manager is well-suited for the job.
comparatively easy	6	It is comparatively easy to switch off some Internet sites.
densely populated	9	The Netherlands is the most densely populated country in Europe.
exceptionally talented	10	Relatively few children are exceptionally talented musically.
fundamentally sound	14	NASA is confident that spacecrafts are fundamentally sound.
perilously close	15	The world came perilously close to losing the panda in the 1980s.
aptly named	27	The ship was aptly named after the Titans, who ruled the universe.
prominently displayed	29	The electronic bar code is not prominently displayed on a product.
severely punished	30	In some countries, high-speed driving is severely punished.
PREPOSITIONS + NOUNS		
to its core	7	Patients view the medical profession as selfish to its core.
on impulse	25	Psychology has explored why purchases are made on impulse.
COMPARATIVE ADJECTIVE		
more prevalent than	11	Sports utility vehicles are more prevalent than compact cars.
PHRASAL PREPOSITION		
in conjunction with	5	Good road design in conjunction with effective driver education makes roads safer.
in opposition to	19	There is growing sentiment in opposition to sea bass fishing.

LESSON 1

- **abroad**
- **abrupt**
- **acceptable**
- **acclaim**
- **adverse**
- **aspect**
- **attractive**
- **autonomous**
- **chronic**
- **disapproval**
- **disruptive**
- **haphazardly**
- **intervention**
- **persistent**
- **postpone**
- **valid**
- **withdraw**

---

abroad *adv.* to or in another country
syn. overseas; internationally

Louis Armstrong often traveled *abroad.*

Living *abroad* can be an educational experience.

abrupt *adj.* quick; without warning
syn. sudden

adv. abruptly
n. abruptness

There was an *abrupt* change in the weather.

After the incident everyone left *abruptly.*

acceptable *adj.* allowable or satisfactory
syn. permissible

v. accept
adv. acceptably
n. acceptability
adj. accepting

The idea was *acceptable* to everyone.

The registrar *accepted* more applicants than he should have.

acclaim *n.* enthusiastic approval; applause
syn. praise

adj. acclaimed
n. acclamation

Leonardo DiCaprio has earned *acclaim* abroad as an actor.

Acclaimed authors often win Pulitzer Prizes.

adverse *adj.* displeasing, objectionable, or bad
syn. unfavorable

adv. adversely
n. adversity
n. adversary

The game was cancelled by officials due to the *adverse* weather conditions.

His indecision *adversely* affected his job performance.

aspect *n.* a part or characteristic of something; an element
syn. facet

I would trust the professional's advice in that *aspect* of economics.
There are many fascinating *aspects* to the complex procedure.

attractive *adj.* calling attention to; pleasing; creating interest; pretty
syn. appealing

v. attract
n. attraction
n. attractiveness
adv. attractively

The idea of working four, ten-hour work days was *attractive* to many employees.
The major *attraction* of the show was a speech by the president.

autonomous *adj.* by itself; with no association
syn. independent

adv. autonomously

Mexico became an *autonomous* state in 1817.
Although working closely with the government, all businesses function *autonomously*.

chronic *adj.* always present; continual
syn. constant

adv. chronically

The author's *chronic* headache prevented her from finishing the chapter.
He is *chronically* late to class.

disapproval *n.* the act of disagreeing; not giving approval
syn. objection

v. disapprove
adv. disapprovingly

Their *disapproval* of the plan caused the experiment to be abandoned.
The students *disapproved* of the level of difficulty of the test.

disruptive *adj.* causing confusion and interruption
syn. disturbing

v. disrupt
n. disruption
adv. disruptively

Frequent questions during lectures can be *disruptive*.
The storm caused a *disruption* in bus service.

haphazardly *adv.* having no order or pattern; by chance

adj. haphazard
n. haphazardness

syn. arbitrarily; carelessly

It was obvious that the house was built *haphazardly.*

Susan completed the assignment in a *haphazard* way.

intervention *n.* taking action; be involved

v. intervene

syn. involvement

The tutor's *intervention* helped him improve his grade.

Some world leaders decide to not *intervene* in the affairs of other nations.

persistent *adj.* continuous; refusing to give up; firm in action or decision

v. persist
n. persistence
adv. persistently

syn. constant

The attorney's *persistent* questioning unsettled the witness.

Her *persistence* earned her a spot on the team.

postpone *v.* to change to a later time; to delay

adj. postponable
n. postponement

syn. reschedule

The referees decided to *postpone* the soccer match.

The *postponement* of the meeting upset the impatient club members.

valid *adj.* producing a desired result based on truths or facts

n. validity
adv. validly

syn. convincing

The students had a *valid* reason for missing class.

The professor questioned the *validity* of the test results.

withdraw *v.* to remove, take out, or take back

n. withdrawal

syn. extract

The player *withdrew* from the competition.

Gloria had to make a *withdrawal* from her savings to pay tuition.

MATCHING

Choose the synonym.

1. withdraw
   - Ⓐ extract
   - Ⓑ describe
   - Ⓒ copy
   - Ⓓ convince

2. autonomous
   - Ⓐ independent
   - Ⓑ sudden
   - Ⓒ international
   - Ⓓ abrupt

3. chronic
   - Ⓐ famous
   - Ⓑ visible
   - Ⓒ constant
   - Ⓓ ordinary

4. intervene
   - Ⓐ involve
   - Ⓑ oppose
   - Ⓒ interrupt
   - Ⓓ create

5. aspect
   - Ⓐ attraction
   - Ⓑ talent
   - Ⓒ characteristic
   - Ⓓ objection

6. haphazardly
   - Ⓐ suddenly
   - Ⓑ secretly
   - Ⓒ carelessly
   - Ⓓ constantly

7. constant
   - Ⓐ disruption
   - Ⓑ acceptable
   - Ⓒ abrupt
   - Ⓓ persistent

8. valid
   - Ⓐ attractive
   - Ⓑ convincing
   - Ⓒ normal
   - Ⓓ abrupt

9. unfavorably
   - Ⓐ attractively
   - Ⓑ haphazardly
   - Ⓒ acceptably
   - Ⓓ adversely

10. postpone
    - Ⓐ respond
    - Ⓑ reschedule
    - Ⓒ assert
    - Ⓓ reveal

LESSON 1—MULTIPLE-CHOICE TEST QUESTIONS

1. A customs union is an organization of **autonomous** countries that agree that international trade between member states is free of restrictions. They place a tariff or other restriction on products entering the customs union from nonmember states. One of the best-known customs unions is the European Union, or EU.

   The word **autonomous** in the passage is closest in meaning to

   Ⓐ massive
   Ⓑ acclaimed
   Ⓒ prosperous
   Ⓓ independent

2. The search to hide natural body odors led to the discovery and use of musk. Musk is a scent used in perfumes. It is obtained from the sex glands of the male musk deer, a small deer native to the mountainous regions of the Himalayas. The odor of musk, penetrating and **persistent**, is believed to act as an aphrodisiac. In animals, musk serves the functions of defining territory, providing recognition, and attracting mates.

   The word **persistent** in the passage is closest in meaning to

   Ⓐ attractive
   Ⓑ disruptive
   Ⓒ constant
   Ⓓ pleasant

3. Until the late ninteenth century all rubber was extracted **haphazardly** from trees found in the jungles of South America. It was expensive and the supply was uncertain. However, during the 1860s the idea of transporting rubber trees to the British colonies in Asia was conceived. This led to the larger-scale cultivation of rubber trees on organized plantations.

   The word **haphazardly** in the passage is closest in meaning to

   Ⓐ carelessly
   Ⓑ secretly
   Ⓒ constantly
   Ⓓ dangerously

4. Some animals use bold coloration to **disrupt** a would-be predator's perception. Other animals have color patterns that blend with their surroundings. Such coloration serves for protection, to attract mates, or to distract enemies. Called cryptic coloration, it uses the animals' living place, habits, and means of defense. Cryptic coloration may blend an animal so well with its environment that it is virtually invisible.

   The word **disrupt** in the passage is closest in meaning to

   Ⓐ disturb
   Ⓑ distinctive
   Ⓒ brilliant
   Ⓓ unfavorable

5. Cognitive approaches to therapy assume that emotional disorders are the result of irrational beliefs or perceptions. The mind may interpret an event as scary or calming, happy or sad. The emotionally disordered person may perceive **adverse** events as personal failures. Cognitive psychotherapies seek to make the patient aware of the irrationality of this perception and to substitute more rational evaluations of such events.

   The word **adverse** in the passage is closest in meaning to

   Ⓐ monotonous
   Ⓑ threatening
   Ⓒ inoffensive
   Ⓓ unfavorable

6. Increasingly, authorities are uneasy about teenagers who talk or text on their phones while driving. For many, phone use and driving are perfectly compatible; others, however, are more easily distracted, especially while listening to music. The growing number of accidents associated with phone use supports this claim. Many communities now **disapprove of** this habit so much that they have forbidden anyone of any age to use cell phones while driving.

   In stating that many communities now **disapprove of** these phones, the author means that they

   Ⓐ fully endorse their popularity.
   Ⓑ condemn or oppose their use.
   Ⓒ favor their use only by adults.
   Ⓓ agree to their unrestricted use.

7. Fans are used to circulate air in rooms and buildings and for cooling and drying people, materials, or products. Even though air that is circulated by a fan is comforting, no fan actually cools the air. Air conditioners use a complicated process to cool the air and create changes in temperature. While repairing a fan is relatively simple, a professional repairman will often have **to intervene** when home owners face problems with their air conditioning units.

   The words **to intervene** in the passage is closest in meaning to

   Ⓐ to be interested in
   Ⓑ to learn about
   Ⓒ to get involved
   Ⓓ to be prepared

8. Tornadoes strike in many areas of the world, but nowhere are they as frequent or as devastating as in the United States. A vast "tornado belt" embraces large portions of the Great Plains of the United States and the southeastern portion of the country. Tornadoes pose the greatest threats to these areas, which are especially vulnerable to **abrupt** changes in weather conditions.

   The word **abrupt** in the passage is closest in meaning to

   Ⓐ sudden
   Ⓑ vivid
   Ⓒ sharp
   Ⓓ direct

9. For women in the 1920s, freedom in dress reflected their new freedom to take up careers. Only a small percentage of women pursued such opportunities, but the revolutionary change affected the types of clothes worn by most women. For example, trousers became **acceptable** attire for almost all activities. This milestone in the fashion world favored more stylish and comfortable clothing instead of more formal modes of dress.

   The word **acceptable** in the passage is closest in meaning to

   Ⓐ usable
   Ⓑ endurable
   Ⓒ believable
   Ⓓ permissible

10. The National Film Board of Canada was established in 1939 to produce films that reflect Canadian life and thought, and to distribute them both domestically and abroad. By winning awards from film festivals around the world, it has earned international **acclaim** for the artistic and technical excellence of its work.

    The word **acclaim** in the passage is closest in meaning to

    Ⓐ fascination
    Ⓑ praise
    Ⓒ acceptance
    Ⓓ attraction

LESSON 2

- **advantage**
- **advent**
- **agile**
- **albeit**
- **appealing**
- **celebrated**
- **circumvent**
- **collide**
- **contemporary**
- **distribute**
- **encourage**
- **energetic**
- **frail**
- **heyday**
- **myth**
- **refine**
- **worthwhile**

---

advantage *n.* something that may help one to be successful or to gain something
syn. benefit

adv. advantageously
adj. advantageous

Is there any *advantage* in arriving early?
He was *advantageously* born into a rich family.

advent *n.* the coming or appearance of something
syn. arrival

With the *advent* of computers, many tasks have been made easier.
The orchestra's latest newsletter announced the *advent* of the upcoming concert season.

agile *adj.* able to move in a quick and easy way
syn. nimble

adv. agilely
n. agileness
n. agility

Deer are very *agile* animals.
She moved *agilely* across the stage.

albeit *conj.* in spite of the facts, regardless of the fact
syn. although

His trip was successful, *albeit* tiring.
Albeit difficult at times, speaking another language is rewarding.

appealing *adj.* attractive or interesting
syn. alluring

v. appeal
n. appeal
adv. appealingly

Working abroad is *appealing* to many people.
Through his speeches, the candidate *appealed* to the voters.

celebrated — *adj.* acclaimed; well-known and popular
syn. renowned

The *celebrated* pianist will be giving a concert this weekend.
San Francisco is *celebrated* for its multicultural makeup.

circumvent — *v.* to go around; avoid
n. circumvention
syn. evade

The hacker attempted to *circumvent* the computer's security system.
Circumvention of the freshman math requirement is possible.

collide — *v.* to hit one object against another with violent force; to be in opposition
n. collision
syn. crash

The *collision* caused major damage to both cars.
Moon craters were caused when large asteroids *collided* with the moon.

contemporary — *adj.* modern, up-to-date, or (*n.*) a person living at the same time as another person
n. contemporary
syn. current

Contemporary architecture makes very good use of space.
Cervantes was a *contemporary* of Shakespeare.

distribute — *v.* to divide among people or to give out
n. distribution
syn. dispense

Many publishers now *distribute* their newspapers via the Internet.
The *distribution* of seeds is very quick with this new machine.

encourage — *v.* to promote, help, or support
n. encouragement
n. encourager
adv. encouragingly
adv. encouraging
syn. stimulate

The government cut taxes in order to *encourage* spending.
The professor gave each student the *encouragement* that was needed to learn the material.

energetic *adj.* full of life, action, or power

n. energy *syn.* vigorous

adv. energetically

Sam hasn't been as *energetic* as he usually is.

There's a lot of *energy* in these batteries.

frail *adj.* weak in health or in body

n. frailty *syn.* fragile

The *frail* wings of the newborn bird could not lift it off the ground.

One of the *frailties* of human beings is laziness.

heyday *n.* a high point of success or abundance

syn. pinnacle

Many settlers became rich during the *heyday* of the California gold rush of the 1800s.

We are living in the *heyday* of digital communications.

myth *n.* an invented story or idea

adj. mythological *syn.* legend

n. mythology

Throughout history *myths* were created in an attempt to explain many common natural occurrences.

Mythology is the study of legends and fables.

refine *v.* to make pure; to improve

n. refinement *syn.* perfect (verb)

adj. refined

Factories must *refine* oil before it can be used as fuel.

A squirt of lime juice is the perfect *refinement* to cola.

worthwhile *adj.* value in doing something

syn. rewarding

It was *worthwhile* waiting ten hours in line for the tickets.

It's *worthwhile* to prepare for the TOEFL.

MATCHING

Choose the synonym.

1. circumvent
   Ⓐ celebrate
   Ⓑ attract
   Ⓒ evade
   Ⓓ appeal

2. advantage
   Ⓐ benefit
   Ⓑ persistence
   Ⓒ nimbleness
   Ⓓ allure

3. fragile
   Ⓐ modern
   Ⓑ famous
   Ⓒ refined
   Ⓓ frail

4. contemporary
   Ⓐ timing
   Ⓑ current
   Ⓒ well-known
   Ⓓ perfect

5. appealing
   Ⓐ refined
   Ⓑ encouraging
   Ⓒ alluring
   Ⓓ popular

6. renowned
   Ⓐ unknown
   Ⓑ celebrated
   Ⓒ adverse
   Ⓓ disapprove

7. worthwhile
   Ⓐ rewarding
   Ⓑ acceptable
   Ⓒ agile
   Ⓓ permitted

8. vigorous
   Ⓐ attractive
   Ⓑ beautiful
   Ⓒ energetic
   Ⓓ advantageous

9. refine
   Ⓐ persist
   Ⓑ value
   Ⓒ perfect
   Ⓓ divide

10. heyday
   Ⓐ agreement
   Ⓑ acclaim
   Ⓒ postponement
   Ⓓ pinnacle

LESSON 2—MULTIPLE-CHOICE TEST QUESTIONS

1. Over the years, investigators have evaluated the local folklore of areas where sightings of the **celebrated** Abominable Snowman have been reported. The same scientists have collected physical evidence, such as footprints, body parts, and photographs, but this evidence remains unconvincing. In 1960 the renowned mountaineer Sir Edmund Hillary of New Zealand conducted an investigation of the reports of the creature, but found no evidence of its existence.

   The word **celebrated** in the passage is closest in meaning to

   Ⓐ elusive
   Ⓑ ambiguous
   Ⓒ renowned
   Ⓓ indistinct

2. Exercises that demand total body involvement improve and maintain fitness. The most effective way to feel more mentally alert and **energetic** is to engage in aerobic activity at least three times a week for 30 minutes. Such activities may include jogging, running, swimming, dancing, and fast walking.

   The word **energetic** in the passage is closest in meaning to

   Ⓐ vigorous
   Ⓑ frail
   Ⓒ agile
   Ⓓ appealing

3. Most people do not appreciate the importance of packaging. Packages maintain the purity and freshness of their contents and protect them from elements outside. If the contents are harmful, corrosive, or poisonous, the package must also protect the outside environment. A package must identify its contents, which facilitates **distribution** of the product.

   The word **distribution** in the passage is closest in meaning to

   Ⓐ usage
   Ⓑ disruption
   Ⓒ dispensing
   Ⓓ advertising

4. A **contemporary** issue among psychologists is the activation or cause of emotion, its structure or components, and its functions and consequences. Each of these aspects can be considered from a biosocial view. Generally, biosocial theory focuses on the neurophysiological aspects of emotions and their roles as organizers of cognition and motivators of action.

   The word **contemporary** in the passage is closest in meaning to

   Ⓐ current
   Ⓑ acclaimed
   Ⓒ contemptuous
   Ⓓ favored

5. The early artists of the Hudson River school were Thomas Doughty, Asher Durand, and Thomas Cole. They found the wilderness in the Hudson River valley **appealing.** Although these painters studied in Europe, they first achieved a measure of success at home, and chose the common theme of the remoteness and splendor of the American interior.

   The word **appealing** in the passage is closest in meaning to

   Ⓐ annoying
   Ⓑ ongoing
   Ⓒ spectacular
   Ⓓ alluring

6. Recent polls suggest that fewer people see an **advantage in** moving to the city than they used to. There was a time when cities attracted country dwellers like powerful magnets: cities had more jobs, better schools, more services. Today, people often see pollution, crime, stress, and unemployment where they once saw opportunity. Instead of advantages, they see disadvantages in uprooting their families for the uncertainty of urban life.

   In stating that fewer people see an **advantage in** moving to the city, the author means that fewer people

   Ⓐ consider cities a poor option.
   Ⓑ prefer to relocate to big cities.
   Ⓒ take a positive view of cities.
   Ⓓ view city life as advantageous.

7. The growing popularity of television in the 1950s marked an important turning point in the entertainment world. This development created vast new entertainment choices for people who lived within the signal areas of TV stations. Later, with the **advent** of satellite and cable TV, almost everyone, regardless of location, was able to experience this entertainment medium.

   The word **advent** in the passage is closest in meaning to

   Ⓐ dependence
   Ⓑ allowance
   Ⓒ explosion
   Ⓓ arrival

8. Passerines form the dominant avian group on Earth today. They are regarded as the most highly evolved of all birds and occur in abundance. Humans have long enjoyed passerines for their songs and their almost infinite variety of colors, patterns, and behavioral traits. Many passerines are considered to be quite **agile**. Among the most energetic of them is the swallow, whose small body is designed for effortless maneuvering.

   The word **agile** in the passage is closest in meaning to

   Ⓐ nimble
   Ⓑ detectible
   Ⓒ broad
   Ⓓ fast

9. In part because seafood tends to spoil rapidly, in certain areas of the United States, shrimping is allowed only during specific predetermined seasons. For example, in Mississippi tidal waters, shrimping is allowed only between October and May. In the past, this short season made it difficult to find shrimp out of season. However, the development of freezing techniques in the 1940s **encouraged** the shrimping industry to expand, making it a global industry. The United States now imports shrimp from over sixty countries and shrimp can be bought at any time of the year.

   The word **encouraged** in the passage is closest in meaning to

   Ⓐ advanced
   Ⓑ accepted
   Ⓒ stimulated
   Ⓓ wanted

10. Scientific disciplines, such as genetic engineering, are exploding with possibilities. As a result of new technologies and procedures to treat health conditions, new treatments for many diseases have been developed. Although the development of advanced methods will continue to change the face of healthcare, moral beliefs often **collide with** scientific advancements, slowing down the progress of some healthcare treatments.

    The phrase **collide with** in the passage is closest in meaning to

    Ⓐ are in opposition to
    Ⓑ are absent from
    Ⓒ are associated with
    Ⓓ are concerned about

LESSON 3

- **alter**
- **analyze**
- **ancient**
- **annoying**
- **anticipate**
- **ascertain**
- **benign**
- **conform**
- **enrich**
- **intensify**
- **intolerable**
- **ongoing**
- **potential**
- **propose**
- **restore**
- **turbulent**
- **vital**

---

alter *v.* to change or make different
syn. modify

v. altered
n. alteration
adj. alterable
adv. alterably

Will the storm *alter* its course and miss the coast?
Gloria hasn't *altered* her plans to return to school.

analyze *v.* to study something carefully; to separate into parts for study
syn. examine

v. analyzed
n. analysis

Scientists must *analyze* problems thoroughly.
Analysis of the substance confirms the presence of nitrogen.

ancient *adj.* something from a long time ago; very old
syn. old

Archaeologists analyze *ancient* civilizations.
Dave found an *ancient* Roman coin.

annoying *adj.* a slight bother; disturbing to a person
syn. bothersome

n. annoyance
v. annoy
adv. annoyingly

Mosquitoes can be an *annoying* part of a vacation at the beach.
She *annoyed* her parents by coming home late.

anticipate *v.* to think about or prepare for something ahead of time

adj. anticipatory
n. anticipation

syn. predict

No one can *anticipate* the results of the games.

They planned their vacation with *anticipation.*

ascertain *v.* to discover; find out

adj. ascertainable
adv. ascertainably
n. ascertainment

syn. determine

I tried to *ascertain* if he was telling the truth.

The jury made a decision based on its *ascertainment* of the facts.

benign *adj.* doing no harm or damage; gentle

syn. harmless

He has a warm, *benign* smile that makes everyone comfortable.

The mold on the plants proved to be *benign.*

conform *v.* to follow established rules or patterns of behavior

n. conformity
n. conformist

syn. adapt

You must *conform* to the rules or leave the club.

She has always been a *conformist.*

enrich *v.* to make rich; to make something of greater value

n. enrichment
adj. enriching

syn. enhance

The fine arts *enrich* our lives.

The discovery of oil was an *enrichment* for the country.

intensify *v.* to make stronger in feeling or quality

n. intensity
adj. intense
adj. intensive
adv. intensely
adv. intensively

syn. heighten

The importance of the test will sometimes *intensify* the nervousness of the students.

The chess match was played with great *intensity.*

intolerable *adj.* difficult or painful to experience; not able to accept different ways of thought or behavior

n. intolerance
adv. intolerably
adv. intolerantly
adj. intolerant

syn. unbearable

Any opposition to the rules is *intolerable.*

His boss was *intolerant* of his tardiness.

ongoing *adj.* continuing

syn. current

The tutoring project is an *ongoing* program of the school.

Maintaining roads is an *ongoing* job.

potential *n.* an ability, happening, or opportunity that has not occurred or been developed

adj. potential
adv. potentially

syn. possibility

The medical students have shown great *potential* to become doctors.

Small space heaters are a *potential* fire hazard.

propose *v.* to suggest or plan to do something

n. proposal
n. proposition
adj. proposed

syn. suggest

The governor is going to *propose* new taxes.

Her *proposal* was well accepted.

restore *v.* to give back or bring back something; to return to the original condition

n. restoration
adj. restored

syn. revitalize

He *restored* my confidence in him.

It is a beautiful *restoration* of the old table.

turbulent *adj.* to be in a disordered, disturbed, or unstable condition

n. turbulence
adv. turbulently

syn. chaotic

The plane flew through an area of *turbulence.*

The *turbulent* crowd insisted on a meeting with the prime minister.

vital *adj.* of great importance; full of life

n. vitality *syn.* indispensable
adv. vitally

Money is *vital* to the success of the program.

His intense *vitality* was easily observable.

MATCHING

Choose the synonym.

1. indispensable
   Ⓐ abrupt
   Ⓑ abroad
   Ⓒ vital
   Ⓓ frail

2. restore
   Ⓐ appeal
   Ⓑ revitalize
   Ⓒ attract
   Ⓓ disrupt

3. conform
   Ⓐ annoy
   Ⓑ divide
   Ⓒ encourage
   Ⓓ adapt

4. turbulent
   Ⓐ chaotic
   Ⓑ intolerant
   Ⓒ annoying
   Ⓓ adverse

5. ascertain
   Ⓐ delay
   Ⓑ render
   Ⓒ determine
   Ⓓ assert

6. potential
   Ⓐ attraction
   Ⓑ possibility
   Ⓒ anticipation
   Ⓓ persistence

7. benign
   Ⓐ harmless
   Ⓑ weak
   Ⓒ essential
   Ⓓ minuscule

8. enrich
   Ⓐ alter
   Ⓑ dispense
   Ⓒ disrupt
   Ⓓ enhance

9. unbearable
   Ⓐ inspiring
   Ⓑ unfavorable
   Ⓒ intolerable
   Ⓓ ancient

10. proposal
    Ⓐ question
    Ⓑ attention
    Ⓒ benefit
    Ⓓ suggestion

LESSON 3—MULTIPLE-CHOICE TEST QUESTIONS

1. The point at which pain becomes **intolerable** is known as the pain perception threshold. Studies have found this point to be similar among different social and cultural groups. However, the pain tolerance threshold varies significantly among these groups. A stoical, unemotional response to pain may be seen as a sign of braveness in certain cultural or social environments. However, this behavior can also mask the seriousness of an injury to an examining physician.

   The word **intolerable** in the passage is closest in meaning to

   Ⓐ elusive
   Ⓑ altered
   Ⓒ intense
   Ⓓ unbearable

2. Nutritional additives are utilized to restore nutrients lost during production, to **enrich** certain foods in order to correct dietary deficiencies, or to add nutrients to food substitutes. Nowadays, vitamins are commonly added to many foods in order to increase their nutritional value. For example, vitamins A and D are added to dairy and cereal products, and several of the B vitamins are added to cereals.

   The word **enrich** in the passage is closest in meaning to

   Ⓐ alter
   Ⓑ enhance
   Ⓒ produce
   Ⓓ restore

3. In modern manufacturing production facilities that produce equipment sensitive to environmental contamination, a dust-free working area with strict temperature and humidity controls is of **vital** importance. Seamless plastic walls and ceilings, external lighting, a continuous flow of dust-free air, and daily cleaning are features of this "clean room." Workers wear special clothing, including head coverings. When entering this room, they pass through a "shower" to remove contaminants.

   The word **vital** in the passage is closest in meaning to

   Ⓐ indispensable
   Ⓑ lively
   Ⓒ extreme
   Ⓓ dubious

4. Human populations are classified in terms of genetically transmitted traits. For groups that have lived for generations in certain locations, research illustrates the long-term genetic effects of environmental factors such as climate and diet. **Ongoing** investigations track the history of evolution and its genetic changes and help to explain the origin of genetically determined diseases and their long-term influence.

   The word **ongoing** in the passage is closest in meaning to

   Ⓐ current
   Ⓑ thorough
   Ⓒ proposed
   Ⓓ temporary

5. In the 1890s, a rising generation of young antiorganization leaders came on the political scene. These leaders transformed the art and practice of politics in the United States, by exercising strong leadership and by bringing about institutional changes that helped **revitalize** political democracy. Most important was their achievement of economic and social objectives, such as legislation to prevent child labor, and accident insurance systems to provide compensation to injured workers.

   The word **revitalize** in the passage is closest in meaning to

   Ⓐ intensify
   Ⓑ establish
   Ⓒ reform
   Ⓓ restore

6. There are more than 100 types or species of chameleon. A member of the lizard family, the chameleon lives in countries as diverse as Madagascar, Spain, and Sri Lanka. It is thought to change color to **conform to** its surroundings, but that is rarely true. While changes do occur with changes in light or temperature, especially when the chameleon is frightened, its new color rarely matches its immediate surroundings.

   In stating that the chameleon's color **conforms to** its surroundings, the author means that it

   Ⓐ differs from the color of its setting.
   Ⓑ contrasts with its surroundings.
   Ⓒ clashes with the colors around it.
   Ⓓ looks the same as its environment.

7. Infrared light emission photographs are particularly helpful to astronomers. The composition and temperature of heavenly bodies can often be determined by **analysis** of photos taken with a camera that is sensitive to infrared light emissions. Using infrared detectors, astronomers can observe cooler celestial objects than they can with optical devices, since infrared radiation is less affected by interstellar dust than is light.

   The word **analysis** in the passage is closest in meaning to

   Ⓐ intensification
   Ⓑ examination
   Ⓒ dispersion
   Ⓓ production

8. Working environments in which loud noise is frequent can be harmful to the employee. Aside from simply being **annoying**, the most measurable physical effect of noise pollution is damage to hearing. This may be either temporary or permanent and may cause disruption of normal activities. In work areas where noise is a problem, care should be taken to protect the ears with earplugs.

   The word **annoying** in the passage is closest in meaning to

   Ⓐ difficult
   Ⓑ ongoing
   Ⓒ bothersome
   Ⓓ refined

9. The construction of shelter, found among the first stable human societies about 5,000 years ago, is considered to be among the most important of all **ancient** human activities. The systematic placement of groups of housing marked a momentous cultural transition toward the formation of towns. It generated new needs and resources and was accompanied by a significant increase in technological innovation.

   The word **ancient** in the passage is closest in meaning to

   Ⓐ old
   Ⓑ actual
   Ⓒ distinct
   Ⓓ dated

10. Seeking to take advantage of new economic trends of the late 1800s, Manitoba's leaders made important changes in economic policies. These changes, which **anticipated** new directions in economic development of the region, took advantage of the unique business attributes of the province. During the early 1900s, these policies gave the province an advantage over other prairie provinces.

    The word **anticipated** in the passage is closest in meaning to

    Ⓐ encouraged
    Ⓑ analyzed
    Ⓒ modified
    Ⓓ predicted

LESSON 4

- **ambiguous**
- **arbitrary**
- **assert**
- **astounding**
- **astute**
- **concur**
- **deceptively**
- **designate**
- **determined**
- **elicit**
- **embody**
- **instigate**
- **mundane**
- **petition**
- **relinquish**
- **resilient**
- **stagnant**

---

ambiguous *adj.* of unclear meaning; something that can be understood in more than one way

adv. ambiguously
n. ambiguity

syn. vague

The men received an *ambiguous* message from their boss.

Her letter was full of *ambiguities.*

arbitrary *adj.* an action or decision made with little thought, order, or reason

adv. arbitrarily
n. arbitrariness

syn. haphazard

Her choice of clothing seemed *arbitrary.*

The teacher *arbitrarily* decided to give the class a test.

assert *v.* to express or defend oneself strongly; to state positively

adv. assertively
n. assertiveness
n. assertion
adj. assertive

syn. declare

The government *asserted* its control over the banking system.

The company president is an *assertive* individual.

astounding *adj.* very surprising

v. astound
adv. astoundingly

syn. astonishing

The scientists made an *astounding* discovery.

The fans were *astounded* by their team's success.

astute — *adj.* very intelligent, smart, clever
syn. perceptive

adj. astutely
n. astuteness

He was an *astute* worker, finishing in half the time it took the others to finish.

They *astutely* determined that there would be no chance to finish on time.

concur — *v.* to have the same opinion or draw the same conclusion
syn. agree

n. concurrence

The director *concurred* with the conclusions of the committee's report.

Do you *concur* with the details of the business plan?

deceptively — *adv.* making something appear true or good when it is false or bad
syn. misleadingly

adj. deceptive
v. deceive
n. deception

The magician *deceptively* made the rabbit disappear.

Richard *deceived* Joe about the cost of the coat.

designate — *v.* to specify, name, or select to do a task; to indicate
syn. assign

n. designation
n. designator

The president *designated* the vice president to represent him at the meeting.

The *designated* driver drove every one home after the party.

determined — *adj.* strong in one's opinion, firm in conviction, to find out
syn. resolute

n. determination
v. determine

They were *determined* to go to graduate school.

The judge *determined* that the man was lying.

elicit *v.* to get the facts or draw out the truth
n. elicitation *syn.* extract

A lawyer will *elicit* all the facts necessary to prove her case.
Elicitation of the truth can be difficult at times.

embody *v.* to be a good example of a concept or idea
n. embodiment *syn.* exemplify

The constitution is an *embodiment* of American ideals.
Charlotte *embodies* all of the qualities of a good leader.

instigate *v.* to cause a conflict or argument
n. instigator *syn.* initiate
adj. instigative
adv. instigatively

No one knew who had *instigated* the demonstration.
Dissatisfaction with government policies *instigated* the revolution.

mundane *adj.* common or routine
adv. mundanely *syn.* ordinary
n. mundaneness
n. mundanity

The student's *mundane* summer job frustrated her.
His mother asked him to do all the *mundane* household chores.

petition *v.* to make a request
n. petition *syn.* appeal

Canada *petitioned* the United Nations to consider its case.
The student's *petition* was denied.

relinquish *v.* to give up control
n. relinquishment *syn.* abdicate

The troubled executive *relinquished* her control of the company.
The *relinquishment* of his claim to the building will allow the building to be sold.

resilient *adj.* strong enough to recover from difficulty or disease

adv. resiliently
n. resilience

syn. tenacious

She has a *resilient* personality and will soon feel better.
The doctor was surprised by his patient's *resilience.*

stagnant *adj.* not moving or developing

n. stagnation
v. stagnate

syn. still

The *stagnant* water was a perfect home for frogs.
Some say that television causes the mind to *stagnate.*

MATCHING

Choose the synonym.

1. appeal
   Ⓐ enrich
   Ⓑ assert
   Ⓒ petition
   Ⓓ restore

2. mundane
   Ⓐ celebrated
   Ⓑ ordinary
   Ⓒ astounding
   Ⓓ alterable

3. instigate
   Ⓐ initiate
   Ⓑ empower
   Ⓒ intensify
   Ⓓ restore

4. elicit
   Ⓐ declare
   Ⓑ withdraw
   Ⓒ conform
   Ⓓ extract

5. abdicate
   Ⓐ relinquish
   Ⓑ alter
   Ⓒ encourage
   Ⓓ heighten

6. misleadingly
   Ⓐ abruptly
   Ⓑ deceptively
   Ⓒ progressively
   Ⓓ truly

7. stagnant
   Ⓐ still
   Ⓑ flowing
   Ⓒ angry
   Ⓓ enormous

8. resilient
   Ⓐ bothersome
   Ⓑ vital
   Ⓒ unbearable
   Ⓓ tenacious

9. embody
   Ⓐ exemplify
   Ⓑ entice
   Ⓒ notice
   Ⓓ enrich

10. vague
    Ⓐ intolerable
    Ⓑ adverse
    Ⓒ beautiful
    Ⓓ ambiguous

LESSON 4—MULTIPLE-CHOICE TEST QUESTIONS

1. The creation and analysis of optical illusions involve mathematical and geometric principles, such as the proportionality between the areas of similar figures. Optical illusions and their effects are often created through careful physical attributes, such as a nonstandard use of perspective, distorted angles, **deceptive** shading, unusual juxtaposition, and color effects.

   The word **deceptive** in the passage is closest in meaning to

   Ⓐ elusive
   Ⓑ misleading
   Ⓒ altered
   Ⓓ ambiguous

2. The Seneca Falls Convention, held in 1848, started the woman's suffrage movement in the United States. A "Declaration of Sentiments," which called upon women to organize and to **petition** for their rights, was passed. However, one controversial resolution, calling for the right of women to vote, narrowly passed. The ridicule of that provision of the Declaration caused many backers of women's rights to withdraw their support later on.

   The word **petition** in the passage is closest in meaning to

   Ⓐ vote
   Ⓑ demand
   Ⓒ appeal
   Ⓓ persist

3. Space law is concerned with the proper uses of outer space. The most important treaty of space laws was the 1967 Outer Space Treaty. The participants who crafted the treaty concluded that the moon and all other celestial bodies were to be free for exploration and use by all nations. They also **concurred** that the use of weapons of mass destruction was to be forbidden in space.

   The word **concurred** in the passage is closest in meaning to

   Ⓐ assumed
   Ⓑ agreed
   Ⓒ anticipated
   Ⓓ observed

4. It is a common misconception that the U.S. Congress has the constitutional power to legislate nearly anything for the general welfare. The Constitution gives Congress many powers, but it does not give Congress the power to legislate freely for the general welfare. In many instances, Congress may try to cause the states to do something by means of offers of subsidies or grants, but it cannot compel them to accept the incentives. The lawmaking process can **become stagnant** if the states do not agree with the proposed legislation.

   The phrase **become stagnant** in the passage is closest in meaning to

   Ⓐ continue flowing
   Ⓑ stop progressing
   Ⓒ be cancelled
   Ⓓ create arguments

5. Due to the **astounding** progress of integrated-circuit technology, an enormous number of transistors can be placed onto a single integrated-circuit chip. The first commercially successful microprocessor chip had only 4,800 transistors, but by the beginning of the 2000s, the newest high-end chips had 7.2 billion.

   The word **astounding** in the passage is closest in meaning to

   Ⓐ astonishing
   Ⓑ rapid
   Ⓒ solid
   Ⓓ resilient

6. Deer populations have grown dramatically in the northeast United States in the last 20 years. Many residents are happy to have deer in their communities, but many others see them as a menace. Deer often wander into traffic, cause automobile accidents, trample lawns, eat flowers, and host insects that carry disease. Therefore, many residents are **determined to** restrict their movements, fence them out, or even eliminate them altogether.

   In stating that many people are **determined to** eliminate the deer, the author means that they

   Ⓐ want to decide what to do.
   Ⓑ support their increase.
   Ⓒ insist on reducing them.
   Ⓓ favor enlarging the herd.

7. The game of chess was not well organized until 1946, when the world chess governing body, FIDE, **asserted** its control over international play. At that time, national chess groups immediately welcomed the chance to join the new federation. However, FIDE's authority has not been universally recognized, and even today there is no general agreement as to the status of the world championship.

   The word **asserted** in the passage is closest in meaning to

   Ⓐ enhanced
   Ⓑ empowered
   Ⓒ permitted
   Ⓓ declared

8. Social anthropologists attempt to illustrate the social emergence and evolution of the human race and to determine differences between human social organization and that of other primates. Despite the fact that all classifications of human societies and cultures are **arbitrary**, they also attempt to note differences between various human societies. In spite of these difficulties, anthropologists have made great advances in the identification and grouping of human civilizations.

   The word **arbitrary** in the passage is closest in meaning to

   Ⓐ vague
   Ⓑ haphazard
   Ⓒ disputed
   Ⓓ elusive

9. The Monroe Doctrine allowed the United States to intervene in the affairs of Latin American countries in case of foreign invasion. Once the United States was **designated** to act on behalf of its neighbors to the south, episodes of foreign interference decreased until the 1960s, when Cuba wanted the support and economic aid of the former Union of Soviet Socialist Republics.

   The word **designated** in the passage is closest in meaning to

   Ⓐ authorized
   Ⓑ accustomed
   Ⓒ determined
   Ⓓ tempted

10. J. Edgar Hoover was an **astute** professional who served as Director of the FBI for 48 years. A resilient and determined government official, Hoover's tenure spanned one of the most important eras of modern U.S. history. His policies helped to shape and create what has now become a highly respected modern investigative organization.

    The word **astute** in the passage is closest in meaning to

    Ⓐ acclaimed
    Ⓑ celebrated
    Ⓒ perceptive
    Ⓓ eminent

LESSON 5

- **baffle**
- **bear**
- **blur**
- **brilliant**
- **caution**
- **enhance**
- **facilitate**
- **incessant**
- **in conjunction with**
- **intrigue**
- **obstruct**
- **persuade**
- **recompense**
- **shed**
- **unique**
- **well-suited**
- **work out**

---

baffle — *v.* to confuse to a point at which no progress can be made
adj. baffling
n. bafflement
syn. puzzle

The causes of many harmful diseases have *baffled* doctors for centuries.
That was a *baffling* question.

bear — *v.* to produce, to carry; to show; to endure
adv. bearably
adj. bearable
syn. yield

This orchard *bears* many fine harvests of apples.
Although stock prices declined, losses have been *bearable* for most investors.

blur — *v.* to make something difficult to see
adj. blurred
n. blur
syn. cloud

The rain *blurred* everyone's view of the valley.
The whole accident is just a *blur* in my mind.

brilliant — *adj.* intensely bright or colorful; intelligent
adv. brilliantly
n. brilliance
syn. radiant

Einstein was a *brilliant* thinker.
She *brilliantly* produced a solution to the problem.

caution — *v.* to alert someone of danger, warn someone to take care or pay attention to something

adj. cautious
adj. cautionary
adv. cautiously
n. caution

syn. warn

The officer *cautioned* the motorist to slow down.
They entered into the negotiations *cautiously*.

enhance — *v.* to increase in a positive way, such as in value, power, or beauty

n. enhancement
adj. enhanced

syn. strengthen

Passing the exam should *enhance* your chances of being admitted to college.
The computer *enhanced* our productivity.

facilitate — *v.* to make easier; to ease the progress of

adv. facilitative

syn. assist

His careful planning *facilitated* the completion of the project.
Good teaching strategies *facilitate* student learning.

incessant — *adj.* nonstop, continual, or never-ending

adv. incessantly

syn. constant

The woman's *incessant* talking disturbed everyone watching the movie.
The dogs' *incessant* barking kept the whole neighborhood up all night.

in conjunction with — *prep. ph.* in addition to, alongside

syn. along with

Exercise, *in conjunction with* a nourishing diet, contributes to a healthy lifestyle.
The architects planned the building *in conjunction with* the engineers.

intrigue — *v.* to interest greatly

adj. intriguing
adv. intriguingly
n. intrigue

syn. fascinate

He was *intrigued* by the acclaim that he received.
The *intriguing* question baffled historians.

obstruct *v.* to prevent movement, progress, or success

n. obstruction
adj. obstructive
adv. obstructively

syn. block

Just after the storm, downed trees *obstructed* many roads in the community.

A huge building *obstructed* the ocean view from the apartment.

persuade *v.* to change a belief or behavior by argument or reason

adv. persuasively
adj. persuasive
n. persuasion

syn. convince

They couldn't *persuade* their critics to see their point of view.

John presented a *persuasive* argument for his salary increase.

recompense *n.* a repayment or reward for a deed

adv. recompensable
v. recompense

syn. compensation

The knight received gold as *recompense* for saving the kingdom.

His boss assured him that he'd be *recompensed* for his extra efforts.

shed *v.* to throw off naturally; to give out

syn. discard

In order to grow, crabs must *shed* their shells.

The experiments *shed* no new information on the cause of the disease.

unique *adj.* to be the only one of a kind; special

adv. uniquely
n. uniqueness

syn. rare

He was presented with a *unique* opportunity to attend the conference.

His style of writing is *uniquely* his own.

well-suited *adj.* to be complementary or appropriate; a good match

syn. compatible

The design of the house is *well-suited* to its surroundings.

The experienced principal was *well-suited* for the job of superintendent of schools.

work out *v.* to end or cause to end successfully; to develop
syn. solve

Their ambitious plan will likely *work out.*
The two groups *worked out* a compromise that benefited them both.

MATCHING

Choose the synonym.

1. incessant
   Ⓐ unique
   Ⓑ constant
   Ⓒ blocked
   Ⓓ baffled

2. obstruct
   Ⓐ warn
   Ⓑ tempt
   Ⓒ enhance
   Ⓓ block

3. intrigue
   Ⓐ fascinate
   Ⓑ elicit
   Ⓒ intensify
   Ⓓ enrich

4. well-suited to
   Ⓐ unique to
   Ⓑ compatible with
   Ⓒ enhanced with
   Ⓓ dedicated to

5. work out
   Ⓐ finalize
   Ⓑ compensate
   Ⓒ solve
   Ⓓ oppose

6. convince
   Ⓐ assert
   Ⓑ persuade
   Ⓒ restore
   Ⓓ yield

7. rare
   Ⓐ determined
   Ⓑ warned
   Ⓒ vague
   Ⓓ unique

8. facilitate
   Ⓐ assist
   Ⓑ refine
   Ⓒ alter
   Ⓓ discard

9. enhance
   Ⓐ entice
   Ⓑ strengthen
   Ⓒ relinquish
   Ⓓ encourage

10. puzzled
   Ⓐ valid
   Ⓑ assertive
   Ⓒ baffled
   Ⓓ astute

LESSON 5—MULTIPLE-CHOICE TEST QUESTIONS

1. A newborn chick uses its egg tooth to break the shell of its egg and escape from it at hatching. This toothlike structure is then **shed** since its only use is to help the bird break the eggshell. Some animals, such as lizards and snakes, develop a true tooth that projects outside the row of other teeth. This tooth helps adults hatch their young.

   The word **shed** in the passage is closest in meaning to

   Ⓐ guarded
   Ⓑ preserved
   Ⓒ discarded
   Ⓓ enhanced

2. Imitation gems are usually made of glass or plastics. In recent years, an enormous array of plastics has become available for imitations, but these materials are soft and lack the clarity present in real gemstones. Therefore, they are less satisfactory for the purpose than glass. Flint glasses, containing lead oxide, have higher refractive indices and therefore possess a **brilliance** not found in plastics. This makes flint glasses more suitable than plastic for imitation gems.

   The word **brilliance** in the passage is closest in meaning to

   Ⓐ radiance
   Ⓑ lightness
   Ⓒ enhancement
   Ⓓ appeal

3. During a shower, meteors appear to spread from a point in the sky, called the radiant. These radiant points give each shower its name. For example, the Perseids shower appears to radiate from the constellation Perseus. During the heaviest showers, 30 to 70 meteors may be seen every hour, but on **unique** occasions in a spectacular display, that number may be visible every second.

   The word **unique** in the passage is closest in meaning to

   Ⓐ intriguing
   Ⓑ amazing
   Ⓒ celebrated
   Ⓓ rare

4. Sometimes, advertisers impact society by the use of advocacy ads, whose purpose is not to **persuade** the public to buy a product, but to change the public's view about a specific issue. Companies use this advertising to influence public opinion. Critics say that such ads are unfairly one-sided; advertisers say that the mass media have been equally one-sided in failing to report company views.

   The word **persuade** in the passage is closest in meaning to

   Ⓐ convince
   Ⓑ dissuade
   Ⓒ solicit
   Ⓓ encourage

5. In the mid-1800s, gold and silver were common components of dentures. As a result, they were very expensive. However, in 1851, a process to harden the juices of certain tropical plants into rubber was discovered. This new product could be molded to a model of a patient's mouth and artificial teeth could be made. As a result, when used **in conjunction with** new manufacturing methods, these molds caused the cost of dentures to fall dramatically.

   The phrase **in conjunction with** in the passage is closest in meaning to

   Ⓐ along with
   Ⓑ under
   Ⓒ throughout
   Ⓓ within limits of

6. The issue of where human life first arose has always been an **intriguing question** for science. Many guesses, or hypotheses, have been advanced, ranging from Asia to Europe. However, the oldest known human bones, or fossils, were discovered in East Africa in 1972. They are nearly 2 million years old. Their age was determined by measuring the age of the rocks surrounding them and comparing them to other fossils.

   In stating that the origin of human life is an **intriguing question**, the author means that it

   Ⓐ interests a lot of scientists.
   Ⓑ can never be answered.
   Ⓒ receives too much attention.
   Ⓓ will always be a mystery.

7. The Sioux and Cheyenne peoples told outsiders not to look for gold on Indian land. Eventually, the Sioux and Cheyenne had to defend their land against a U.S. army force in the Battle of Little Bighorn. This battle, also known as "Custer's Last Stand," was led by General George Custer. Custer was **cautioned** by his advisors not to underestimate the strength of his opponent, but ignored their advice, resulting in the defeat of the U.S. force.

   The word **cautioned** in the passage is closest in meaning to

   Ⓐ warned
   Ⓑ discarded
   Ⓒ advised
   Ⓓ convinced

8. Clothing and adornments used among certain cultures often reflect the social status of an individual. Body painting and tattooing are common methods used to distinguish social status. Other methods include the use of lip, ear, and nose rings, in addition to bracelets, arm bands, necklaces, and head ornaments made of delicate, colorful feathers. It is common for groups of people to use the natural resources around them to **work out** a way of visually designating social rank.

   The verb **work out** in the passage is closest in meaning to

   Ⓐ restore
   Ⓑ discard
   Ⓒ argue
   Ⓓ develop

9. Species of alyssum are particularly suitable as edging plants for flower gardens. Alyssum is generally grayish with yellow or white flowers. One popular species is sweet alyssum, a perennial that grows up to nine inches tall. The narrow, green-gray leaf of the sweet alyssum usually **bears** many silvery hairs.

   The word **bears** in the passage is closest in meaning to

   Ⓐ produces
   Ⓑ elicits
   Ⓒ attracts
   Ⓓ inspires

10. In ancient times, the labyrinth was a structure composed of a complex series of passageways and chambers, probably at first designed to **baffle** enemies. A labyrinth either had branched paths with misleading ends, or it contained one long meandering path that led to a central end.

    The word **baffle** in the passage is closest in meaning to

    Ⓐ obstruct
    Ⓑ puzzle
    Ⓒ discard
    Ⓓ astound

LESSON 6

- **chiefly**
- **coarse**
- **commonplace**
- **complex**
- **conventional**
- **curious**
- **emit**
- **exceedingly**
- **exclusively**
- **extinguish**
- **immense**
- **instantaneous**
- **rigid**
- **routinely**
- **stamina**
- **sufficiently**
- **visibly**

---

chiefly *adv.* the most important or most common
adj. chief *syn.* mostly

Houses are made *chiefly* of wood products.
Corn is the *chief* crop of the Midwest.

coarse *adj.* not fine or smooth; not delicate
adv. coarsely *syn.* rough
n. coarseness

Sandpaper is an extremely *coarse* material.
Wool clothing has a certain *coarseness* in texture.

commonplace *adj.* ordinary
syn. frequent

In some parts of the world, text messaging is more *commonplace* than voice calling.
Female lawyers are *commonplace* in the United States.

complex *adj.* difficult to understand or explain; having many parts
n. complexity *syn.* complicated

The businessmen astutely approached the *complex* production problem.
The universe has a *complexity* beyond comprehension.

conventional *adj.* following accepted rules or standards

adv. conventionally
n. convention

syn. traditional

Professor Canfield agreed with the *conventional* theory about the origin of the Basque language.

To become integrated into a society, you must learn the *conventions* of that society.

curious *adj.* odd or strange; eager to learn

adv. curiously
n. curiosity

syn. peculiar

A *curious* object was discovered in the remains.

Sally was *curiously* interested in the history of Alaska.

emit *v.* to send out; give off

n. emission
n. emitter

syn. release

The raging forest fire *emitted* a dense, white smoke.

Modern telescopes can detect the faintest light *emitted* by distant stars.

exceedingly *adv.* very; to an unusual degree

v. exceed
n. excess
adj. excessive
adv. excessively

syn. extremely

In tropical zones, it is *exceedingly* hot and humid.

It is not safe to *exceed* the speed limit.

exclusively *adv.* no one else; nothing else; not shared with others

adj. exclusive
n. exclusion
v. exclude

syn. restrictively

This room is used *exclusively* by the faculty.

They *excluded* everyone under 21 from the contest.

extinguish *v.* to bring about the end of something

adj. extinguishable *syn.* terminate
n. extinguishment

The firefighters quickly *extinguished* the flames.
Modern medicine has *extinguished* many previously serious illnesses.

immense *adj.* extremely large

adv. immensely *syn.* massive
n. immensity

From the mountaintop you can see the *immense* valley.
She was *immensely* interested in the idea of teaching a foreign language.

instantaneous *adj.* occurring in an instant

adv. instantly *syn.* immediate
n. instant

A lightbulb turns on nearly *instantaneously* when you flip the switch.
The teacher was *instantly* met with complaints when he announced the test.

rigid *adj.* not easy to bend; firm; inflexible

adv. rigidly *syn.* stiff

The teacher was very *rigid* in his ideas about class attendance.
He adhered *rigidly* to his opinions about economic growth.

routinely *adv.* regularly; usually done

adj. routine *syn.* ordinarily
n. routine

She *routinely* gets a physical examination.
It is *routine* for students to become homesick at times.

stamina *n.* lasting physical or mental strength

syn. endurance

The Olympic runner demonstrated incredible *stamina.*
The horse lacked the *stamina* to win the race.

sufficiently *adv.* enough; in a satisfying manner

n. sufficiency
adj. sufficient
v. suffice

syn. adequately

Jenny is *sufficiently* mature to make her own decisions.

Her income is *sufficient* for her needs.

visibly *adv.* can be seen

adj. visible
n. vision*
v. view
adj. visionary*

*power of imagination or wisdom, especially with regard to the future

syn. noticeably

Ken was *visibly* upset about his performance evaluation.

Stars are more *visible* on a clear fall evening.

MATCHING

Choose the synonym.

1. instantaneous
   - Ⓐ angry
   - Ⓑ interesting
   - Ⓒ immediate
   - Ⓓ gigantic

2. traditional
   - Ⓐ arbitrary
   - Ⓑ astounding
   - Ⓒ conventional
   - Ⓓ frequent

3. extinguish
   - Ⓐ terminate
   - Ⓑ discard
   - Ⓒ emit
   - Ⓓ deceive

4. curious
   - Ⓐ annoying
   - Ⓑ brilliant
   - Ⓒ peculiar
   - Ⓓ enhanced

5. adequately
   - Ⓐ sufficiently
   - Ⓑ deceptively
   - Ⓒ intensely
   - Ⓓ amazingly

6. immense
   - Ⓐ abrupt
   - Ⓑ massive
   - Ⓒ ongoing
   - Ⓓ complicated

7. exceedingly
   - Ⓐ resiliently
   - Ⓑ extremely
   - Ⓒ assertively
   - Ⓓ resolutely

8. visibly
   - Ⓐ noticeably
   - Ⓑ frequently
   - Ⓒ persuasively
   - Ⓓ encouragingly

9. stamina
   - Ⓐ courage
   - Ⓑ indulgence
   - Ⓒ weakness
   - Ⓓ endurance

10. restrictively
    - Ⓐ exclusively
    - Ⓑ adversely
    - Ⓒ roughly
    - Ⓓ relatively

LESSON 6—MULTIPLE-CHOICE TEST QUESTIONS

1. North American trade patterns offer remarkable contrasts. Canada has a small population but with vast resources and high productivity. It has a low home consumption and depends on foreign trade more than any other developed country on the North American continent. The United States, on the other hand, has an **immense** domestic market and the highest per capita consumption of goods in the world. It depends mainly on trade within its national borders.

   The word **immense** in the passage is closest in meaning to

   Ⓐ massive
   Ⓑ successful
   Ⓒ prominent
   Ⓓ significant

2. By the end of the 20th century, computers had greatly influenced the way in which we produced and printed documents. Letters and reports could be easily prepared on personal computers, because the user could see on the monitor what the text would look like when printed. The task of writing was made even easier with the advent of more advanced word processing programs that checked spelling and grammar before printing. A wide range of fonts became available to the public, and their number was far greater than that of **conventional** printing processes. Thanks to progress in laser printing technology, the quality of text printed by laser printer soon surpassed that of commercially typeset material.

   The word **conventional** in the passage is closest in meaning to

   Ⓐ restricted
   Ⓑ available
   Ⓒ traditional
   Ⓓ competing

3. Contour mapping is the process by which a map is formed by constructing lines of equal values of that property from available data points. For example, a topographic map reveals the relief of an area by means of contour lines that represent elevation. In addition to topography, there are examples of geophysical, geochemical, meteorological, sociological, and other variables that are **routinely** mapped by the method. The availability of plotting devices has permitted mapping by computer, which reduces the effect of human bias on the final product.

   The word **routinely** in the passage is closest in meaning to

   Ⓐ ordinarily
   Ⓑ effectively
   Ⓒ sluggishly
   Ⓓ efficiently

4. Motion-picture technology is a **curious** blend of the old and the new. In much of the equipment, state-of-the-art digital electronics may be working with a mechanical system invented in 1895. Moreover, the technology of motion pictures is based not only on the invention of still photography but also on a combination of several more or less independent technologies: camera and projector design, film manufacture and processing, sound recording and reproduction, and lighting and light measurement.

   The word **curious** in the passage is closest in meaning to

   Ⓐ productive
   Ⓑ peculiar
   Ⓒ coveted
   Ⓓ appealing

5. The durable surfacing of a road, airstrip, or similar area is known as a pavement. Its primary function is to transmit loads to the sub-base and underlying soil. Modern flexible pavements contain sand and gravel or crushed stone. These are compacted with a binder of bituminous material, such as asphalt or tar. Such a pavement demonstrates enough plasticity to absorb shocks. **Rigid** pavements are made of concrete, composed of coarse and fine aggregate and portland cement, and usually reinforced with steel rod or mesh.

   The word **rigid** in the passage is closest in meaning to

   Ⓐ strong
   Ⓑ stiff
   Ⓒ pliable
   Ⓓ complex

6. The Internet is a source of accessible entertainment, but research indicates that constant Internet use may cause a person's attention span to shorten. Some experts estimate that the habitual user's span can drop to as little as that of a goldfish, roughly nine seconds. Many blame this effect on the **instantaneous** nature of Internet content. Of course, attention depends as much on content as delivery. It is comparatively easy to switch off some images, but comparatively hard to abandon others. For example, computer games usually hold a user's attention longer than advertising.

   In stating that Internet entertainment is **instantaneous**, the author means that it is

   Ⓐ constantly being viewed
   Ⓑ available without delay
   Ⓒ difficult to find
   Ⓓ of low quality

7. Water is a powerful solvent that acts as a catalyst for many reactions. It also stores heat and cold well. In terms of its composition, water has an unusually high boiling and freezing point. It also shows unusual volume changes with temperature. Water is easily the most **complex** of all common substances that are single chemical compounds.

   The word **complex** in the passage is closest in meaning to

   Ⓐ renown
   Ⓑ peculiar
   Ⓒ nimble
   Ⓓ intricate

8. Over several decades, scientists and engineers have confronted the issue of pollutants **emitted** by motor vehicles. Some of the waste products of the combustion process include carbon dioxide, nitrogen gas, and water vapor. Though these by-products are not really harmful, many scientists theorize that carbon dioxide may contribute to the problem of global warming. However, the combustion process also produces carbon monoxide, nitrogen oxides, and hydrocarbons, all of which are known threats to human health. Due to government regulations that set emission standards, motor vehicle companies have significantly reduced the amount of harmful gases that are discharged by installing catalytic converters in vehicles.

   The word **emitted** in the passage is closest in meaning to

   Ⓐ released
   Ⓑ created
   Ⓒ converted
   Ⓓ maintained

9. The cotton gin, invented by Eli Whitney, was **commonplace** on many nineteenth-century farms. Although patented in 1794, the ingenious design was imitated so much by others that Whitney gained only a modest financial reward from his simple invention. The cotton gin soon revolutionized farming in many parts of the South.

   The word **commonplace** in the passage is closest in meaning to

   Ⓐ noticeable
   Ⓑ standard
   Ⓒ celebrated
   Ⓓ refined

10. The delicate look and feel of silk are deceptive. It is a strong, natural fiber, ranked in strength with synthetic nylon. To the naked eye, it appears to be smooth, but under the microscope, cultivated silk fiber looks **coarse**. It is the coolest of hot-weather fabrics, and it can absorb up to 30 percent of its weight in moisture without feeling wet.

    The word **coarse** in the passage is closest in meaning to

    Ⓐ stiff
    Ⓑ strong
    Ⓒ rough
    Ⓓ refined

LESSON 7

- **brash**
- **clarify**
- **conceal**
- **confirm**
- **convenient**
- **core**
- **critical**
- **discrepancy**
- **distort**
- **diverse**
- **eventually**
- **prosperous**
- **purposefully**
- **reveal**
- **scarcely**
- **simultaneous**
- **theoretically**

---

brash *adj.* confident or aggressive; lacking regard for consequences

adv. brashly
n. brashness

syn. reckless

The *brash* young man made many poor business decisions.
Lucy's *brashness* often got her into trouble at school.

clarify *v.* to make more easily understood; to make clear

n. clarification

syn. explain

Chapter 2 in the textbook *clarifies* the process of osmosis.
A *clarification* of the government's position on this matter is necessary.

conceal *v.* to prevent from being seen or discovered

n. concealment

syn. hide

The students *concealed* their feelings about the course.
His *concealment* of the evidence made his case more difficult to prove.

confirm *v.* to make certain; give support

adj. confirmed
n. confirmation

syn. prove

The director *confirmed* that the meeting would be on the tenth.
We have just received *confirmation* of your reservation on the flight to Los Angeles.

convenient *adj.* easy to reach; near; suitable to one's needs

adv. conveniently
n. convenience

syn. practical

The investigator suspected that the disappearance of the evidence was too *convenient* to be accidental.

For the *convenience* of the student body, the library is located in a central location.

core *adj.* the central or most important part of something

n. core

syn. chief

The *core* curriculum consists of courses that are required of all students.

The *core* of an apple is not edible.

critical *adj.* very serious or unsafe; finding fault

v. critique
n. criticism
n. critic
adv. critically

syn. dangerous

It is *critical* to follow the directions for the experiment exactly as the instructor indicates.

The runner accepted *criticism* from his coach very well.

discrepancy *n.* a difference between things that should be similar or equal

syn. inconsistency

The *discrepancy* in her experiment data led her to believe that she had made a mistake.

There is usually a *discrepancy* between how coffee smells and how it tastes.

distort *v.* to change from the original shape or condition, usually in an unnatural way

adj. distorted
n. distortion

syn. deform

Time and space are *distorted* when traveling at the speed of light.

Distortion of the image from a microscope can be caused by low light.

diverse *adj.* various; distinct from others

adv. diversely
n. diversity
v. diversify

syn. different

Freud had many *diverse* interests in psychology.

The *diversity* of life forms on the earth makes zoology an interesting area of study.

eventually *adv.* to happen at some time in the future, usually gradually

syn. finally

A good education will *eventually* pay big dividends.

Eventually the couple will pay off their mortgage and own their house.

prosperous *adj.* successful, wealthy

adv. prosperously
v. prosper
n. prosperity

syn. thriving

In the early 1900s, San Francisco was a *prosperous* city.

Bacteria *prosper* under the proper conditions.

purposefully *adv.* done for a special reason

adj. purposeful
adv. purposely
n. purpose

syn. deliberately

The course syllabus was designed *purposefully* to be easy to follow.

He was authorized to spend the money for business *purposes*.

reveal *v.* to uncover; to expose

adv. revealingly
adj. revealing
n. revelation

syn. disclose

The president *revealed* some of his ideas before he gave his speech.

The report made some *revelations* about the nature of the conflict.

scarcely *adv.* almost not

adj. scarce
n. scarcity

syn. hardly

The woman *scarcely* spoke a word of English.

Due to a *scarcity* of water, a rationing plan was established.

simultaneous *adj.* occurring at the same time

adv. simultaneously *syn.* concurrent

The boys *simultaneously* screamed, "Ice cream!"

This student is skilled at performing many tasks *simultaneously*.

theoretically *adv.* according to a reasoned, but not proven, point of view

adj. theoretical
n. theory
v. theorize

syn. hypothetically

His argument was *theoretically* appealing, but not realistic.

Leonardo da Vinci *theorized* that Earth was not the center of the universe.

MATCHING

Choose the synonym.

1. deform
   - Ⓐ hide
   - Ⓑ distort
   - Ⓒ concur
   - Ⓓ block

2. simultaneous
   - Ⓐ instant
   - Ⓑ permanent
   - Ⓒ coincidental
   - Ⓓ concurrent

3. eventually
   - Ⓐ finally
   - Ⓑ soon
   - Ⓒ once
   - Ⓓ consequently

4. clarify
   - Ⓐ shed
   - Ⓑ enhance
   - Ⓒ explain
   - Ⓓ elicit

5. brash
   - Ⓐ distorted
   - Ⓑ thoughtful
   - Ⓒ reckless
   - Ⓓ deceptive

6. thriving
   - Ⓐ prosperous
   - Ⓑ resilient
   - Ⓒ convenient
   - Ⓓ tolerable

7. inconsistency
   - Ⓐ critique
   - Ⓑ discrepancy
   - Ⓒ deliberation
   - Ⓓ sufficiently

8. different
   - Ⓐ noticeable
   - Ⓑ diverse
   - Ⓒ conventional
   - Ⓓ curious

9. hypothetically
   - Ⓐ exceedingly
   - Ⓑ haphazardly
   - Ⓒ theoretically
   - Ⓓ routinely

10. reveal
    - Ⓐ disclose
    - Ⓑ baffle
    - Ⓒ conceal
    - Ⓓ confirm

LESSON 7—MULTIPLE-CHOICE TEST QUESTIONS

1. The geologic history of Earth **reveals** much information about the evolution of the continents, oceans, atmosphere, and biosphere. The layers of rock at Earth's surface contain evidence of the evolutionary processes these components underwent when each layer was formed. By studying this rock record from the beginning, it is possible to track their development through time.

   The word **reveals** in the passage is closest in meaning to

   Ⓐ teaches
   Ⓑ discloses
   Ⓒ traces
   Ⓓ donates

2. Day-to-day weather constitutes a major element of the environment and an important factor in human well-being and activity. Agriculture, animal husbandry, transportation, and public health and safety are all greatly influenced by weather. It is not surprising that one of humanity's oldest environment-related interests has been to manage the weather **purposefully**.

   The word **purposefully** in the passage is closest in meaning to

   Ⓐ prosperously
   Ⓑ eventually
   Ⓒ exceedingly
   Ⓓ deliberately

3. Illumination plays a great role in our psychological and physical well-being. Light can model objects or flatten them, reveal colors or **distort** them, provide a cheerful environment or a gloomy one. Glare and reflected glare can cause discomfort and reduce visibility. In addition to calculating illumination, a lighting engineer must deal with all of these problems through the choice of light sources and fixtures.

   The word **distort** in the passage is closest in meaning to

   Ⓐ hide
   Ⓑ accentuate
   Ⓒ deform
   Ⓓ highlight

4. The different appearance of animals is chiefly superficial; the **diverse** variety of known forms can be assorted among only a half-dozen basic body plans. These plans are established during the embryonic stages of development and limit the size and complexity of the animals. Symmetry, number, and development of tissue, presence, and nature of body cavities, and several aspects of early development define these fundamental plans of organization.

   The word **diverse** in the passage is closest in meaning to

   Ⓐ recognized
   Ⓑ acknowledged
   Ⓒ different
   Ⓓ critical

5. When the settlers of the western United States abandoned their original log cabins, sod houses, and dugouts, they built small, wood-framed dwellings of one or two rooms without a basement. Rooms were usually added as **prosperous** families grew larger. This usually resulted in a series of large, open rooms laid end to end so that each would have an equal amount of sunlight.

   The word **prosperous** in the passage is closest in meaning to

   Ⓐ numerous
   Ⓑ thriving
   Ⓒ prominent
   Ⓓ courageous

6. The medical profession is sometimes accused of being more interested in itself than the quality of care it delivers. Many patients feel they don't get the attention they deserve; many see the profession as selfish **to its core**. Doctors rarely agree, as a recent survey comparing their attitudes and that of the public shows. Seventy percent of the public were disappointed in the quality of care; only 35 percent of the doctors agreed.

   In stating that the medical profession is selfish **to its core**, the author means that it

   Ⓐ is entirely interested only in itself.
   Ⓑ contains a group of bad doctors.
   Ⓒ has wide support among patients.
   Ⓓ includes good and bad physicians.

7. Industrial cities appeared after the full development of industrial capitalism in the core nation-states of the eighteenth century. As a result, one of the dramatic features of the industrial revolution **eventually** developed, a remarkable increase in production. This increase was made possible by the improved methods of manufacturing that were adopted by factories.

   The word **eventually** in the passage is closest in meaning to

   Ⓐ quickly
   Ⓑ carefully
   Ⓒ instantaneously
   Ⓓ gradually

8. The earliest complete calendars were probably based on lunar observations. But lunar years were not **convenient** for agricultural purposes. Therefore, to keep in step with the Sun, lunar-solar calendars were formed by adding an additional "leap" month when the observation of crops made it seem necessary. Eventually the Gregorian civil calendar, a solar calendar that is calculated without reference to the Moon, became the most popular method of measuring years.

   The word **convenient** in the passage is closest in meaning to

   Ⓐ useful
   Ⓑ ideal
   Ⓒ proper
   Ⓓ practical

9. Mollusks have existed for some 500 million years, and about 10,000 extinct species are known. There are 350 or more living species of cephalopods from the Mollusk family. One of these is the cuttlefish. Fossil evidence **confirms** that the ancient cuttlefish has existed in its present form for more than 20 million years. When we compare the modern-day cuttlefish to the ancient fossils, we see evidence that the well-developed head, the many arms, two gills, two kidneys, and three hearts of the contemporary cuttlefish were also present in the cuttlefish of long ago.

   The word **confirms** in the passage is closest in meaning to

   Ⓐ discloses
   Ⓑ asserts
   Ⓒ proves
   Ⓓ reveals

10. The first swimsuits **concealed** the shape of the human body. Over the decades, attitudes relaxed regarding the public display of one's body shape. Designers could move away from conservative styles and promote those that revealed a body's physical attributes.

    The word **concealed** in the passage is closest in meaning to

    Ⓐ hid
    Ⓑ distorted
    Ⓒ enhanced
    Ⓓ disrupted

Lesson 8

- **accelerate**
- **crush**
- **cultivate**
- **derive**
- **dictate**
- **distinguish**
- **docile**
- **engender**
- **engross**
- **flaw**
- **harvest**
- **mammoth**
- **mirror**
- **negotiate**
- **obtain**
- **particle**
- **transport**

---

accelerate — *v.* to go faster

syn. hasten

n. acceleration
n. accelerator

The action of molecules *accelerates* when they are heated.

The poor condition of the motor made *acceleration* difficult.

crush — *v.* to press together so as to completely distort the shape or nature of the object

syn. grind

adj. crushing
n. crush

The machine *crushes* corn to produce cornmeal.

Passage of the legislation was a *crushing* blow to the president's program.

cultivate — *v.* to plant and raise a crop; to encourage growth of a relationship or friendship

syn. grow

adj. cultivated
n. cultivation

The professionals had common interests that allowed them to *cultivate* a working relationship with each other.

The *cultivation* of diverse crops in pre-Columbian America is well documented.

derive — *v.* to come from or find something from its starting point

syn. obtain

The English word "decadent" is *derived* from the Latin word "decadere."

He *derives* great joy from growing vegetables in his backyard.

dictate *v.* to state demands with the power to enforce

adj. dictatorial *syn.* impose
n. dictator

The workers were not in a position to *dictate* demands to management.

His boss resembled a *dictator*.

distinguish *v.* to hear, see, or recognize differences

adj. distinguishable *syn.* discriminate
adj. distinguished
adj. distinguishing

Some people cannot *distinguish* colors well.

Anteaters are *distinguished* by their long noses.

docile *adj.* easy to control or train

adv. docilely *syn.* manageable
n. docility

The moose is typically a very *docile* animal.

Many rebellious young people see *docility* as a weakness.

engender *v.* to cause something new to exist; to create

syn. produce

The politician's charisma *engendered* enthusiasm.

Economic conditions in the 1950s *engendered* an era of industrial growth.

engross *v.* to become completely occupied or involved in an activity

n. engrossment
adj. engrossing *syn.* engage

The teacher's lecture *engrossed* the entire class.

O. Henry's short stories *engross* readers all the way to their surprise endings.

flaw — *n.* a small sign of damage that makes an item imperfect
adj. flawed
syn. defect

There is a *flaw* in his theory.
They noticed that the contract was *flawed.*

harvest — *n.* the act of collecting a crop; the crops gathered
adj. harvested
v. harvest
syn. gather

The United States had a comparatively good grain *harvest* this year.
They were able to *harvest* the crop before the rain.

mammoth — *adj.* very large
n. mammoth
syn. enormous

The successful entrepreneur is now known as a *mammoth* in the computer world.
The physics teacher required the students to purchase a *mammoth* textbook.

mirror — *v.* to show, as in a mirror
n. mirror
syn. reflect

The results of the study *mirror* public opinion.
The strength of the economy is *mirrored* in the standard of living of the people.

negotiate — *v.* to find a middle ground, come to an agreement
n. negotiation
n. negotiator
syn. bargain

He *negotiated* with his teacher for an extension on the project.
The *negotiations* brought about an end to the conflict.

obtain — *v.* to gain or secure something
adj. obtainable
syn. gain

The university *obtained* a new particle accelerator.
The painting by Whistler was not *obtainable.*

particle *n.* a very small piece of something
syn. fragment

Particles of dust can destroy electronic instruments.

Small *particles* of matter hold the keys to understanding the origin of life.

transport *v.* to move from one place to another
syn. carry

adj. transportable
adj. transported
n. transportation

Flying is not always the fastest way to *transport* passengers to their destination.

The *transportation* expenses of products increase the final cost of the item.

MATCHING

Choose the synonym.

1. flaw
   Ⓐ particle
   Ⓑ agile
   Ⓒ defect
   Ⓓ creation

2. dictate
   Ⓐ transport
   Ⓑ engender
   Ⓒ grow
   Ⓓ impose

3. hasten
   Ⓐ crawl
   Ⓑ crush
   Ⓒ conceal
   Ⓓ accelerate

4. crop
   Ⓐ harvest
   Ⓑ advice
   Ⓒ mirror
   Ⓓ settlement

5. fragment
   Ⓐ authorization
   Ⓑ particle
   Ⓒ cultivation
   Ⓓ advantage

6. mammoth
   Ⓐ assertive
   Ⓑ enormous
   Ⓒ chronic
   Ⓓ minuscule

7. manageable
   Ⓐ docile
   Ⓑ relaxed
   Ⓒ lovable
   Ⓓ mundane

8. discriminate
   Ⓐ enhance
   Ⓑ persuade
   Ⓒ distinguish
   Ⓓ distort

9. reflect
   Ⓐ mirror
   Ⓑ confirm
   Ⓒ produce
   Ⓓ grind

10. derive
   Ⓐ confirm
   Ⓑ bargain
   Ⓒ deduce
   Ⓓ obtain

LESSON 8—MULTIPLE-CHOICE TEST QUESTIONS

1. Testing metals for quality assurance can be accomplished by several methods. One common nondestructive technique, used to locate surface cracks and **flaws** in metals, employs a penetrating liquid. Normally this fluid is brightly dyed or fluorescent. After being spread over the surface of the material, it soaks into any tiny cracks. The liquid is cleaned off, allowing cracks and blemishes to be easily seen.

   The word **flaws** in the passage is closest in meaning to

   Ⓐ bends
   Ⓑ defects
   Ⓒ cavities
   Ⓓ dents

2. An important task of management is to motivate individual workers to coordinate their collective efforts to achieve an organization's goals. The concepts and methods used to structure work and to design organizations have changed considerably. An organization's age can often be predicted by the way work is structured. Work practices tend to **reflect** the organization's design theory present at the time the organization was founded.

   The word **reflect** in the passage is closest in meaning to

   Ⓐ influence
   Ⓑ mirror
   Ⓒ cultivate
   Ⓓ accelerate

3. The Mayflower Compact was a document signed by 41 of the male passengers on the *Mayflower* before their landing at Plymouth, Massachusetts. The passengers, concerned that some members of the company might leave the group and settle on their own, **negotiated** laws amongst themselves to create the document. The Mayflower Compact created a political body whose purpose was to form a simple government. Those who signed the compact pledged to abide by any future laws and regulations.

   In stating that the settlers **negotiated**, the author means that

   Ⓐ they traded livestock
   Ⓑ they fought a war
   Ⓒ they agreed immediately
   Ⓓ they reached a compromise

4. Before the invention of electroacoustic equipment that generates and measures sound, the available hearing tests gave approximate results in the best cases. A person's hearing could be explained in terms of the ability to **distinguish** between the ticking of a watch and the clicking of coins or to determine the distance at which conversational speech or a whispered voice could no longer be understood.

   The word **distinguish** in the passage is closest in meaning to

   Ⓐ discriminate
   Ⓑ listen
   Ⓒ clarify
   Ⓓ conceal

5. When DNA is subjected to restriction-enzyme activity, **fragments** of various sizes are formed. This process reveals a unique pattern of restriction-enzyme DNA. This specific DNA pattern found in each human genetic lineage is unique, because each person, except for identical twins, is formed from different combinations of the genetic material from two family lines. The pattern of sizes of the DNA from an individual is unique and can serve as a "DNA fingerprint" of that person.

   The word **fragments** in the passage is closest in meaning to

   Ⓐ growths
   Ⓑ modifications
   Ⓒ flaws
   Ⓓ particles

6. The invention of the airplane was a **crushing blow** for proponents of hot air ballooning. Early advocates of ballooning such as Jean-Pierre Blanchard and John Jeffries thought it would transform international travel. Instead, the cost of launching a balloon, the problem of controlling a balloon in high winds, and the instant attractiveness of more stable airplane travel have kept ballooning from becoming more than a hobby for a limited number of wealthy adventurers.

   In stating that the airplane's invention was a **crushing blow** for proponents of ballooning, the author means that it

   Ⓐ led directly to the invention of the airplane.
   Ⓑ caught on immediately among the public.
   Ⓒ promoted hot air ballooning internationally.
   Ⓓ kept ballooning from becoming more popular.

7. Farming continues to be an important activity on the eastern shore of Maryland. The eastern shore specializes in chickens for urban markets along the East Coast. Although market vegetables are also produced for the same urban markets, corn and soybeans continue to be the two most important crops **cultivated** on Maryland's eastern shore.

   The word **cultivated** in the passage is closest in meaning to

   Ⓐ grown
   Ⓑ gathered
   Ⓒ developed
   Ⓓ extracted

8. The earliest grain mills were hand-powered devices. Querns, which have been used for centuries to **crush** grains, are examples of such milling devices. A quern has an upper grinding stone with a handle. This handle rotates inside another stone, which contains the grain.

   The word **crush** in the passage is closest in meaning to

   Ⓐ produce
   Ⓑ roughen
   Ⓒ grind
   Ⓓ elicit

9. Creating chocolate is an involved process. First, the cacao beans must be meticulously harvested from the cacao tree. The irresistible chocolate candies we are familiar with are **derived** from these beans. The cacao beans must be crushed and then go through a process known as tempering—a repeating cycle of warming and cooling of the liquefied product.

   The word **derived** in the passage is closest in meaning to

   Ⓐ distinct
   Ⓑ theoretically
   Ⓒ separated
   Ⓓ obtained

10. The economic depression that plagued the United States in the 1930s was unique in its size and its consequences. During the worst period of the Depression, in 1933, one in every four American workers was out of a job. The great industrial slump **engendered** extreme hardship throughout the world that persisted throughout the 1930s.

    The word **engendered** in the passage is closest in meaning to

    Ⓐ accelerated
    Ⓑ produced
    Ⓒ omitted
    Ⓓ developed

LESSON 9

- **account for**
- **accurate**
- **acute**
- **classify**
- **currency**
- **dense**
- **dim**
- **display**
- **exports**
- **gigantic**
- **impressive**
- **install**
- **jargon**
- **saturate**
- **straightforward**
- **uniform**
- **vibrant**

---

account for — *ph. v.* to take something into consideration; to provide reasons for an event
syn. explain

He did not *account for* Earth's gravity in his physics calculations.
Her intense studying *accounts for* her excellent grades.

accurate — *adj.* careful and exact
adv. accurately
n. accuracy
syn. precise

She was able to make *accurate* observations with the new telescope.
Experiments must be conducted with *accuracy*.

acute — *adj.* having a sudden consequence or severe effect
adv. acutely
n. acuteness
syn. intense

The president was *acutely* aware of the fact that her decision would be unpopular.
He was suffering from an *acute* headache.

classify — *v.* to place into groups according to type
adj. classified
n. classification
syn. arrange

Biologists *classify* life forms into many phylla.
The library's catalog is a *classification* of books in the library.

currency *n.* monetary unit; cash
syn. money

Most purchases in foreign countries must be made in the local *currency*.
The Japanese *currency* is gaining strength against the dollar.

dense *adj.* closely packed or crowded; difficult to see through
syn. thick

adv. densely
n. density

The boating accident was caused by the *dense* fog.
Hong Kong is one of the most *densely* populated cities in the world.

dim *adj.* not bright or clear
syn. faint

adv. dimly
v. dim
n. dimness

The light was too *dim* for studying.
The stars *dimly* lit the evening sky.

display *v.* to show; reveal
syn. exhibit

n. display

The model *displayed* the details of the human hand.
The candidate's *display* of anger was unfortunate.

exports *n.* products sold abroad
syn. foreign sales

adj. exported
v. export

The United States' imports now exceed its *exports*.
Exported goods are usually high in quality.

gigantic *adj.* very large
syn. enormous

adv. gigantically

Reaching the moon was a *gigantic* step in space exploration for mankind.
New methods of farming offer *gigantic* advantages over the old methods.

impressive *adj.* causing admiration because of an object's importance, size, or quality

adv. impressively
v. impress
n. impression

syn. imposing

Lincoln's power of persuasion was *impressive.*
Everyone left with a good *impression* of the play.

install *v.* to set up or create an office; to place in a fixed position

n. installation
n. installer

syn. establish

The software we needed was already *installed* on the computer.
Antonia was *installed* as president of the art club last week.

jargon *n.* language specific to a profession or activity

adj. jargony

syn. terminology

The legal *jargon* in the contract was confusing.
Science fiction *jargon* used in television shows and movies often comes from real science.

saturate *v.* to fill or occupy to the maximum level

n. saturation
adj. saturated

syn. overflow

In order to paint, you must *saturate* a brush with a hue of your choice.
In order to obtain food, the sponge *saturates* itself with sea water.

straightforward *adj.* easy to understand; simple; honest

adv. straightforwardly
n. straightforwardness

syn. uncomplicated

The assembly directions were *straightforward.*
His *straightforward* approach to his business dealings earned him respect.

uniform *adj.* every part being the same

adv. uniformly *syn.* consistent
n. uniformity

Bread has a *uniform* texture.

The grades on the test were *uniformly* poor.

vibrant *adj.* lively; powerful; full of action; bright

adv. vibrantly *syn.* brilliant
n. vibrance

His *vibrant* personality made him well liked by everyone.

The *vibrance* of the city is attractive to many individuals.

MATCHING

Choose the synonym.

1. enormous
   - Ⓐ prosperous
   - Ⓑ autonomous
   - Ⓒ gigantic
   - Ⓓ classified

2. dialect
   - Ⓐ terminology
   - Ⓑ flaws
   - Ⓒ exports
   - Ⓓ jargon

3. vibrant
   - Ⓐ brilliant
   - Ⓑ critical
   - Ⓒ paint
   - Ⓓ deep

4. straightforward
   - Ⓐ agreeable
   - Ⓑ honest
   - Ⓒ useful
   - Ⓓ dependable

5. imposing
   - Ⓐ impressive
   - Ⓑ creative
   - Ⓒ intriguing
   - Ⓓ ambiguous

6. uniform
   - Ⓐ rigid
   - Ⓑ diverse
   - Ⓒ complex
   - Ⓓ consistent

7. install
   - Ⓐ hand in
   - Ⓑ set up
   - Ⓒ put on
   - Ⓓ get in

8. saturate
   - Ⓐ overflow
   - Ⓑ seek
   - Ⓒ stagnate
   - Ⓓ surpass

9. acute
   - Ⓐ intense
   - Ⓑ accurate
   - Ⓒ precise
   - Ⓓ gigantic

10. classify
   - Ⓐ trust
   - Ⓑ learn
   - Ⓒ clarify
   - Ⓓ arrange

LESSON 9—MULTIPLE-CHOICE TEST QUESTIONS

1. Written by Adam Smith in 1776, *The Wealth of Nations* is a **vibrant** attack against mercantilism and one of the most influential books ever written on economics. One of its main ideas is that when people pursue their own selfish interests, society as a whole benefits. Competition, rather than private or government monopoly, should regulate prices and wages. He also believed that competition produces socially beneficial consequences and that government should not interfere with market forces.

   The word **vibrant** in the passage is closest in meaning to

   Ⓐ critical
   Ⓑ brilliant
   Ⓒ intriguing
   Ⓓ convincing

2. Despite its weaknesses and inner conflicts, the humanistic movement was heroic in its scope and energy, and exceptional in its aspirations. For human development in all fields, it created a context of seldom-equaled fertility. This era was **saturated** with advancements in both science and the liberal arts. Its characteristic modalities of thought, speech, and vision lent themselves to bring on the genius of humankind and provide a path for enduring achievement.

   By saying that the era was **saturated** with advancements, the author means that

   Ⓐ there were too many new ideas.
   Ⓑ society was filled with geniuses.
   Ⓒ people became very rich.
   Ⓓ there was an abundance of progress.

3. The **gigantic**, intricately formed chasm of the Grand Canyon contains a great many impressive peaks, canyons, and ravines between its outer walls. The canyon includes a number of side canyons and surrounding plateaus. The deepest and most impressively beautiful section is within Grand Canyon National Park, which encompasses the Colorado River's length from Lake Powell to Lake Mead.

   The word **gigantic** in the passage is closest in meaning to

   Ⓐ deep
   Ⓑ turbulent
   Ⓒ enormous
   Ⓓ thrilling

4. The unified classical architectural style of the 1893 World's Columbian Exposition buildings proved to be the most **impressive** and influential style of its time. A committee of East Coast architects and firms gathered in December 1890 to plan the fair buildings. The collective result was the construction of a group of 150 buildings known as the White City. Their design established white, columnar architecture as the only acceptable public style in the United States for 40 years thereafter.

   The word **impressive** in the passage is closest in meaning to

   Ⓐ imposing
   Ⓑ critical
   Ⓒ massive
   Ⓓ enduring

5. The position of President of the United States has, in the past decade, expanded in its diversity. There were forty-two Caucasian presidents of the United States prior to President Barack Obama's election. His **installation** as president inspired countless Americans to pursue their dreams regardless of race.

   The noun **installation** in the passage is closest in meaning to

   Ⓐ establishment
   Ⓑ term
   Ⓒ triumph
   Ⓓ energy

6. England is the second-most **densely populated** country in Europe, preceded only by Malta. It has 255 inhabitants per square kilometer. In comparison, Italy has 200 inhabitants and Spain 87. Many European countries have agricultural economies, and their populations are unevenly distributed. For example, Paris has 3,550 people per square kilometer, while many parts of the rest of France contain fewer than 30 people per square kilometer.

   In stating that England is **densely populated**, the author means that its

   Ⓐ population is the most unevenly distributed.
   Ⓑ population is the largest in Europe.
   Ⓒ population is the largest per square kilometer.
   Ⓓ population is largest in its cities.

7. In the field of artificial intelligence, scientists are studying methods for developing computer programs that **display** aspects of intelligent behavior. Research into all aspects of artificial intelligence is vigorous. However, some researchers doubt that artificial intelligence can truly replicate forms of intelligent behavior like that observed in intelligent living organisms. Indeed, artificial intelligence programs are simple when compared to the intuitive reasoning and induction capabilities of the human brain.

   The word **display** in the passage is closest in meaning to

   Ⓐ exhibit
   Ⓑ narrate
   Ⓒ declare
   Ⓓ arrange

8. Canadian thistle is a bothersome North American weed that grows in clusters. However, some species such as the Scotch, or cotton thistle, which have **dense** heads of small pink or purple flowers, can make attractive garden plants and are widely cultivated for ornamental purposes throughout the Northeast.

   The word **dense** in the passage is closest in meaning to

   Ⓐ small
   Ⓑ many
   Ⓒ beautiful
   Ⓓ thick

9. The Sun is not the only star known to be accompanied by an extensive planetary system. A few nearby stars are now known to be encircled by particles of undetermined size. This opens the strong hypothesis that the universe is filled with many solar systems similar to that of our sun. No deep understanding of the Solar System can be achieved without an appreciation of the basic properties of the Sun, which in part **accounts for** the existence of life on Earth.

   The phrase **accounts for** is closest in meaning to

   Ⓐ brings about
   Ⓑ comes from
   Ⓒ gives details for
   Ⓓ stems from

10. An exchange rate is the rate at which one country's **currency** may be exchanged for that of another. Exchange rates have been governed in recent years primarily by the forces of supply and demand. The exchange rate normally changes, depending upon the strength of a country's economy and its trade balance.

    The word **currency** in the passage is closest in meaning to

    Ⓐ exports
    Ⓑ goods
    Ⓒ gains
    Ⓓ money

LESSON 10

- **distinct**
- **dominant**
- **dormant**
- **drab**
- **dramatic**
- **eclectic**
- **elaborate**
- **exceptional**
- **genuine**
- **hazardous**
- **minuscule**
- **prime**
- **rudimentary**
- **skeptical**
- **stoic**
- **superficial**
- **vigorous**

---

distinct *adj.* clearly noticed; different

adv. distinctly
adj. distinctive
n. distinction

syn. definite

There was a *distinct* aroma of coffee in the restaurant.

The two theories are *distinctly* different from each other.

dominant *adj.* primary or principal; having or exercising control over something

adv. dominantly
v. dominate
n. domination

syn. major

The *dominant* life forms of the Paleozoic era lived in the water.

The skyscraper *dominated* the skyline.

dormant *adj.* not growing or producing; asleep

n. dormitory

syn. inactive

The volcano had been *dormant* for hundreds of years before the eruption last month.

The seniors live in the new *dormitory*.

drab *adj.* lacking color; uninteresting, boring

adv. drably
n. drabness

syn. colorless

Their clothing was quite *drab*.

The *drabness* of the desert made driving less interesting.

dramatic — *adj.* something that captures the imagination; exciting

adv. dramatically
v. dramatize
n. drama

syn. emotional

The *dramatic* finish to the game left us speechless.
The hurricane *dramatically* changed the coastline.

eclectic — *adj.* to select or represent something chosen from many sources or places

adv. eclectically

syn. diverse

He has an *eclectic* taste in music, from hard rock to classical.
The *eclectic* group of students came from fifteen different countries.

elaborate — *adj.* something with a large number of parts; full of details

adv. elaborately
v. elaborate
n. elaboration

syn. complex

An *elaborate* head dress indicated rank within the Aztec community.
His *elaboration* of the issue was quite thorough.

exceptional — *adj.* unusual in a positive way

adv. exceptionally

syn. phenomenal

The orchestra's performance was *exceptional.*
The North Star is *exceptionally* bright.

genuine — *adj.* honest or true; real

adv. genuinely
n. genuineness

syn. authentic

She was *genuinely* concerned about world hunger.
This is a *genuine* artifact from the American Civil War.

hazardous — *adj.* very risky, unsafe

adv. hazardously
n. hazard

syn. dangerous

Handling flammable liquids is *hazardous.*
There are many *hazards* involved with starting a business.

minuscule *adj.* of little consequence; very small

adj. minute
n. minutia

syn. tiny

The sale of the building had a *minuscule* effect on the profits of the corporation.

Some leaves are covered with *minute* hairs.

prime *v.* to make ready;
*first in importance or in time

adj. primed
adj. prime*
n. prime

syn. prepare

The directors *primed* the actors before the performance.

Mozart passed away in the *prime* of his life.

rudimentary *adj.* simple; not complex

n. rudiment

syn. basic

He has a *rudimentary* knowledge of computers.

The *rudiments* of grammar are taught in all English classes.

skeptical *adj.* to question the truthfulness of information presented as fact; to not trust

adv. skeptically
n. skeptic

syn. unconvinced

The professor was *skeptical* about the theories of climate change.

To answer his *skeptics*, the scientist presented proof of his conclusions at the conference.

stoic *adj.* showing no emotion; appearing disinterested

adv. stoically
n. stoicism

syn. indifferent

His *stoic* reaction to the event surprised his friends.

His *stoicism* was unusual, since he is normally an emotional boy.

superficial *adj.* simple; not deep; near the surface
adv. superficially *syn.* shallow

The inspector determined that the crack in the bridge was only *superficial.*

You should not try to answer the question *superficially.*

vigorous *adj.* powerful, full of action
adv. vigorously *syn.* strong
n. vigor

His *vigorous* defense of the issues impressed everyone.

He approached his work with *vigor.*

MATCHING

Choose the synonym.

1. exceptional
   - Ⓐ dominant
   - Ⓑ dense
   - Ⓒ phenomenal
   - Ⓓ acceptable

2. stoic
   - Ⓐ distorted
   - Ⓑ indifferent
   - Ⓒ hazardous
   - Ⓓ straightforward

3. prepare
   - Ⓐ concur
   - Ⓑ display
   - Ⓒ depend
   - Ⓓ prime

4. eclectic
   - Ⓐ vibrant
   - Ⓑ energized
   - Ⓒ limited
   - Ⓓ diverse

5. dangerous
   - Ⓐ hazardous
   - Ⓑ rigid
   - Ⓒ commonplace
   - Ⓓ intolerable

6. elaborate
   - Ⓐ gigantic
   - Ⓑ impressive
   - Ⓒ complex
   - Ⓓ dramatic

7. minuscule
   - Ⓐ tiny
   - Ⓑ dim
   - Ⓒ drab
   - Ⓓ major

8. superficial
   - Ⓐ emotional
   - Ⓑ lasting
   - Ⓒ shallow
   - Ⓓ curious

9. authentic
   - Ⓐ basic
   - Ⓑ valid
   - Ⓒ genuine
   - Ⓓ rudimentary

10. vigorous
    - Ⓐ dominant
    - Ⓑ convenient
    - Ⓒ uniform
    - Ⓓ strong

LESSON 10—MULTIPLE-CHOICE TEST QUESTIONS

1. The development of centralized governments was not accompanied by centralized responsibility for road maintenance. One important development in the construction and maintenance of public transportation systems was the establishment of turnpike trusts. Entrepreneurs would join together to obtain government permission to take over a length of road for 21 years or build a new one and pay for its maintenance by collecting tolls. However, in its early years, road engineering was **rudimentary**, and many trusts did not know how to preserve the roads.

   The word **rudimentary** in the passage is closest in meaning to

   Ⓐ elaborate
   Ⓑ haphazard
   Ⓒ flawed
   Ⓓ basic

2. Language is a system of communication specific to the human race. It is primarily oral-aural, since all naturally evolved large-scale linguistic systems have orderly patterns of sound produced by the human voice and perceived and processed by the ear. Despite the great variety of languages spoken throughout the world and the **superficial** differences among them, most linguists agree that all languages are essentially similar in structure and function.

   The word **superficial** in the passage is closest in meaning to

   Ⓐ certain
   Ⓑ frightening
   Ⓒ exceptional
   Ⓓ shallow

3. The layers of volatile gases and liquids near and above the surface of the Earth are of **prime** importance, along with solar energy, to maintaining life on Earth. They are distributed and recycled throughout the relatively thin atmosphere of the Earth. This atmosphere is a mixture of gases, primarily nitrogen and oxygen. However, the atmosphere also contains much smaller amounts of gases such as argon, carbon dioxide, methane, and water vapor along with minute solid and liquid particles in suspension.

   The word **prime** in the passage is closest in meaning to

   Ⓐ chief
   Ⓑ dubious
   Ⓒ superficial
   Ⓓ dramatic

4. Avoidance is the most common form of defense in reptiles. At the first sign of danger, most snakes and lizards slither or dart away under cover; turtles and crocodiles plunge out of sight into water. But, in cases where danger presents itself abruptly and flight may be **hazardous**, reptiles may attack.

   The word **hazardous** in the passage is closest in meaning to

   Ⓐ harmless
   Ⓑ dangerous
   Ⓒ arbitrary
   Ⓓ unacceptable

5. As the Industrial Revolution developed in the nineteenth century, the era of wooden-hulled sailing ships gave way to that of steam-powered iron ships. **Phenomenal** changes took place in nearly every facet of ship design and operation. By the mid-1800s, these changes caused the end of the majestic wooden-hulled ship line. Despite its demise, another half century would elapse before it was clear what form its replacement would take.

   The word **phenomenal** in the passage is closest in meaning to

   Ⓐ vigorous
   Ⓑ definite
   Ⓒ exceptional
   Ⓓ debilitating

6. Research suggests that musical ability is genetic. Twins have the same genetic makeup. Therefore, researchers asked more than 500 children to sing along with recorded popular songs and discovered that 80 percent were equally able or unable to duplicate the melody. These results support the claim that musical talent is inherited—many children have some talent, but few are **exceptionally talented**, and only they have any hope of becoming concert pianists.

   In stating that few children are **exceptionally talented**, the author means that

   Ⓐ musical ability is evenly distributed.
   Ⓑ almost everyone should study music.
   Ⓒ the most talented are few in number.
   Ⓓ twins cannot sing along with a song.

7. In the social sciences, conflict theory refers to the theoretical approach that views social phenomena as the result of conflict between individuals or groups. Conflict theory has developed at both micro and macro levels. Since much of the documented behavior is **dramatic** and unpredictable, theories of such behavior are more evaluative than analytic.

   The word **dramatic** in the passage is closest in meaning to

   Ⓐ frightening
   Ⓑ distinctive
   Ⓒ emotional
   Ⓓ distorted

8. Feathers serve as an adaptable cover for the body of a bird. They form a smooth surface that reduces friction with the air, and they furnish flexible strong wings for flight and tails for steering. Feathers also act as superb insulation to conserve body heat and are relatively waterproof. Many songbirds in temperate zones reveal a **drab** plumage during the winter, in contrast to their brilliant springtime mating plumage.

   The word **drab** in the passage is closest in meaning to

   Ⓐ soft
   Ⓑ colorless
   Ⓒ bright
   Ⓓ basic

9. Comic books began as collections of newspaper comic strips and took on a life of their own in the 1930s. The favorite reading matter of several generations of children, comic books often dealt with heroic characters who fought crime or terror. The newspaper strip and the comic book represent the **dominant** graphic mythology of the twentieth century.

   The word **dominant** in the passage is closest in meaning to

   Ⓐ major
   Ⓑ elaborate
   Ⓒ lasting
   Ⓓ critical

10. The vast majority of animals exhibit a symmetrical form, therefore making form a fundamental, representative characteristic for most animals. All animals with a bilateral symmetry, those that have a **distinct** right and left side and a front and rear end, are classified together as Bilateria, a division of multicellular animals. Bilateria contrast with multicellular animals, which have a radial symmetry. An example is the jellyfish, which has no right or left sides.

    The word **distinct** in the passage is closest in meaning to

    Ⓐ dominant
    Ⓑ uniform
    Ⓒ definite
    Ⓓ conventional

LESSON 11

- **amenity**
- **disperse**
- **element**
- **elementary**
- **eliminate**
- **emerge**
- **emphasize**
- **encircle**
- **erratic**
- **exaggerate**
- **integral**
- **justify**
- **mortify**
- **overbearing**
- **precipitate**
- **prevalent**
- **release**

---

amenity

n. something that makes life easier or more enjoyable

syn. convenience

She missed all the *amenities* of home when she went camping.

One expects many *amenities* at a five-star hotel.

disperse

adj. dispersed

v. to cause to move in many different directions

syn. circulate

The high winds and rain *dispersed* the crowd.

After the hurricane, *dispersed* belongings cluttered the street.

element

adj. elemental
n. element*

n. a part of the whole
*environment

syn. component

Her presence added an *element* of humor to the group.

Hard work and perseverance are the basic *elements* of success.

elementary

adj. simple in structure, easy to do

syn. primary

The solution to the problem was actually quite *elementary*.

You must take *Elementary* Physics before you can enroll in the advanced course.

eliminate *v.* to remove, free oneself of something

adj. eliminated
n. elimination

syn. delete

Mistakes must be *eliminated* before you hand in a term paper.
The *elimination* of the runner from the race was decided by the judge.

emerge *v.* to come into view, or existence

n. emergence

syn. appear

It took an hour for the newborn chick to *emerge* from its egg.
The sun *emerged* from the thick rain clouds, giving hope that the game would be played.

emphasize *v.* to show that something is especially important or exceptional

adv. emphatically
adj. emphatic
n. emphasis

syn. highlight

The professor *emphasized* certain aspects of the historical period.
When asked if they would like to leave class early, the students answered with an *emphatic* "yes."

encircle *v.* to make a circle around

adj. encircled

syn. surround

The players *encircled* their coach after winning the big game.
The *encircled* celebrity actually became afraid of her fans.

erratic *adj.* no regular pattern in thinking or movement; changeable without reason

adv. erratically

syn. inconsistent

The artist's paintings have an *erratic* quality, some being excellent, and others mediocre.
The unstable chemical reacted *erratically*.

exaggerate *v.* to make something more than what it is

adj. exaggerated
n. exaggeration

syn. overstate

The federal government *exaggerated* the success of its programs.
To say that his business is successful would be a slight *exaggeration*.

integral — *adj.* to be an essential or basic part of something

adv. integrally
n. integrallity

syn. vital

Knowledge of spelling is an *integral* part of writing in any language.

A film's music is *integral* to drawing the viewers into the story.

justify — *v.* to show to be right or reasonable; to support

n. justification
adj. justifiably

syn. defend

The young boy could not *justify* his rude behavior.

There was no *justification* for the criminal's attack.

mortify — *v.* to embarrass

n. mortification

syn. humiliate

He was *mortified* upon forgetting his lines during the play.

She *mortified* her son by showing Alice his baby pictures.

overbearing — *adj.* persistently overconfident or controlling

syn. oppressive

The old woman's *overbearing* demeanor did not make her approachable.

The teacher tried his best to not be *overbearing* when speaking to his students.

precipitate — *v.* to speed up the occurrence or development of something

syn. hasten

Romeo and Juliet's relationship *precipitated* a violent conflict.

Trade with other cultures was the main *precipitant* for the advent of the Renaissance.

prevalent *adj.* existing widely or commonly
n. prevalence *syn.* commonplace

Comfortable trade winds are *prevalent* in the Caribbean islands.
There is a *prevalence* of disease where poor sanitation conditions exist.

release *v.* to allow to come out; to give freedom
n. release *syn.* free

A new movie was just *released.*
The *release* of the Supreme Court's decision was expected today.

MATCHING

Choose the synonym

1. amenity
   Ⓐ advice
   Ⓑ convenience
   Ⓒ element
   Ⓓ emphasis

2. justify
   Ⓐ defend
   Ⓑ conform
   Ⓒ disperse
   Ⓓ forbid

3. overbearing
   Ⓐ consistent
   Ⓑ oppressive
   Ⓒ unstable
   Ⓓ benign

4. mortify
   Ⓐ frighten
   Ⓑ humiliate
   Ⓒ criticize
   Ⓓ extinguish

5. exaggerate
   Ⓐ impress
   Ⓑ dominate
   Ⓒ elaborate
   Ⓓ overstate

6. disperse
   Ⓐ circulate
   Ⓑ classify
   Ⓒ distort
   Ⓓ encircle

7. release
   Ⓐ free
   Ⓑ restore
   Ⓒ settle
   Ⓓ block

8. vital
   Ⓐ rigid
   Ⓑ complex
   Ⓒ erratic
   Ⓓ integral

9. commonplace
   Ⓐ elementary
   Ⓑ rudimentary
   Ⓒ prevalent
   Ⓓ uniform

10. emerge
   Ⓐ join
   Ⓑ distort
   Ⓒ appear
   Ⓓ release

LESSON 11—MULTIPLE-CHOICE TEST QUESTIONS

1. Kapok is made from the silky fiber that **encircles** the seeds of the tropical silk-cotton tree. This dense mat of cottony fibers surrounds each seed within the fruit. However, unlike cotton fibers, kapok fibers do not lend themselves to spinning. Since they are water resistant and buoyant, kapok fibers were extensively used for padding and insulation until the development of synthetic fibers.

   The word **encircles** in the passage is closest in meaning to

   Ⓐ releases
   Ⓑ circulates
   Ⓒ surrounds
   Ⓓ disperses

2. Lewis and Clark's expedition's central objective, the discovery of the "water communication," was not realized. However, a huge blank space on the map of North America had been filled as a result of the expedition. The rumor and myth related to the American West had been **eliminated** and new knowledge about the Wild West was made known to the American people.

   The word **eliminated** in the passage is closest in meaning to

   Ⓐ released
   Ⓑ circulated
   Ⓒ deleted
   Ⓓ exaggerated

3. The most **elementary** type of convection can be explained by the fact that heat rises. Convection currents permit buildings to be heated without the use of circulatory devices. The heated air moves solely by gravity. In the atmosphere, convection causes the wind to blow. Most severe weather conditions, such as tornadoes, result from particularly sharp convection currents.

   The word **elementary** in the passage is closest in meaning to

   Ⓐ dispersed
   Ⓑ erratic
   Ⓒ prevalent
   Ⓓ primary

4. The key **element** of the air conditioner is a fluorocarbon refrigerant that flows constantly through the conditioner's mechanisms. It becomes a liquid and gives off heat when it is compressed, and becomes a gas and absorbs heat when the pressure is removed. The mechanisms that evaporate and compress the refrigerant are divided into two areas, one on the interior, which includes an air filter, fan, and cooling coil, and one on the exterior, which includes a compressor, condenser coil, and fan.

   The word **element** in the passage is closest in meaning to

   Ⓐ amenity
   Ⓑ component
   Ⓒ purpose
   Ⓓ advantage

5. A common inhabitant of the southwest United States, the prairie dog lives in groups called *coteries*. A breeding coterie contains one male, one to four females, and the young of the past two years. Several coteries form large groups called *wards*, which are determined by the structure of the terrain. The wards in turn are united into *towns*—complex dwellings of interconnecting burrows and many entrances. The towns may cover as many as 65 to 160 acres, which contain thousands of individuals. While the prairie dog population is thought to have once been in the billions, urban development of the southwestern region has **precipitated** a population decline of nearly 95 percent.

   The word **precipitated** in the passage is closest in meaning to

   Ⓐ hastened
   Ⓑ halted
   Ⓒ avoided
   Ⓓ altered

6. The sport utility vehicle, or SUV, is the most popular type of automobile in the United States today. SUVs are spacious, powerful, and rugged; they have more room for passengers, equipment, groceries, and boxes than ordinary cars. Therefore, they are more commonly found in the country than in the city, and in some suburban neighborhoods they are **more prevalent than** compact cars or vans. Even their high consumption of gas has little effect on their popularity.

   In stating that SUVs are **more prevalent than** compact cars, the author means that they

   Ⓐ cost more than compact cars.
   Ⓑ are more numerous than compacts.
   Ⓒ take up more parking space.
   Ⓓ use more gas than other vehicles.

7. Water whirlwinds, commonly called waterspouts, are whirling columns of air and watery mist. Brief whirlwinds are **erratic** in motion, but the longer-lasting ones move slowly with the prevailing winds and are more regular in their movement. Storms generate most waterspouts, but tornado spouts, generated in thunderstorms, in association with tropical cyclones, are the most dangerous.

   The word **erratic** in the passage is closest in meaning to

   Ⓐ unique
   Ⓑ inconsistent
   Ⓒ arbitrary
   Ⓓ complex

8. Partly because it has promoted U.S. interests, the Monroe Doctrine has had considerable effect and enjoyed strong support in the United States. It has been used to justify intervention in the internal affairs of other American nations. However, U.S. diplomatic relations are strained due to growing anxiety over the **prevalent** instability of Latin American politics and recent controversial interventions.

   The word **prevalent** in the passage is closest in meaning to

   Ⓐ definite
   Ⓑ determined
   Ⓒ constant
   Ⓓ commonplace

9. A caricature is a picture or other representation that **exaggerates** a particular physical, facial appearance, dress, or the manners of an individual to produce a distinct comical effect. It is used to ridicule political, social, or religious situations and institutions, or actions by individuals, groups, or classes of a society. The latter types of caricature are usually done with satirical rather than humorous intent, in order to encourage political or social change.

   The word **exaggerates** in the passage is closest in meaning to

   Ⓐ emphasizes
   Ⓑ astonishes
   Ⓒ embellishes
   Ⓓ fabricates

10. Geologic changes provide a convincing explanation for the puzzling way that plant species are spread around the world. The conifers of the genus *Araucaria*, for example, have large seeds that do not float in seawater and are **dispersed** only short distances. However, they have been found either as fossils or as actively growing plants on all continents and on some islands that appear to be fragments of continents.

    The word **dispersed** in the passage is closest in meaning to

    Ⓐ scattered
    Ⓑ discarded
    Ⓒ arranged
    Ⓓ released

LESSON 12

- **benefit**
- **blind**
- **broaden**
- **burgeon**
- **carry out**
- **conspicuously**
- **deficient**
- **eloquent**
- **endorse**
- **enormous**
- **entirely**
- **erode**
- **evaporate**
- **recover**
- **reportedly**
- **shift**
- **susceptible**

---

benefit

v. to be useful or helpful

syn. assist

adv. beneficially
adj. beneficial
n. benefit
n. beneficiary

Use of solar power will *benefit* all mankind.

It is extremely *beneficial* to prepare for a test.

blind

adj. unable to see or understand; to conceal; showing poor judgment or understanding

syn. unaware

adv. blindly
n. blindness

They were *blind* to the fact that they had little chance to succeed.

He went into the job *blindly*, with no previous experience.

broaden

v. to make larger or greater

syn. enlarge

adv. broadly
adj. broad
n. breadth

Education will *broaden* your opportunities to land a good job.

The *breadth* of his knowledge is impressive.

burgeon

v. growing at a fast pace

syn. thrive

adj. burgeoning

His talent as a pianist *burgeoned* at the age of 14.

The *burgeoning* population of major cities is creating a demand for more services.

carry out *v.* to perform a task, often for someone else
syn. accomplish

The boss required her team to *carry out* their plan.
The prime minister asked for his order to be *carried out* immediately.

conspicuously *adv.* attracting attention
adj. conspicuous
syn. noticeably

His name was *conspicuously* absent from the list of winners.
The attorneys were *conspicuous* for their aggressive manner in the courtroom.

deficient *adj.* not having enough of something
adv. deficiently
n. deficiency
syn. lacking

A diet *deficient* in calcium can lead to bad health.
There is a *deficiency* of qualified engineers in the country.

eloquent *adj.* expressing clearly, effectively, and convincingly
adv. eloquently
n. eloquence
syn. articulate (*adj.*)

Successful politicians are usually *eloquent* speakers.
That student's essay is *eloquently* written.

endorse *v.* to express approval
n. endorsement
syn. support

The union *endorsed* the new contract.
The president's *endorsement* of the project guaranteed its funding.

enormous *adj.* very large
adv. enormously
n. enormity
syn. tremendous

His *enormous* wealth allows him to contribute to many charities.
A diet with many fruits and vegetables is *enormously* beneficial to the body.

entirely *adv.* completely

adj. entire
n. entirety

syn. thoroughly

The economist was *entirely* right in his analysis.

The president released the speech in its *entirety* before the news conference.

erode *v.* to wear away; disappear slowly

n. erosion

syn. deteriorate

The senator's support is *eroding* because of his unpopular positions on the major issues.

It took millions of years of *erosion* for nature to form the Grand Canyon.

evaporate *v.* to vanish

n. evaporation

syn. disappear

The chances of the two sides reaching an agreement have *evaporated.*

The *evaporation* of the funds was unexplainable.

recover *v.* to get back; to have something returned

adj. recovered
adj. recoverable
n. recovery

syn. retrieve

The NASA team was unable to *recover* the space capsule.

The *recovered* objects had not been damaged.

reportedly *adv.* to know by report; unconfirmed; supposedly

adj. reported
v. report
n. report

syn. rumored

The students *reportedly* sent a representative, but she has not yet arrived.

The *reported* tornado has not been confirmed.

shift *n.* a change in position or direction

adj. shifting
v. shift
adj. shifty

syn. switch

The *shift* in the wind was helpful to the sailors.

Earthquakes are caused by the *shifting* of the Earth's crust along tectonic faults.

susceptible *adj.* to be subject to influence; capable of being affected by a person or thing

n. susceptibleness
adj. susceptibly

syn. vulnerable

When traveling in tropical climates, travelers are *susceptible* to malaria.

Adolescents are especially *susceptible* to the influence of their friends.

MATCHING

Choose the synonym.

1. benefit
   - Ⓐ prosper
   - Ⓑ demand
   - Ⓒ assist
   - Ⓓ distinguish

2. carry out
   - Ⓐ discern
   - Ⓑ hasten
   - Ⓒ accomplish
   - Ⓓ lift

3. rumored
   - Ⓐ routinely
   - Ⓑ purposefully
   - Ⓒ comparatively
   - Ⓓ reportedly

4. lacking
   - Ⓐ deficient
   - Ⓑ unaware
   - Ⓒ slim
   - Ⓓ enjoyable

5. thrive
   - Ⓐ exaggerate
   - Ⓑ burgeon
   - Ⓒ dominate
   - Ⓓ endorse

6. susceptible
   - Ⓐ vulnerable
   - Ⓑ conspicuous
   - Ⓒ exaggerated
   - Ⓓ released

7. broaden
   - Ⓐ impress
   - Ⓑ elicit
   - Ⓒ reveal
   - Ⓓ enlarge

8. switch
   - Ⓐ enrich
   - Ⓑ shift
   - Ⓒ propose
   - Ⓓ support

9. retrieve
   - Ⓐ recover
   - Ⓑ deteriorate
   - Ⓒ disperse
   - Ⓓ relinquish

10. eloquent
    - Ⓐ articulate
    - Ⓑ remarkable
    - Ⓒ enduring
    - Ⓓ conspicuous

LESSON 12—MULTIPLE-CHOICE TEST QUESTIONS

1. Politics are an integral aspect of modern sports. In many places, political decisions determine which sports will be encouraged, how much public support will be available to promote recreational sports, and whether or not athletes will be free to compete in certain international competitions. Bitter controversies have arisen as some political support for popular sporting events has **evaporated** in various parts of the world.

   The word **evaporated** in the passage is closest in meaning to

   Ⓐ burgeoned
   Ⓑ intensified
   Ⓒ broadened
   Ⓓ disappeared

2. Rolltop desks are named after their sliding roll tops, or tambours, that cover the working surface of the upper part and can be locked. First introduced into England from France in the late eighteenth century, the rolltop desk had become a standard piece of office equipment by the end of the nineteenth century. It was mass-produced in large quantities. Shortly after this period of mass production, its popularity **eroded**.

   The word **eroded** in the passage is closest in meaning to

   Ⓐ recovered
   Ⓑ shifted
   Ⓒ intensified
   Ⓓ deteriorated

3. The American architect Frank Lloyd Wright designed furniture, but its distinctive appearance defies categorization. The furniture design was **entirely** dependent on the design of the building; the same motifs appear in both. He consistently favored built-in furniture because then the furniture was part of the architecture.

   The word **entirely** in the passage is closest in meaning to

   Ⓐ slowly
   Ⓑ reportedly
   Ⓒ completely
   Ⓓ conspicuously

4. While the potential **benefit** of genetic engineering is substantial, the potential dangers may be equivalent. Improper handling could pose a health hazard to the public. For example, the introduction of cancer-causing genes into common infectious organisms like the influenza virus could be one of these dangers.

   The word **benefit** in the passage is closest in meaning to

   Ⓐ cost
   Ⓑ assistance
   Ⓒ endorsement
   Ⓓ recovery

5. Jogging has been **endorsed** by many medical authorities as valuable exercise for the heart and for general physical conditioning. It should be conducted every other day. Other medical authorities, however, warn that fallen arches and other ailments can result from jogging. Warm-up exercises before jogging, properly designed shoes, proper jogging technique, loose clothing, and general good health are vital for safe participation in this activity.

   The word **endorsed** in the passage is closest in meaning to

   Ⓐ reported
   Ⓑ supported
   Ⓒ criticized
   Ⓓ exaggerated

6. In 1900, when countries such as Russia, Italy, and Japan claimed an exclusive right to trade with China, the secret society of "Boxers" was formed to oppose this intrusion into Chinese affairs. Members of the group were **reported to** have magical powers that protected them in attacks from invading foreigners. Nevertheless, more than 20,000 foreign troops eventually landed in China, successfully attacked Beijing, established their right to remain, and disbanded the Boxers.

   In stating that the Boxers were **reported to** have magical powers, the author means that their magical powers

   Ⓐ were an established fact.
   Ⓑ were alleged to exist.
   Ⓒ had been reported as false.
   Ⓓ had been verified as true.

7. From 1890 to 1940, Los Angeles was the core orange-growing area. The city was inland from any potential port, but city leaders persuaded the U.S. Congress to finance a breakwater at the city of San Pedro. The territory between the two cities was annexed, and a great harbor was constructed between 1899 and 1914. As a result, Los Angeles experienced **burgeoning** economic growth.

   The word **burgeoning** in the passage is closest in meaning to

   Ⓐ enduring
   Ⓑ hastened
   Ⓒ ideal
   Ⓓ thriving

8. Normal schools were established chiefly to train elementary-school teachers. They were commonly state-supported and offered a two-year course beyond high school. In the twentieth century, schools **broadened** their teacher-training requirements to at least four years. Therefore, after World War II, teacher-training institutions lengthened their programs. By the 1960s, most former normal schools had been absorbed into colleges or universities as departments or schools of education.

   The word **broadened** in the passage is closest in meaning to

   Ⓐ replaced
   Ⓑ shifted
   Ⓒ enlarged
   Ⓓ advanced

9. Experiments are underway to prove the usefulness of new oil discovery technology. They will enable vast accumulations of crude oil to be **recovered** along both the Athabasca River in northcentral Alberta, Canada, and along the Orinoco River in eastern Venezuela. If these experiments are successful and a significant volume of crude is found, the world's petroleum supply may be extended by several decades.

   The word **recovered** in the passage is closest in meaning to

   Ⓐ retrieved
   Ⓑ exported
   Ⓒ reported
   Ⓓ extracted

10. The Internet is a powerful tool available to students around the world. Thanks to its rapid growth, researching any topic is now as easy as a mouse click. It is no longer commonplace to see students using information from books in a library because the Internet is far more convenient. Students can carry an **enormous** amount of information in their backpacks or briefcases just by having a laptop computer with access to the worldwide web. Some people claim that digital books will soon replace physical books. Others believe that libraries will become obsolete and that scholars will turn to online sources to conduct research.

    The word **enormous** in the passage is closest in meaning to

    Ⓐ astounding
    Ⓑ exceptional
    Ⓒ advantageous
    Ⓓ tremendous

LESSON 13

- **accolade**
- **crucial**
- **elude**
- **evident**
- **exhaust**
- **extensive**
- **face**
- **facet**
- **idol**
- **inaccessible**
- **oblivious**
- **obviously**
- **offensive**
- **predictably**
- **suitable**
- **surpass**
- **uphold**

---

accolade *n.* an award or distinction
syn. honor

She received many *accolades* during her academic career.
A Nobel Prize is just one of his many *accolades*.

crucial *adj.* of great importance; extremely necessary
adv. crucially *syn.* critical

Favorable weather is *crucial* to a good harvest.
Having all the information necessary to make a good decision is *crucially* important.

elude *v.* to escape in a tricky way
adj. elusive *syn.* evade
n. elusiveness

The criminal has *eluded* the police for months.
Success has been *elusive* for the team.

evident *adj.* easy to see, usually because of some proof
adv. evidently *syn.* apparent
n. evidence

It is *evident* that you are not feeling well.
All the *evidence* points to the presence of hydrogen.

exhaust — *v.* to use completely; to expend all energy; very thorough

syn. deplete

adv. exhaustively
adj. exhaustive
adj. exhausting
adj. exhausted
n. exhaustion

They *exhausted* their energy in ten minutes.

The *exhaustive* report was acclaimed by everyone.

extensive — *adj.* large in area or number

*to offer; to make longer

syn. comprehensive

adv. extensively
v. extend*
n. extension*

The *extensive* snowfall caused problems throughout the city.

The professor *extended* a warm welcome to the new student.

face — *v.* to be in the presence of and oppose

syn. confront

The mountain climbers *faced* grave danger on the cliff.

He finds it difficult to *face* his problems.

facet — *n.* element or component

syn. aspect

adj. faceted

The proposal had many beneficial *facets*.

It was a *multifaceted* problem that challenged the entire student body.

idol — *n.* a person or image that is loyally admired or respected

syn. hero

n. idolatry
adj. idolatrous

The Beatles, a famous singing group of the 1960s, were the *idols* of many teenage girls.

Sports fans often *idolize* famous athletes.

inaccessible *adj.* something that cannot be reached or communicated with

n. inaccessibility
adv. inaccessibly

syn. remote

The summit of the mountain was *inaccessible.*

The dignitary's *inaccessibility* frustrated the reporter.

oblivious *adj.* to be unaware of or forgetful

n. obliviousness
adj. obliviously

syn. ignorant

The students were *oblivious* to the fact that the test would cover the entire chapter.

The coastal inhabitants were *oblivious* to the dangers of the approaching hurricane.

obviously *adv.* in a clear, easy-to-understand way

adj. obvious

syn. evidently

It had *obviously* rained.

It was *obvious* that he had not practiced his oral report.

offensive *adj.* causing anger; rude; being unpleasant

n. offensiveness
adv. offensively

syn. insulting

Rotten eggs emit an *offensive* odor.

Her *offensive* remarks angered the entire audience.

predictably *adv.* in a way that foretells future events

adj. predictable
v. predict
n. prediction

syn. expectedly

She *predictably* forgot to do her assignment.

The government's *predictions* were accurate.

suitable *adj.* appropriate; correct; convenient

adv. suitably
v. suit

syn. appropriate

Her dress was not *suitable* for the occasion.

The agreement *suits* all the members of the negotiating team.

surpass *v.* to go beyond

adj. surpassable *syn.* exceed
n. surpasser

The movie *surpassed* even the film critics' high expectations.

The soccer player will probably *surpass* the scoring record set last year.

uphold *v.* to support or maintain

n. upholder *syn.* sustain

The tree house was *upheld* by three thick tree branches.

Each president of the United States must promise to *uphold* the Constitution.

MATCHING

Choose the synonym.

1. oblivious
   - Ⓐ elusive
   - Ⓑ blind
   - Ⓒ eclectic
   - Ⓓ valid

2. critical
   - Ⓐ prevalent
   - Ⓑ elusive
   - Ⓒ prime
   - Ⓓ crucial

3. predictably
   - Ⓐ obliviously
   - Ⓑ expectedly
   - Ⓒ conspicuously
   - Ⓓ extensively

4. sustain
   - Ⓐ uphold
   - Ⓑ emit
   - Ⓒ creep
   - Ⓓ distinguish

5. inaccessible
   - Ⓐ depleted
   - Ⓑ incessant
   - Ⓒ remote
   - Ⓓ enormous

6. elude
   - Ⓐ erode
   - Ⓑ evade
   - Ⓒ endorse
   - Ⓓ enrich

7. extensive
   - Ⓐ delicate
   - Ⓑ impressive
   - Ⓒ comprehensive
   - Ⓓ disruptive

8. honor
   - Ⓐ recompense
   - Ⓑ accolade
   - Ⓒ instruction
   - Ⓓ enlargement

9. evidently
   - Ⓐ routinely
   - Ⓑ entirely
   - Ⓒ exceptionally
   - Ⓓ obviously

10. exceed
   - Ⓐ surpass
   - Ⓑ benefit
   - Ⓒ ascertain
   - Ⓓ recompense

LESSON 13—MULTIPLE-CHOICE TEST QUESTIONS

1. Engineering geologists survey the geology of an area, and then prepare a geological map. One of their main responsibilities is to determine whether the geological structure of a location is **suitable** for the building of huge structures such as dams.

   The word **suitable** in the passage is closest in meaning to

   Ⓐ appropriate
   Ⓑ extensive
   Ⓒ recoverable
   Ⓓ perfect

2. Experts believe that a child's family experiences are **crucial** for personality development. The ways that basic needs are met in infancy, along with later techniques of child rearing, can leave a permanent mark on personality. Children learn behavior appropriate to their sex by identifying with the parent of the same sex. A warm, caring relationship with that parent helps such learning.

   The word **crucial** in the passage is closest in meaning to

   Ⓐ evident
   Ⓑ extensive
   Ⓒ critical
   Ⓓ obvious

3. The Everglades comprises one of the wildest and most **inaccessible** areas in the United States. Its wildlife is plentiful and is largely protected within the Everglades National Park. The only inhabitants of the Everglades are several hundred Seminole Indians.

   The word **inaccessible** in the passage is closest in meaning to

   Ⓐ remote
   Ⓑ indiscriminate
   Ⓒ inactive
   Ⓓ immense

4. Bank credit and debit cards, now used worldwide, are examples of general purpose bank cards. Establishments offering almost every kind of product or service now honor such cards. These cards are designed to give customers access to credit, savings, and checking accounts, eliminating the need to purchase items with cash. It is **predicted** that, in the future, these cards will completely eliminate the need for carrying cash.

   The word **predicted** in the passage is closest in meaning to

   Ⓐ inconceivable
   Ⓑ evident
   Ⓒ justified
   Ⓓ anticipated

5. In Western culture, until about the middle of the seventeenth century, biographies were generally tributes to famous individuals. Their purpose was to enlighten and motivate. They often dealt with the exemplary lives of people who became heroes and **heroines** to the public, but sometimes also glorified the lives of infamous doers of bad deeds.

   The word **heroines** in the passage is closest in meaning to

   Ⓐ dignitaries
   Ⓑ idols
   Ⓒ benefactors
   Ⓓ philanthropists

6. Kinesics is the name given to the study of nonverbal interactions such as facial expressions, gestures, and eye contact. In many cultures, direct eye contact is seen as a sign of disrespect in **face-to-face encounters**. Students, for example, are expected to lower their eyes while addressing a teacher. In other cultures, lowered eyes are construed as an indication of shame, embarrassment, or dishonesty. Kinesics focuses on many such cultural differences.

   In discussing **face-to-face encounters**, the author is referring to social interactions in which two people are

   Ⓐ sitting back to back.
   Ⓑ in front of each other.
   Ⓒ keeping their eyes down.
   Ⓓ staring into space.

7. High standards and rigorous early training are **evident** where dance is an art performed before an audience. In early cultures, dance was something in which everyone participated; dancers were not singled out and trained because of their skill or charm. Once religious worship developed into ritual, it became important for dancers to be as skilled as possible.

   The word **evident** in the passage is closest in meaning to

   Ⓐ rumored
   Ⓑ apparent
   Ⓒ vibrant
   Ⓓ enhanced

8. Mineral deposits form because there is a transporting agent for the ore minerals. The transporting agent removes the minerals it carries from one area and deposits them in another. Groundwater and seawater are examples of transporting agents. The transporting agent process is involved in the creation of deposits of both abundant and **exhausted** metals.

   The word **exhausted** in the passage is closest in meaning to

   Ⓐ depleted
   Ⓑ eroded
   Ⓒ released
   Ⓓ restricted

9. The independent African states encounter numerous problems implementing an educational policy that will encourage economic and social development. The difficulties most governments **face** are basically political. There is also concern about the financial problems of the different states. The lack of communication between educational policy makers and economic and social planners may also create hardships.

   The word **face** in the passage is closest in meaning to

   Ⓐ bear
   Ⓑ resolve
   Ⓒ confront
   Ⓓ endorse

10. Pop artists seek to portray modern culture. Their art emphasizes modern social values, the sprawl of urban life, and the flashy, frivolous, transitory, and offensive **facets** of modern life. These values are the very opposites of the values cherished by artists of the past.

    The word **facets** in the passage is closest in meaning to

    Ⓐ aspects
    Ⓑ ideals
    Ⓒ facts
    Ⓓ particles

LESSON 14

- **ample**
- **arduous**
- **arid**
- **avert**
- **defy**
- **diligent**
- **enact**
- **feign**
- **fertile**
- **freshly**
- **function**
- **fundamental**
- **indiscriminate**
- **pinpoint**
- **selective**
- **spacious**
- **withstand**

---

ample — *adj.* more than enough
adv. amply
syn. sufficient

There is *ample* evidence that the young man was speeding when the accident occurred.

She was *amply* paid for the work she completed.

arduous — *adj.* very difficult or challenging; requiring hard work
adv. arduously
n. arduousness
syn. demanding

The mountain tour guides climbed the mountain at an *arduous* pace.

The farmer's crops survived despite the *arduous* summer heat.

arid — *adj.* being of little rain or water
syn. dry

The area known as the Sahara Desert is one of the most *arid* places in the world.

The valley on the leeward side of the mountain was extremely *arid.*

avert — *v.* to stop from occurring; to turn away or aside
n. aversion
adj. avertable
syn. prevent

She could have *averted* the accident if she had not been texting while driving.

The citizens packed sandbags along the river bank to *avert* the flooding of their streets.

defy — *v.* to show little fear or regard for rules or established norms; to challenge

adv. defyingly
adj. defying

syn. resist

I *defy* you to find that book in the library's collection.

The circus performer demonstrated her death-*defying* routine.

diligent — *adj.* done with persistence and hard work; with attention to details

n. diligence
adv. diligently

syn. conscientious

Stephanie displayed great *diligence* in the completion of her assignments.

The *diligent* worker received recognition for his accomplishments.

enact — *v.* to pass a law

adj. enacted
n. enactment

syn. legislate

Congress *enacted* the legislation during its last session.

The *enactment* of the laws was in the hands of the Senate.

feign — *v.* to pretend; make believe

adj. feigned

syn. simulate

She *feigned* illness when it was time to visit the dentist.

The athlete *feigned* his injury.

fertile — *adj.* able to produce abundantly

v. fertilize
n. fertility
n. fertilizer

syn. rich

The delta areas of rivers are known for their *fertile* soil.

Fertilizers are used on crops to increase yields.

freshly — *adv.* caught or produced not long ago

adj. fresh
v. freshen
n. freshness

syn. recently

Freshly harvested produce is hard to find in the winter months.

The product's *freshness* depends on an efficient transportation system to bring it to market.

function *n.* the normal purpose of something

adv. functionally *syn.* role
adj. functional
v. function

It is the *function* of the director to organize and lead the department.

Most appliances cannot *function* without electricity.

fundamental *adj.* a primary or basic element

adv. fundamentally *syn.* essential

The student government promised *fundamental* changes in the registration process.

He is *fundamentally* strong in his area of expertise.

indiscriminate *adj.* not chosen carefully; unplanned

adv. indiscriminately *syn.* arbitrary

The *indiscriminate* arrangement of the products made the store confusing.

The book's chapters seem to be organized *indiscriminately*.

pinpoint *v.* to find or describe something with precision

adj. pinpoint *syn.* locate

The engineers were immediately able to *pinpoint* the problem with the bridge.

The new, advanced thermometer measures the temperature with *pinpoint* accuracy.

selective *adj.* carefully chosen

adv. selectively *syn.* discriminating
adv. select
v. select
n. selection
n. selectivity

They were very *selective* when they chose the members of the academic team.

He *selected* Spanish as his language class.

spacious *adj.* having a lot of room

adv. spaciously *syn.* expansive
n. space
n. spaciousness

The *spacious* plains of the Midwest make up the nation's breadbasket.
A vacuum is an empty *space.*

withstand *v.* to fight without surrender; to persist
syn. survive

She cannot *withstand* the pressures of her job.
The old building *withstood* the terrible storm.

MATCHING

Choose the synonym.

1. sufficient
   - Ⓐ crucial
   - Ⓑ essential
   - Ⓒ ample
   - Ⓓ extensive

2. survive
   - Ⓐ erode
   - Ⓑ weaken
   - Ⓒ elude
   - Ⓓ withstand

3. defy
   - Ⓐ resist
   - Ⓑ determine
   - Ⓒ simulate
   - Ⓓ discriminate

4. arduous
   - Ⓐ predictable
   - Ⓑ demanding
   - Ⓒ functional
   - Ⓓ chronic

5. arid
   - Ⓐ dry
   - Ⓑ fertile
   - Ⓒ fresh
   - Ⓓ drab

6. avert
   - Ⓐ prevent
   - Ⓑ amaze
   - Ⓒ assert
   - Ⓓ allow

7. selective
   - Ⓐ inaccessible
   - Ⓑ rich
   - Ⓒ recent
   - Ⓓ discriminating

8. diligent
   - Ⓐ fundamental
   - Ⓑ erratic
   - Ⓒ evident
   - Ⓓ conscientious

9. spacious
   - Ⓐ crucial
   - Ⓑ superficial
   - Ⓒ minuscule
   - Ⓓ expansive

10. pinpoint
    - Ⓐ locate
    - Ⓑ enact
    - Ⓒ dictate
    - Ⓓ sustain

LESSON 14—MULTIPLE-CHOICE TEST QUESTIONS

1. Naturally formed caves evolve mainly as a result of the solvent action of water and the chemical compounds it contains. Known as caves of solution, they are most common in regions that have **ample** rainfall.

   The word **ample** in the passage is closest in meaning to

   Ⓐ infrequent
   Ⓑ abundant
   Ⓒ exemplary
   Ⓓ erratic

2. In the early days of gliding, gliders were towed by cars. Today, gliders are towed in the sky by airplanes to a height between 600 and 900 meters above the ground. Flight duration depends on finding updrafts of air along mountain slopes, near cumulus clouds, or over **arid** terrain where rising thermal currents occur.

   The word **arid** in the passage is closest in meaning to

   Ⓐ rocky
   Ⓑ hot
   Ⓒ dry
   Ⓓ high

3. The Conestoga Indians were a powerful people, **defying** the invading Iroquois, until the Iroquois defeated them in about 1675. Part of the tribe fled to the Roanoke River. Others subsequently settled at Conestoga, near what is now Lancaster, Pennsylvania.

   The word **defying** in the passage is closest in meaning to

   Ⓐ ridiculing
   Ⓑ honoring
   Ⓒ resisting
   Ⓓ overthrowing

4. Fasting has been practiced for centuries for many diverse purposes. Some fasts were to induce fertility. Others were intended to **avert** catastrophe or to serve as penance for sin. American Indians held tribal fasts to escape threatening disasters. The Aztecs of Mexico and the Incas of Peru observed penitential fasts to pacify their gods.

   The word **avert** in the passage is closest in meaning to

   Ⓐ overcome
   Ⓑ assert
   Ⓒ confirm
   Ⓓ prevent

5. Monte Albán, near Oaxaca, Mexico, was the center of the Zapotec culture that flourished around the year 100 A.D. Its gigantic stone structures were set around a **spacious** plaza created by leveling the top of a mountain.

   The word **spacious** in the passage is closest in meaning to

   Ⓐ exhaustive
   Ⓑ expansive
   Ⓒ circular
   Ⓓ fertile

6. Space exploration has had its share of problems throughout the years. A flaw in the *Challenger*'s design led to a fatal accident in 1986, the Mir station was often in trouble, and the *Columbia* shuttle crashed on reentry in 2003. Despite these tragedies, the program has profited from its mistakes, and from new engineering and new materials. Today, NASA is confident that spacecraft are **fundamentally sound** and perfectly safe.

   In saying that spacecraft are **fundamentally sound**, the author means that they are

   Ⓐ basically well designed and built.
   Ⓑ equipped with electronic music.
   Ⓒ dangerously old and worn.
   Ⓓ entirely new and experimental.

7. Food serves three **functions** in most living organisms. First, it provides material that is used to sustain the activities of the organism. Second, food supplies the electron donors required for the formative processes that occur within the cell. Third, food provides the materials from which all of the structural components of the living cell can be assembled.

   The word **functions** in the passage is closest in meaning to

   Ⓐ cores
   Ⓑ facets
   Ⓒ resolutions
   Ⓓ roles

8. Harvested wood is dried and preserved as a treatment against insect infestation and rot. These processes ensure that it will last. Some wood products, such as posts and poles, are **freshly** cut. Most other wood products are made up of intermediate materials, which require further processing before they are manufactured into final products.

   The word **freshly** in the passage is closest in meaning to

   Ⓐ hardly
   Ⓑ recently
   Ⓒ routinely
   Ⓓ scarcely

9. Loess is topsoil left by glaciers. Vast deposits of loess make the Midwestern plain of the United States extremely **fertile** and one of the most important farming areas in the world. In addition, the soils in the land along the many rivers and streams of the region also add to its farming potential.

   The word **fertile** in the passage is closest in meaning to

   Ⓐ rich
   Ⓑ hardy
   Ⓒ vital
   Ⓓ adaptable

10. Since opossums are largely arboreal, their homes are often found in hollow trees or under stumps and roots. **Feigning** death is one of the opossum's principal defense mechanisms. This confuses its predators, protecting the opossum from danger.

    The word **feigning** in the passage is closest in meaning to

    Ⓐ imagining
    Ⓑ enacting
    Ⓒ pretending
    Ⓓ displaying

Lesson 15

- adept
- adhere
- foster
- halt
- handle
- harbor
- harmful
- insignificant
- mysterious
- perilous
- promote
- redundant
- reject
- substantial
- trait
- underscore

---

adept *adj.* able to do something well, being talented
syn. skilled

He is *adept* at calming noisy children.
The investigators were *adept* at their jobs.

adhere *v.* to stick to or follow precisely
n. adherence
syn. comply

Travelers must *adhere* to the laws of the country they are visiting.
The referee's excessively strict *adherence* to the rules upset the players.

foster *v.* to promote growth or development
syn. stimulate

The industrial revolution *fostered* the rise of the middle class.
Parents usually *foster* the development of good habits in their children.

halt *v.* to stop or discontinue
adv. haltingly
adj. halting
n. halt
syn. stop

Bus service to the city was *halted* due to poor road conditions.
The supervisor put a *halt* to the tardiness of the employees.

handle *v.* to deal with or control
n. handling
syn. manage

They *handled* themselves very well given the circumstances.
The president's *handling* of the crisis was widely applauded.

harbor *v.* to give protection; to not express a desire or opinion, usually bad

syn. shelter

He *harbors* ill feelings for her.

They *harbored* the political refugee in their home.

harmful *adj.* something that causes pain or damage

adv. harmfully
v. harm
n. harm

syn. unhealthy

Excessive radiation is *harmful* to the body.

Bleach *harms* certain fabrics.

insignificant *adj.* not important; of little value

adv. insignificantly
n. insignificance

syn. meaningless

The amount of rainfall this summer has been *insignificant*.

The *insignificance* of his comment became apparent with the passing of time.

mysterious *adj.* not easily understood or figured out

adv. mysteriously
n. mystery
n. mysteriousness

syn. baffling

He had a *mysterious* effect on everyone who heard him speak.

The man's disappearance was a *mystery*.

perilous *adj.* threatening or risky; harmful

adv. perilously
n. peril

syn. dangerous

It is *perilous* to exceed the speed limit.

There are ample *perils* in the sport of mountain climbing.

promote *v.* to encourage or advertise; to elevate in rank or grade

n. promoter
n. promotion

syn. boost

Many nations *promote* tourism to lure foreign currency.

The customers responded favorably to the half-price *promotion*.

redundant *adj.* being excessive; showing unnecessary repetition
n. redundancy
adv. redundantly
syn. repetitious

Students who ask teachers to "repeat that again" are being *redundant* because "repeat" means "again."

Lush, *redundant* vegetation is common in tropical climates.

reject *v.* to refuse
n. rejection
syn. refuse

The insurance company *rejected* the claim.

The *rejection* of his work was difficult for him to understand.

substantial *adj.* important; strongly made; of value
adv. substantially
adj. substantive
syn. significant

The discovery of a vaccine for smallpox was a *substantial* medical achievement.

This *substantive* article will change your opinion of rock music.

trait *n.* specific qualities that distinguish one from another
syn. characteristic

Her sense of humor and cheerful personality are some of her most impressive *traits.*

Alma's blonde hair is a *trait* inherited from her father.

underscore *v.* to make evident or emphasize
syn. highlight

The high quality of the student's science fair project *underscored* her talent in biology.

The conclusion of the report should *underscore* its main ideas.

MATCHING

Choose the synonym.

1. foster
   - Ⓐ exaggerate
   - Ⓑ stimulate
   - Ⓒ gain
   - Ⓓ enhance

2. halt
   - Ⓐ evaporate
   - Ⓑ avoid
   - Ⓒ defy
   - Ⓓ stop

3. trait
   - Ⓐ dwelling
   - Ⓑ characteristic
   - Ⓒ function
   - Ⓓ abundance

4. adept
   - Ⓐ able
   - Ⓑ honorable
   - Ⓒ content
   - Ⓓ talented

5. redundant
   - Ⓐ repetitious
   - Ⓑ creative
   - Ⓒ round
   - Ⓓ active

6. substantial
   - Ⓐ haphazard
   - Ⓑ diverse
   - Ⓒ significant
   - Ⓓ perilous

7. underscore
   - Ⓐ shelter
   - Ⓑ highlight
   - Ⓒ boost
   - Ⓓ exaggerate

8. mysterious
   - Ⓐ unhealthy
   - Ⓑ dangerous
   - Ⓒ dramatic
   - Ⓓ baffling

9. insignificant
   - Ⓐ meaningless
   - Ⓑ rudimentary
   - Ⓒ vigorous
   - Ⓓ spacious

10. adhere
    - Ⓐ exhaust
    - Ⓑ reject
    - Ⓒ comply
    - Ⓓ withstand

LESSON 15—MULTIPLE-CHOICE TEST QUESTIONS

1. Scientists can only speculate on the possible fate of the Cosmos. If the universe is unbound, there is little possibility that its expansion will **halt.** Thus, eventually the galaxies and stars will all die. The Cosmos then would be a cold, dark, and virtually empty place. If the universe *is* bound, the mass and energy content will come together again in a big fiery squeeze.

   The word **halt** in the passage is closest in meaning to

   Ⓐ continue
   Ⓑ stop
   Ⓒ expand
   Ⓓ intensify

2. The perception of depth and distance depends on information transmitted through various sense organs. Sensory cues indicate the distance at which objects are located from the individual and from each other. The senses of sight and hearing transmit depth and distance cues that are **substantially** independent of one another.

   The word **substantially** in the passage is closest in meaning to

   Ⓐ significantly
   Ⓑ absurdly
   Ⓒ critically
   Ⓓ vigorously

3. Because the needs of human communication are so various, the study of meaning is probably the most difficult and **mysterious** aspect of serious language study. Traditionally, language has been defined as the expression of thought. But this idea is far too narrow an interpretation of language and far too broad a view of thought to be worthwhile. The expression of thought is just one of the many roles of language.

   The word **mysterious** in the passage is closest in meaning to

   Ⓐ substantial
   Ⓑ meaningful
   Ⓒ promising
   Ⓓ baffling

4. The theory of environmental determinism says that the physical surroundings of a people, including natural resources, climate, and geography, are the major determining factors in the development of their culture. Therefore, determinism **rejects** the idea that history and tradition, social and economic factors, and other elements of culture explain social development.

   The word **rejects** in the passage is closest in meaning to

   Ⓐ refuses
   Ⓑ ignores
   Ⓒ promotes
   Ⓓ withstands

5. The greatest benefit of a regular exercise program is an improvement in overall fitness. Appropriate exercise **boosts** muscular strength and endurance, flexibility, and cardiorespiratory endurance. The level of maximum oxygen intake or cardiorespiratory endurance is usually not of great importance to most individuals. The most important thing is to attain their maximum level of performance.

   The word **boosts** in the passage is closest in meaning to

   Ⓐ harms
   Ⓑ manages
   Ⓒ promotes
   Ⓓ alters

6. The number of giant pandas in the world is dwindling. The chief reason is that their natural habitat in China has been reduced as bamboo forests have been cleared to increase available land for China's vast human population. In fact, the world came **perilously close** to losing the panda altogether in the 1980s as a result. Today, the panda's future is brighter. The Chinese government now protects most of the panda's natural habitat.

   In saying that the world came **perilously close** to losing the panda, the author means that the giant panda

   Ⓐ has been set free from zoos.
   Ⓑ endangered human beings.
   Ⓒ threatened the extinction of bamboo.
   Ⓓ was nearly entirely eliminated.

7. Several pilots were killed during the competition for the Orteig Prize, which was promised to the first pilot to fly nonstop from New York to Paris. Charles Lindbergh believed he could win it if he had the right airplane, and he was right. He received the $25,000 prize in 1927 for being the first to make the **perilous** flight across the Atlantic.

   The word **perilous** in the passage is closest in meaning to

   Ⓐ substantial
   Ⓑ dangerous
   Ⓒ haphazard
   Ⓓ prosperous

8. In parts of the world that lack modern sewage treatment plants, water carrying human waste can flow into drinking water supplies. Disease-carrying bacteria in the waste can make the drinking water **harmful**. Even in certain U.S. cities, such contaminants have been found in urban water supplies.

   The word **harmful** in the passage is closest in meaning to

   Ⓐ frail
   Ⓑ adverse
   Ⓒ conspicuous
   Ⓓ unhealthy

9. Commercial arbitration has been practiced in European countries for many years. In the United States, commercial arbitration to **handle** disputes is gaining in popularity. The American Arbitration Association hires panels of arbitrators who mediate disagreements and propose solutions. The decisions of these panels have been enforced by the courts of many states.

   The word **handle** in the passage is closest in meaning to

   Ⓐ face
   Ⓑ manage
   Ⓒ enact
   Ⓓ promote

10. Martin Luther King Jr. had a magnificent speaking ability. This quality enabled him to **adeptly** express African-Americans' need for social justice. He gained the support of millions of people of all races through his eloquent pleas for nonviolent social action in the face of acute opposition. He received international accolades when he was awarded the 1964 Nobel Peace Prize, after many years of struggle to assure basic civil rights for all citizens.

    The word **adeptly** in the passage is closest in meaning to

    Ⓐ constantly
    Ⓑ extremely
    Ⓒ passionately
    Ⓓ skillfully

LESSON 16

- **conscientious**
- **convey**
- **encompass**
- **expansion**
- **heighten**
- **highlight**
- **inadvertently**
- **inevitable**
- **infancy**
- **mimic**
- **paramount**
- **proficient**
- **retrieve**
- **systematically**
- **unlikely**
- **unwarranted**
- **zenith**

---

conscientious *adj.* showing serious purpose; one who works carefully and with enthusiasm

adv. conscientiously

syn. meticulous

She is a *conscientious* representative of the student body.

They approached the task *conscientiously*.

convey *v.* to make something known to others; to communicate

syn. communicate

The manager of the store *conveyed* his displeasure directly to the workers.

He was able to *convey* his message to the audience with ease.

encompass *v.* to surround completely; to envelop

syn. include

Her plan of study *encompasses* every aspect of computer science.

The course *encompasses* all the literature of the nineteenth century.

expansion *n.* the act of making larger

adj. expandable
v. expand

syn. growth

Expansion occurs when matter is heated.

The laboratory is *expanding* its capacity to produce computer chips.

heighten *v.* to cause to become greater

adj. heightened *syn.* intensify
n. height

A very successful interview can *heighten* a candidate's chances to get a job.

The public was in a *heightened* state of nervousness as the hurricane approached.

highlight *v.* to emphasize the part of a greater whole

n. highlight *syn.* emphasize

The owner's manual *highlights* the basic functions of the camera.

The final goal was the *highlight* of the game.

inadvertently *adv.* by accident; without paying attention; unexpectedly

adj. inadvertent *syn.* carelessly

The reporters had *inadvertently* failed to include the name of one of the dignitaries.

His *inadvertent* calculation caused him to derive the wrong answer.

inevitable *adj.* something that cannot be prevented from happening

adv. inevitably
n. inevitability *syn.* unavoidable

When two weather systems meet, unpredictable weather conditions are *inevitable.*

The *inevitability* of the outcome made the challenge less exciting.

infancy *n.* in the beginning stages of development

adj. infantile *syn.* beginning
n. infant

The new theory is in its *infancy* and will be thoroughly tested by its critics.

The author's *infantile* writing style appeals to young readers.

mimic — *v.* to copy an action

n. mimicker — *syn.* imitate

The comedian *mimicked* the president's gestures.

Parrots *mimic* the speech that they hear in their surroundings.

paramount — *adj.* to be of highest importance

adv. paramountly — *syn.* foremost
n. paramountcy

The club's *paramount* goal is to raise awareness of the importance of community service.

Being quiet is of *paramount* importance while watching a movie at the theater.

proficient — *adj.* to be skilled or experienced in something

adv. proficiently — *syn.* competent
n. proficiency

The exam will test the students' *proficiency* in the Portuguese language.

Highly *proficient* athletes earn the privilege of competing in the Olympics.

retrieve — *v.* to find and bring back

adj. retrieved — *syn.* recover
n. retrieval

Will Detroit *retrieve* its status as the car manufacturing center of the world?

This computerized information *retrieval* system is the most up-to-date system available.

systematically — *adv.* done according to a plan

adj. systematic — *syn.* methodically
n. system

The plan was developed *systematically* by a team of experts.

Systematic changes in foreign policy have been proposed.

unlikely *adj.* not probable
syn. doubtful

Rain is *unlikely* to occur during the dry season.
It is *unlikely* that he will want to attend the conference.

unwarranted *adj.* without good reason or cause; inappropriate
syn. unjustified

His negative reaction was *unwarranted.*
The motorist felt that the ticket for the infraction was *unwarranted.*

zenith *n.* the highest point
syn. apex

He reached the *zenith* of his profession at a very young age.
The publication of the book represented the *zenith* of his career.

MATCHING

Choose the synonym.

1. convey
   Ⓐ intensify
   Ⓑ promote
   Ⓒ communicate
   Ⓓ engender

2. proficient
   Ⓐ suitable
   Ⓑ persistent
   Ⓒ competent
   Ⓓ inevitable

3. growth
   Ⓐ expansion
   Ⓑ function
   Ⓒ highlight
   Ⓓ recover

4. meticulously
   Ⓐ haphazardly
   Ⓑ conscientiously
   Ⓒ inadvertently
   Ⓓ conspicuously

5. retrieve
   Ⓐ disperse
   Ⓑ recover
   Ⓒ accelerate
   Ⓓ broaden

6. encompass
   Ⓐ emphasize
   Ⓑ gain
   Ⓒ heighten
   Ⓓ include

7. apex
   Ⓐ facet
   Ⓑ zenith
   Ⓒ trait
   Ⓓ flaw

8. systematically
   Ⓐ unexpectedly
   Ⓑ persuasively
   Ⓒ astoundingly
   Ⓓ methodically

9. paramount
   Ⓐ likely
   Ⓑ foremost
   Ⓒ appealing
   Ⓓ meticulous

10. mimic
    Ⓐ exceed
    Ⓑ imitate
    Ⓒ astonish
    Ⓓ highlight

LESSON 16—MULTIPLE-CHOICE TEST QUESTIONS

1. The first elevated rail system was successfully operated in New York City in 1871, using steam power. Because steam power had many disadvantages, the lines were later electrified. An extensive network of elevated lines was built in New York City. It was in service for many years, but was **systematically** eliminated because of its antiquated appearance and because it contributed to traffic congestion.

   The word **systematically** in the passage is closest in meaning to

   Ⓐ inadvertently
   Ⓑ appropriately
   Ⓒ meticulously
   Ⓓ methodically

2. Municipal solid waste must be collected and treated in order to reduce the total volume and weight of the material that requires final disposal. Treatment changes the form of the waste and makes it easier to handle. It can also be used to **recover** certain materials, as well as heat energy, for recycling or reuse.

   The word **recover** in the passage is closest in meaning to

   Ⓐ retrieve
   Ⓑ convey
   Ⓒ deplete
   Ⓓ develop

3. American biographer and historian Samuel Eliot Morrison colorfully recreated notable stories of modern history. Combining a gift for storytelling with **meticulous** scholarship, he took the reader back into history to relive the adventures of such characters as Ferdinand Magellan, Christopher Columbus, and Sir Francis Drake. He also recorded the accomplishments of the U.S. Navy during World War II.

   The word **meticulous** in the passage is closest in meaning to

   Ⓐ unwarranted
   Ⓑ infantile
   Ⓒ valid
   Ⓓ conscientious

4. Space medicine protects human beings from the environment of space and studies their reactions to that environment. The foundations of space medicine can be traced to aviation medicine. The term aerospace medicine has evolved to **encompass** practice in both areas. Aerospace medicine has been a certified subspecialty of the American Board of Preventive Medicine since 1953.

   The word **encompass** in the passage is closest in meaning to

   Ⓐ favor
   Ⓑ promote
   Ⓒ emphasize
   Ⓓ include

5. If some motion is possible according to physical laws, then a motion in which events appear in reverse order is also possible. For example, it would be unusual to observe a real process in which a vase broken on the floor collects itself and flies up whole into a person's hand. Nevertheless, according to known physical laws, such a process is not impossible, although it is too **unlikely** to expect it to actually happen.

   The word **unlikely** in the passage is closest in meaning to

   Ⓐ difficult
   Ⓑ doubtful
   Ⓒ astonishing
   Ⓓ superficial

6. In 1896 a Swedish chemist first assessed the effects of greenhouse gases. He showed that activities such as burning coal, destroying forests, and even raising cattle dangerously increase atmospheric concentrations of such gases as carbon dioxide, methane, and nitrous oxide. Since then, **heightened awareness** of the effects cars and factories have on the environment has led to more concern about these gas concentrations. Recently they have been blamed for an apparent warming trend in Earth's atmosphere.

   In referring to **heightened awareness**, the author means that people are

   Ⓐ ignorant of the situation.
   Ⓑ more conscious of the situation.
   Ⓒ unconcerned about the problem.
   Ⓓ ashamed that the problem exists.

7. Great technological advances were made during the **infancy** of the United States' industrial growth. But the modern trends of the 1920s brought about problems as well as benefits. Many Americans had trouble adjusting to the impersonal, fast-paced life of cities. The complex life in cities tended to weaken the strong family ties that had always been part of American society.

   The word **infancy** in the passage is closest in meaning to

   Ⓐ prime
   Ⓑ beginnings
   Ⓒ miracle
   Ⓓ ambiguity

8. Careful testing is one of a pharmaceutical company's most important responsibilities. Pharmaceutical companies and the Food and Drug Administration constantly guard against the possibility of a harmful drug being sold to the public. But even the most careful testing cannot always reveal the possibility that a drug may produce an **inadvertent** harmful effect.

   The word **inadvertent** in the passage is closest in meaning to

   Ⓐ acute
   Ⓑ unlikely
   Ⓒ agilely
   Ⓓ unexpected

9. Basketball was invented by James Naismith, a Canadian-American, in 1891. Today, it is the world's most popular indoor sport. Basketball **emphasizes** teamwork and the athletic qualities of endurance, speed, and agility. Tall players have an advantage because they can reach closer to the basket or above other players to shoot and rebound the ball. Smaller players make contributions to their teams as shooters and ball handlers.

   The word **emphasizes** in the passage is closest in meaning to

   Ⓐ encompasses
   Ⓑ elaborates
   Ⓒ highlights
   Ⓓ enhances

10. Daniel Webster was a well-known American speaker, and one of the most capable lawyers and statesmen of his time. He used his speaking ability to establish a strong national government in the Senate. He also applied the speaking skills he had mastered as a lawyer to **heighten** his appeal for the end to slavery.

    The word **heighten** in the passage is closest in meaning to

    Ⓐ intensify
    Ⓑ persuade
    Ⓒ promote
    Ⓓ convey

LESSON 17

- **abysmal**
- **agitate**
- **comply**
- **confidential**
- **delighted**
- **discreetly**
- **documented**
- **endemic**
- **evoke**
- **gradually**
- **impartial**
- **inordinate**
- **intentionally**
- **intrinsic**
- **inundate**
- **mindset**
- **nominal**

---

abysmal *adj.* very bad; awful
syn. appalling

Her performance on the test was *abysmal.*

He made an *abysmal* attempt to lift the heavy couch.

agitate *v.* to shake or move; to cause worry
syn. disturb

n. agitation
n. agitator

The fact that she had not arrived by midnight *agitated* her parents.

He was known as a political *agitator*.

comply *v.* to agree to follow a request or command; to adhere to specific standards
syn. acquiesce

adj. compliant
n. compliance

A well-trained dog will *comply* when told to sit.

Students must maintain a B average to remain in *compliance* with the scholarship's rules.

confidential *adj.* to be said or written in secret
syn. secret

v. confide
adv. confidentially
n. confidant

We were told that the information is strictly *confidential.*

She *confided* to me that she had always wanted to be a movie star.

delighted *adj.* to be satisfied; very happy

adj. delightfully
adj. delightful
n. delight

syn. elated

He was *delighted* with the results of the experiment.

It was a *delightful* afternoon.

discreetly *adv.* in a careful, polite manner

adj. discreet

syn. cautiously

The teacher *discreetly* told the parents about their child's inappropriate behavior.

You can count on me to be *discreet.*

documented *adj.* proven with written evidence

adj. documentary
v. document
n. documentation

syn. proven

He had *documented* proof that the bank had made an error.

The car's *documentation* was in order.

endemic *adj.* native to or commonly found in a specific place

syn. indigenous

Kiwi birds are *endemic* only to Australia.

The use of English is by no means *endemic* to English-speaking countries.

evoke *v.* to call up or produce memories or feelings; to cause to remember

syn. remind

Hearing her favorite song *evoked* fond memories of her high school years.

Most sounds *evoke* hints of time and place.

gradually *adv.* slowly, but surely
adj. gradual *syn.* steadily

The bay has *gradually* deteriorated over the years.
There has been a *gradual* change in the climate over the past decade.

impartial *adj.* showing no favoritism; being fair or just
n. impartiality *syn.* objective

Teachers must be *impartial* judges of their students' work.
Judges are known for their *impartiality*.

inordinate *adj.* a large amount or quantity; more than reasonable
adv. inordinately *syn.* excessive

The airlines had to cancel an *inordinate* number of flights due to the fog.
There was an *inordinately* large number of whales off the coast.

intentionally *adv.* with definite purpose and planning
adj. intentional *syn.* deliberately
n. intention
n. intent

The machine was left on *intentionally*.
Her action was an indication of her good *intentions*.

intrinsic *adj.* being a primary part of something
adv. intrinsically *syn.* inherent

A penny has little *intrinsic* value.
The forests of the Northwest are *intrinsically* rich in natural resources.

inundate *v.* to flood
n. inundation *syn.* overwhelm

The radio stations were *inundated* with reports of a severe traffic accident.
The charity received an *inundation* of donations after the news story was published.

mindset *n.* an established attitude or mood
syn. mentality

A person is more likely to succeed if he or she approaches projects with a positive *mindset.*

The political *mindset* is different in every region of the country.

nominal *adj.* very small; in form, but not in substance
adv. nominally *syn.* moderate

The office building was sold at a *nominal* price.

She was *nominally* successful as an actress.

MATCHING

Choose the synonym.

1. impartial
   - Ⓐ objective
   - Ⓑ overwhelmed
   - Ⓒ conscientious
   - Ⓓ confident

2. diminutive
   - Ⓐ conscientious
   - Ⓑ minuscule
   - Ⓒ conspicuous
   - Ⓓ obvious

3. documented
   - Ⓐ proven
   - Ⓑ intrinsic
   - Ⓒ substantial
   - Ⓓ durable

4. nominal
   - Ⓐ moderate
   - Ⓑ inherent
   - Ⓒ inevitable
   - Ⓓ harmful

5. excessive
   - Ⓐ impressive
   - Ⓑ lasting
   - Ⓒ deliberate
   - Ⓓ inordinate

6. discreetly
   - Ⓐ obviously
   - Ⓑ cautiously
   - Ⓒ unlikely
   - Ⓓ deceptively

7. agitate
   - Ⓐ heighten
   - Ⓑ reject
   - Ⓒ inundate
   - Ⓓ disturb

8. steadily
   - Ⓐ gradually
   - Ⓑ uniquely
   - Ⓒ intentionally
   - Ⓓ immediately

9. mentality
   - Ⓐ mindset
   - Ⓑ proficiency
   - Ⓒ docility
   - Ⓓ jargon

10. delighted
    - Ⓐ involved
    - Ⓑ elated
    - Ⓒ overwhelmed
    - Ⓓ highlighted

LESSON 17—MULTIPLE-CHOICE TEST QUESTIONS

1. Modes of suggestion, while usually verbal, may be visual or involve other senses. In fact, a mere suggestion may **evoke** a memory that causes a specific reaction. For instance, a person who is allergic to roses may develop an attack of asthma just from looking at a seed catalog. The element of suggestion also plays a significant role in group behavior and hypnosis.

   The word **evoke** in the passage is closest in meaning to

   Ⓐ produce
   Ⓑ engross
   Ⓒ emit
   Ⓓ favor

2. The American actor-director Orson Welles worked on the stage and in films for nearly 50 years. Yet his fame rests principally on two projects. The first, his 1938 radio adaptation of H. G. Wells's *The War of the Worlds*, was a fictitious eyewitness report of a Martian attack. The radio broadcast created a panic among listeners who, believing the attack to be real, **inundated** law enforcement agencies with numerous inquiries.

   The word **inundated** in the passage is closest in meaning to

   Ⓐ agitated
   Ⓑ overwhelmed
   Ⓒ astonished
   Ⓓ delighted

3. The use of cast-metal pieces as a medium of exchange is an ancient tradition. It probably developed out of the use in commerce of ordinary ingots of bronze and other metals that had an **intrinsic** value. Until the development of bills of exchange in medieval Europe and paper currency in medieval China, metal coins were the only means of exchange for goods and services.

   The word **intrinsic** in the passage is closest in meaning to

   Ⓐ inherent
   Ⓑ nominal
   Ⓒ documented
   Ⓓ inordinate

4. The stimuli in a projective test are **intentionally** ambiguous and open to diverse interpretations so that each person will project his unique reactions in his answers. Techniques for evaluating such responses range from the intuitive impressions of the rater to complex schemes for scoring and interpretation that require extensive calculations and interpretation.

   The word **intentionally** in the passage is closest in meaning to

   Ⓐ confidentially
   Ⓑ fundamentally
   Ⓒ arbitrarily
   Ⓓ deliberately

5. The Greek philosopher Anaximander argued that human beings are so **appallingly** helpless at birth that they would instantly die if left on their own. He also believed that known elements are continuously opposing and changing into one another and that, as a result, something different from these elements must underlie and cause changes.

   The word **appallingly** in the passage is closest in meaning to

   Ⓐ completely
   Ⓑ partially
   Ⓒ abysmally
   Ⓓ immediately

6. Some economists resist the notion that cutting taxes is beneficial. Theoretically, decreasing taxes returns money to citizens, therefore increasing jobs and improving conditions for everyone. Some economists say that will happen only with a large, sudden tax reduction. A **gradual decrease**, they say, will not stimulate spending or result in more jobs or a stronger economy. Still others oppose tax reduction altogether.

   In referring to a **gradual decrease** in taxes, the author means one that

   Ⓐ is imposed all at once.
   Ⓑ occurs slowly over time.
   Ⓒ stimulates a lot of jobs.
   Ⓓ affects everyone equally.

7. Traditionally, children of Southwest Indian tribes were treated with warmth and submissiveness during the period of infancy. Weaning was gradual, and training in cleanliness was delayed until a child could walk. Care was taken so that the children were not unduly **agitated**, and that they were protected from harm.

   The word **agitated** in the passage is closest in meaning to

   Ⓐ disturbed
   Ⓑ inundated
   Ⓒ favored
   Ⓓ exhausted

8. Most Latin-American countries achieved **nominal** independence in the ninteenth century. Yet they remained politically, economically, and culturally dependent on U.S. and European powers throughout the first half of the twentieth century. By 1960, people believed that this dependency could best be alleviated through educational reform.

   The word **nominal** in the passage is closest in meaning to

   Ⓐ scarce
   Ⓑ durable
   Ⓒ gradual
   Ⓓ moderate

9. Opinion polls have been developed since the 1930s. Polls are a scientific way of learning what large numbers of people think about various topics. They are used extensively in politics and business. In both fields many polling companies provide political candidates and businesses with **confidential** information about their public image.

   The word **confidential** in the passage is closest in meaning to

   Ⓐ discreet
   Ⓑ mysterious
   Ⓒ secret
   Ⓓ classified

10. At a meeting to discuss the federal Constitution, John Hancock was persuaded to support ratification. To get Hancock's support, some people promised him a nomination for the presidency if George Washington declined. Though appearing to be among the leaders of the revolutionaries, he was not considered an independent figure. Rather, he was a tool of Samuel Adams, who took advantage of Hancock's ambition, vanity, and **inordinate** love of popularity.

    The word **inordinate** in the passage is closest in meaning to

    Ⓐ excessive
    Ⓑ unwarranted
    Ⓒ exhaustive
    Ⓓ overwhelming

LESSON 18

- **absurd**
- **allocation**
- **balanced**
- **brazen**
- **come across**
- **culminate**
- **demeanor**
- **exert**
- **fallacious**
- **feasible**
- **intuition**
- **lack**
- **limber**
- **means**
- **preconception**
- **robust**
- **swift**

---

absurd *adj.* clearly false; without reason
syn. ridiculous

adv. absurdly
n. absurdity

Confidentially, I think his suggestion is *absurd*.
They are *absurdly* irrational about the issue.

allocation *n.* a share; a part set aside for a special purpose; an assignment of portions
syn. distribution

adj. allocated
v. allocate

His *allocation* of materials was gradually used up.
Allocating office space in the building was a difficult task.

balanced *adj.* a state where everything is of the same size or weight; an element on one side that counters an equal element on the other
syn. equalized

v. balance
n. balance

He made a *balanced* presentation of both points of view.
The museum contains a pleasant *balance* of paintings from the eighteenth and nineteenth centuries.

brazen *adj.* defiant or shameless
syn. bold

The student *brazenly* defended her thesis.
The *brazen* politician did not withdraw from the debate.

come across *v.* to find or discover, usually by chance or mistake
syn. encounter

The woman *came across* the old love letters while looking through photos of her youth.

The professor *came across* the article while searching the Internet.

culminate *v.* to finish; to reach a climax or the highest point
n. culmination
adj. culminating
syn. conclude

The rock song *culminated* in a loud guitar solo.

After four years of diligent study, the student's hard work *culminated* in several offers of full scholarships for college.

demeanor *n.* someone's outward appearance or behavior
syn. conduct (*n.*)

The old woman had a pleasant *demeanor*.

The dog was huge, but its friendly *demeanor* eased my fears.

exert *v.* to put into use; to put forth an effort
n. exertion
syn. apply

He had to *exert* all of his strength to move the heavy box.

Your body will be better prepared for physical *exertion* if you exercise daily.

fallacious *adj.* having errors
adv. fallaciously
n. fallacy
syn. incorrect

Her *fallacious* argument could not be defended.

It is a *fallacy* to think that money will bring you happiness.

feasible *adj.* able to be done
adv. feasibly
n. feasibility
syn. possible

It is a *feasible* design for the high-rise building.

Before they begin the project, a study must be done of its *feasibility*.

intuition *n.* a feeling or instinct

adj. intuitive *syn.* hunch

He often relies on his *intuition* rather than analyzing the situation logically.

Her *intuition* told her that there was more to the story than she knew.

lack *n.* a need for; an insufficient amount

adj. lacking *syn.* shortage
v. lack

There was an inordinate *lack* of rain last fall.

The mathematician was *lacking* in communication skills.

limber *adj.* to be stretched; easily shaped

syn. flexible

The dancer has a *limber* body.

He was able to perform the *limber* movements that are required of a gymnast.

means *n.* ways

syn. methods

He was told to finish the job by any *means* available to him.

The most convenient *means* of communicating with someone is by phone.

preconception *n.* an opinion formed in advance without experience or knowledge of something

adj. preconceived *syn.* bias
v. preconceive

It is difficult to overcome *preconceptions* if we are not open to new ideas.

His *preconceived* notions about Los Angeles disappeared after he visited the city.

robust *adj.* showing good health; in good shape

adv. robustly *syn.* energetic
n. robustness

The *robust* economy is expected to continue growing quickly.

The new product is selling *robustly*.

swift *adj.* quick

adv. swiftly *syn.* fast
n. swiftness

The contestants were *swift* thinkers.

They *swiftly* agreed with the conclusion of the report.

MATCHING

Choose the synonym.

1. demeanor
   Ⓐ function
   Ⓑ conduct
   Ⓒ expansion
   Ⓓ bias

2. intuition
   Ⓐ hunch
   Ⓑ decision
   Ⓒ guess
   Ⓓ analysis

3. robust
   Ⓐ energetic
   Ⓑ flexible
   Ⓒ narrow
   Ⓓ ridiculous

4. fast
   Ⓐ swift
   Ⓑ spacious
   Ⓒ intrinsic
   Ⓓ vital

5. balanced
   Ⓐ rigid
   Ⓑ documented
   Ⓒ fundamental
   Ⓓ equalized

6. distribution
   Ⓐ shortage
   Ⓑ allocation
   Ⓒ methods
   Ⓓ disapproval

7. fallacious
   Ⓐ inordinate
   Ⓑ incorrect
   Ⓒ unwarranted
   Ⓓ inevitable

8. apply
   Ⓐ exert
   Ⓑ expand
   Ⓒ conclude
   Ⓓ halt

9. feasible
   Ⓐ absurd
   Ⓑ possible
   Ⓒ limber
   Ⓓ selective

10. come across
    Ⓐ proceed
    Ⓑ travel
    Ⓒ encounter
    Ⓓ transport

LESSON 18—MULTIPLE-CHOICE TEST QUESTIONS

1. Early analog televisions used carrier waves that were picked up by a receiving antenna and then carried to the television receiver. Inside the receiver, the video and audio signals were separated and amplified. They then passed into the picture tube, which used a narrow beam of electrons that bombarded, in a scanning motion, the back of a screen coated with a fluorescent compound. This process **culminated** in the projection of images on the screen.

   The word **culminated** in the passage is closest in meaning to

   Ⓐ proceeded
   Ⓑ began
   Ⓒ resulted
   Ⓓ repeated

2. A simple example of a **means** by which energy is converted from one form to another is demonstrated in the tossing of a ball into the air. When the ball is thrown vertically from the ground, its speed and its kinetic energy decreases steadily until it comes to rest momentarily at its highest point.

   The word **means** in the passage is closest in meaning to

   Ⓐ description
   Ⓑ method
   Ⓒ theory
   Ⓓ benefit

3. The First Continental Congress was formed to protest the British Parliament's intrusion into certain colony affairs. This congress urged the colonies to arm themselves for defense of their rights. It believed that it would be **absurd** not to give a forceful response to England's closing of the port of Boston. By the time the Second Continental Congress convened, the American Revolution had begun.

   The word **absurd** in the passage is closest in meaning to

   Ⓐ ridiculous
   Ⓑ difficult
   Ⓒ feasible
   Ⓓ fallacious

4. The modern sport of gymnastics was essentially the result of the work of the German Friedrich Jahn, in the early nineteenth century. He invented many of the exercises and some of the apparatus of later gymnastics, such as the parallel bars, the rings, and the horizontal bar. Jahn's work was aimed mainly at strengthening the body. The result of gymnastics training is a well-toned, **limber** body.

   The word **limber** in the passage is closest in meaning to

   Ⓐ flexible
   Ⓑ slender
   Ⓒ tiny
   Ⓓ disciplined

5. Many experts believe that in the early years of the twenty-first century the **lack** of water, rather than the availability of fertile land, will be the major obstacle to increased worldwide food production. As with land, the amount of water available for agricultural use cannot easily be increased. Research is now being conducted to improve water availability and thereby increase the amount of land available for farming.

   The word **lack** in the passage is closest in meaning to

   Ⓐ misuse
   Ⓑ abuse
   Ⓒ shortage
   Ⓓ distribution

6. The aim of TV advertising is to motivate viewers to spend money on products; the aim of TV news is to give a **balanced view** of people, products, and events. These aims sometimes conflict with each other. While advertisers stress product features that contribute to a feeling of well-being or enhanced status, reporters have an obligation to describe products more objectively. Reporters have a responsibility to describe both positive and negative product features.

   In referring to a **balanced view**, the author is referring to

   Ⓐ a clearly biased summary.
   Ⓑ information for and against.
   Ⓒ an advocate's point of view.
   Ⓓ factual support for TV ads.

7. A typical cellar may be located beneath a house. It may also be located outdoors, partly underground, with the upper part mounded over with earth. This would protect items from freezing and maintain a fairly uniform temperature and humidity level. Unheated basements or heated and insulated ground-level buildings make it **feasible** to store fruits and vegetables for short periods.

   The word **feasible** in the passage is closest in meaning to

   Ⓐ balanced
   Ⓑ possible
   Ⓒ enacted
   Ⓓ persuasive

8. The operating system of a computer network protects computers from access by illegal users. It also prevents data corruption introduced by unintentional mistakes made by legitimate users. A **robust** security scheme is particularly important for computers that are connected to a communications network, since it has many potential users.

   The word **robust** in the passage is closest in meaning to

   Ⓐ steady
   Ⓑ intrinsic
   Ⓒ strong
   Ⓓ complex

9. Knowledge of how early wheels were constructed is derived from "chariot burials" found in the city-states of Kish and Ur. Wheels were formed from three planks of wood that were clamped by wooden struts and bound with leather tires that were held in place by copper nails. The simplicity of their design allowed for **swift** repairs.

   The word **swift** in the passage is closest in meaning to

   Ⓐ steady
   Ⓑ ample
   Ⓒ suitable
   Ⓓ rapid

10. The law of large numbers, popularly known as "the law of averages," is often thought to require that future outcomes balance past outcomes. This is a **fallacy**. A three-digit lottery number has the same probability of being selected every day. The fact that it has not been selected for a given number of days does not increase this probability.

    The word **fallacy** in the passage is closest in meaning to

    Ⓐ endorsement
    Ⓑ sufficiency
    Ⓒ misconception
    Ⓓ preconception

LESSON 19

- **coherent**
- **emulate**
- **evolve**
- **fabricate**
- **generic**
- **look over**
- **normally**
- **notion**
- **novel**
- **nurture**
- **opposition**
- **relate**
- **suspect**
- **transform**
- **trigger**
- **unbiased**
- **varied**

---

coherent *adj.* well reasoned; ideas that are clearly presented
*sticking together as a group
syn. logical

adv. coherently
v. cohere
n. coherence
adj. cohesive*
n. cohesion*

It was a well-balanced, *coherent* presentation.
There was a *cohesive* feeling among the new workers.

emulate *v.* to match or achieve by imitation
syn. mimic

Young puppies tend to *emulate* the habits of older dogs.
Many authors attempt to *emulate* Hemingway's writing style.

evolve *v.* to grow; to go through a period of change
syn. develop

n. evolution

The management team's idea *evolved* over a period of two years.
The country's hopes for a rapid *evolution* of its economy depend on approval of free trade agreements.

fabricate *v.* to make up, usually with an intent to fool or trick; to lie
syn. invent

adj. fabricated
n. fabrication

The executive *fabricated* the story about the merger.
His alibi is the weakest *fabrication* I have ever heard.

generic *adj.* relating to a whole group or category of things
adv. generically
syn. general

"Bird" is the *generic* term used to describe animals with feathers.

Universities provide students with the *generic* skills needed to compete in the workplace.

look over *ph. v.* to review something; inspect
syn. examine

He asked his mentor to *look over* his essay.

She *looked over* the research in the library's database.

normally *adv.* commonly; usually
adj. normal
v. normalize
n. normalization
n. norm
syn. typically

It is *normally* quite cold this time of the year.

The new treaty led to a *normalization* of relations between the two countries.

notion *n.* an idea, belief, or opinion
syn. concept

She has the *notion* that she wants to become an architect.

Some outlandish *notions* about the origin of the solar system have been disproved.

novel *adj.* something unusual, uncommon; new
syn. original

The physicist had some *novel* ideas about traveling at the speed of light.

The *novel* suggestions were implemented.

nurture *v.* to support and encourage the development of something

adj. nurturing
n. nurture

syn. cultivate

The owner of the vineyard carefully *nurtures* the grapevines in order to produce the best grapes.

That school is well-known for having a *nurturing* learning environment.

opposition *n.* the state of acting against; not being in agreement

adj. opposed
v. oppose

syn. resistance

The students voiced their *opposition* to the rise in tuition.

The government *opposed* price controls.

relate *v.* to tell; to show a connection between two things

adj. related
n. relation
n. relationship

syn. communicate

Although they did not agree with the plan, they did not *relate* their opposition to it.

What is the *relationship* between supply and demand?

suspect *v.* to think that something is true, but having no proof

adj. suspected
n. suspicion
n. suspect

syn. speculate

He *suspected* that the substance was not present in the compound.

I have a *suspicion* that he will want to participate in the investigation.

transform *v.* to change in form or appearance

n. transformation
n. transformer

syn. alter

The leader's policies *transformed* the country in many positive ways.

The student's *transformation* from a "D" student to a "B" student was remarkable.

trigger *v.* to initiate, cause, or start
adj. triggered *syn.* generate

The possibility of being in the path of a hurricane *triggered* fear in the residents of coastal areas.

The town hall meeting *triggered* a lively debate about the need for increased taxes.

unbiased *adj.* with no preconceptions
syn. objective

Her *unbiased* analysis of the problem allowed her to find the solution more rapidly.

Here is *unbiased* proof that nitrogen exists in this compound.

varied *adj.* being of many different types
adv. variably *syn.* diverse
adj. variable
adj. various
v. vary
n. variant
n. variety
n. variation
n. variability

The class expressed *varied* opinions about the movie.

There are *various* ways to solve the problem.

MATCHING

Choose the synonym.

1. nurture
   - Ⓐ function
   - Ⓑ cultivate
   - Ⓒ convey
   - Ⓓ agitate

2. coherent
   - Ⓐ novel
   - Ⓑ original
   - Ⓒ logical
   - Ⓓ robust

3. resistance
   - Ⓐ opposition
   - Ⓑ preservation
   - Ⓒ preconception
   - Ⓓ allocation

4. evolve
   - Ⓐ develop
   - Ⓑ elude
   - Ⓒ involve
   - Ⓓ influence

5. varied
   - Ⓐ diverse
   - Ⓑ feasible
   - Ⓒ hazardous
   - Ⓓ nominal

6. trigger
   - Ⓐ harbor
   - Ⓑ transform
   - Ⓒ encounter
   - Ⓓ generate

7. probe
   - Ⓐ expansion
   - Ⓑ means
   - Ⓒ investigation
   - Ⓓ abuse

8. generic
   - Ⓐ docile
   - Ⓑ original
   - Ⓒ general
   - Ⓓ mundane

9. mimic
   - Ⓐ saturate
   - Ⓑ simulate
   - Ⓒ emulate
   - Ⓓ create

10. unbiased
    - Ⓐ antiquated
    - Ⓑ noteworthy
    - Ⓒ exhausted
    - Ⓓ objective

LESSON 19—MULTIPLE-CHOICE TEST QUESTIONS

1. The capacity among animals to reconstruct body parts is not as common as the ability to compensate for lost tissues. This is due to the complex anatomy of body parts, which requires more elaborate regeneration control mechanisms. If we **look over** only the vertebrates of the animal kingdom, salamanders are the best regenerators of body parts. Because of this characteristic, they are the subject of much folklore. For example, the fire salamander is so called because of an antiquated belief that it could withstand fire.

   The phrasal verb **look over** in the passage is closest in meaning to

   Ⓐ exclude
   Ⓑ examine
   Ⓒ emphasize
   Ⓓ discuss

2. Throughout history, most technological progress has been a result of relatively minor improvements and refinements rather than through major inventions. Organized research is well suited for this kind of development. However, organized research may discourage **novel** approaches and inhibit creativity, so seminal discoveries are still likely to be made by inventors in the classic individualistic tradition.

   The word **novel** in the passage is closest in meaning to

   Ⓐ original
   Ⓑ varied
   Ⓒ coherent
   Ⓓ unbiased

3. Economist Alfred Marshall received acclaim for his economic ideas that integrated modern and classical economic theory. Classicists believed that price was determined by the cost of producing goods, but the modern school believed that price was dependent on the **notion** of marginal utility, or usefulness of the goods. Marshall's theory that price is determined by both cost and utility gained wide acceptance.

   The word **notion** in the passage is closest in meaning to

   Ⓐ investigation
   Ⓑ concept
   Ⓒ effectiveness
   Ⓓ opposition

4. Tidal waves are **triggered** by tectonic displacements. Volcanoes, landslides, or earthquakes on the sea floor can cause a sudden displacement of the water above. This displacement forms a small group of water waves having a wavelength equal to the water depth at the point of origin. In deep water, tidal waves are so long and so slight that ships seldom notice their presence. But as the waves reach shallow water, they increase in amplitude, making them potentially the most catastrophic of all ocean waves.

   The word **triggered** in the passage is closest in meaning to

   Ⓐ fostered
   Ⓑ heightened
   Ⓒ inundated
   Ⓓ generated

5. Throughout the ages, the role of the heart was long considered a mystery. Some thought that it was the source of the soul. Others thought that it was the center of love, courage, happiness, and sadness. Primitive humans were no doubt aware of the heartbeat and probably recognized that the tiny heart, **normally** about the size of a fist, was an organ whose malfunction could cause sudden death.

   The word **normally** in the passage is closest in meaning to

   Ⓐ roughly
   Ⓑ rarely
   Ⓒ scarcely
   Ⓓ typically

6. There is a growing sentiment **in opposition to** sea bass fishing. Most sea bass spawn between May and August, which coincides with the height of the fishing season. Fishing affects the reproductive capacity of the species disproportionately since it does not distinguish between males and females. Instead, it captures both indiscriminately. However, it takes six years longer for a female bass to become fertile than a male.

   In stating that there is a growing sentiment **in opposition to** sea bass fishing, the author means that people

   Ⓐ favor the fishing of sea bass.
   Ⓑ see it as a positive activity.
   Ⓒ dislike sea bass.
   Ⓓ are against its continuation.

7. Gymnastic competitions are judged and scored on both an individual and a team basis. Judges award points to each participant in each event on a 0-to-10 scale, 10 being perfect. The goal of completely **unbiased** judging is very difficult to achieve. Although guidelines are provided, judges seldom agree on the quality of a performance.

   The word **unbiased** in the passage is closest in meaning to

   Ⓐ objective
   Ⓑ balanced
   Ⓒ logical
   Ⓓ suitable

8. Prior to highly advanced weather satellite technology, sounding rockets were used to gather weather intelligence. Sounding rockets were unmanned rockets that recorded atmospheric conditions at heights that were 50–100 miles beyond the reach of airplanes and balloons. **Emulating** weather balloon technology, these rockets usually followed a vertical path as they investigated upper atmospheric conditions with their scientific instruments.

   The word **emulating** in the passage is closest in meaning to

   Ⓐ replacing
   Ⓑ improving
   Ⓒ mimicking
   Ⓓ altering

9. Reality is perceived through appearances. However, appearances are incompatible with reality. If an oar in water looks broken but feels straight to the touch, this must be acknowledged. Thus, a **coherent** picture of reality requires that we acknowledge that appearances can be deceptive.

   The word **coherent** in the passage is closest in meaning to

   Ⓐ logical
   Ⓑ acceptable
   Ⓒ distributed
   Ⓓ vital

10. "Speedwriting" was a writing system devised and patented by Emma Dearborn in 1924. The system used words that were recorded as they sounded, and only employed "long vowels." Thus, "you" is written "u" and "like" is "lik." Some letters were **transformed** to allow for speedy transcription, and the system often employed abbreviations and flourishes.

    The word **transformed** in the passage is closest in meaning to

    Ⓐ illustrated
    Ⓑ altered
    Ⓒ written
    Ⓓ conveyed

LESSON 20

- **accentuate**
- **devise**
- **disguise**
- **embedded**
- **ignite**
- **indifferent**
- **initiate**
- **innovative**
- **narrate**
- **nevertheless**
- **obsolete**
- **omit**
- **outlandish**
- **overcome**
- **partially**
- **portray**
- **streamline**

---

accentuate *v.* to highlight; to give more importance to

adj. accentuated *syn.* emphasize
n. accentuation

The colorful dress *accentuated* the joy of the occasion.

The supervisor *accentuated* her preference for hard-working employees during the performance appraisal.

devise *v.* to brainstorm; to come up with an idea

adj. devisable *syn.* formulate

The firefighters *devised* a plan to safely bring the cat down from the tree.

The scientists had to *devise* an entirely new experiment after the first one failed.

disguise *v.* to hide the usual appearance of something

adj. disguised *syn.* conceal
n. disguise

It is hard to *disguise* the fact that business is slow.

Everyone saw through his *disguise.*

embedded *adj.* included or found inside something

v. embed *syn.* inserted

The archaeologist found a rare fossil *embedded* in the rock face.

The instructions say to *embed* the seeds one inch apart.

ignite — *v.* to set on fire; to give energy or life to something

adj. ignitable
n. ignition

syn. kindle

The jury's decision *ignited* a fierce debate in the legal community.
Wood is difficult to *ignite* if it is damp.

indifferent — *adj.* being uninterested or not caring about something

n. indifference

syn. apathetic

The teacher was *indifferent* to student requests to extend the project's deadline.
The player's *indifference* about his error on the field upset the coach.

initiate — *v.* to begin; to establish; to take decisive action without help

adj. initiated
n. initiation
n. initiative

syn. launch

The newcomers *initiated* the long citizenship process.
Their work shows a lot of *initiative*.

innovative — *adj.* something newly introduced; creative

n. innovator
n. innovation

syn. creative

This *innovative* project is worthy of support.
There have been many *innovations* in the field of genetic engineering.

narrate — *v.* to tell a story; relate

adj. narrative
n. narrative
n. narration
n. narrator

syn. relate

The American actor, Morgan Freeman, *narrated* the documentary film.
Her fabricated *narrative* generated a lot of excitement.

nevertheless *conj.* in spite of that
syn. nonetheless

She was quite sick; *nevertheless*, she attended all of her classes.

His project was flawed; *nevertheless*, it won second prize.

obsolete *adv.* being old fashioned; no longer in general use
n. obsolescence
syn. outdated

Some people believe that writing instruments, such as pencils and pens, will soon be *obsolete*.

Some products are manufactured with planned *obsolescence*.

omit *v.* to leave out; not include
adj. omitted
n. omission
syn. neglect

She inadvertently *omitted* some important data from the report.

His paper had several notable *omissions*.

outlandish *adj.* strange and unpleasant; beyond accepted norms
adv. outlandishly
syn. bizarre

His *outlandish* ideas demonstrated his creativity.

Rebellious youth in many countries dress *outlandishly*.

overcome *v.* to defeat; fight with success; to take control of an individual
syn. conquer

The young woman was *overcome* with emotion when she learned she had won a scholarship.

The family *overcame* many obstacles to purchase the house.

partially *adv.* a part of the whole; incomplete
adv. partly
adj. partial
n. part
syn. somewhat

The clerk was only *partially* responsible for the error.

The business venture was only a *partial* success.

portray *v.* to represent; to act
n. portrayal *syn.* depict

The actress *portrayed* an orphan in the movie.

The book's *portrayal* of Mozart as a calm, mature individual is inaccurate.

streamline *v.* to update; to make more efficient or concise
adj. streamlined *syn.* simplify

The planning process must be *streamlined* in order for it to be more reliable.

Internet stores have *streamlined* the process of finding, buying, and selling merchandise.

MATCHING

Choose the synonym.

1. kindle
   Ⓐ initiate
   Ⓑ ignite
   Ⓒ persuade
   Ⓓ overcome

2. indifferent
   Ⓐ dissimilar
   Ⓑ outlandish
   Ⓒ diverse
   Ⓓ apathetic

3. streamline
   Ⓐ transform
   Ⓑ simplify
   Ⓒ allocate
   Ⓓ navigate

4. embed
   Ⓐ omit
   Ⓑ devise
   Ⓒ insert
   Ⓓ emulate

5. obsolete
   Ⓐ outdated
   Ⓑ current
   Ⓒ omitted
   Ⓓ opposed

6. relate
   Ⓐ restore
   Ⓑ record
   Ⓒ narrate
   Ⓓ balance

7. nevertheless
   Ⓐ nonetheless
   Ⓑ albeit
   Ⓒ although
   Ⓓ presumably

8. formulate
   Ⓐ conceal
   Ⓑ delight
   Ⓒ feign
   Ⓓ devise

9. emphasize
   Ⓐ accentuate
   Ⓑ conquer
   Ⓒ suspect
   Ⓓ select

10. portray
    Ⓐ refine
    Ⓑ depict
    Ⓒ pass
    Ⓓ abuse

LESSON 20—MULTIPLE-CHOICE TEST QUESTIONS

1. In 1982, after years of debate, the Canadian government agreed to extend a constitutional guarantee to their bill of rights. **Embedded** in this Charter of Rights and Freedoms is a reinforcement of the Constitution. Yet Parliament and the provincial legislatures have limited power to pass laws that might conflict with certain provincial rights.

   The word **embedded** in the passage is closest in meaning to

   Ⓐ inserted
   Ⓑ summarized
   Ⓒ outlined
   Ⓓ addressed

2. Although the assertion is at least **partially** true, the citizens of Kansas resent the suggestion that they live in a cultural vacuum. Most of the larger cities have amateur theater groups, while Topeka and Wichita support symphony orchestras. The numerous colleges and universities in the state provide a concentration of art and music in many small communities that otherwise would have no similar activities.

   The word **partially** in the passage is closest in meaning to

   Ⓐ somewhat
   Ⓑ undeniably
   Ⓒ nevertheless
   Ⓓ occasionally

3. Before becoming proficient, sword swallowers must first **overcome** their fear of projecting the sharp sword down their throat. Only after long hours of practice and experience can one swallow the sword comfortably. Beyond their entertainment value, exhibits of sword swallowing have helped to further medicine. By demonstrating to physicians that the pharynx could be accustomed to contact, experimentation and exploration of the involved organs is possible.

   The word **overcome** in the passage is closest in meaning to

   Ⓐ disguise
   Ⓑ conquer
   Ⓒ treat
   Ⓓ accentuate

4. Sun Ra was an important African-American jazz pianist and bandleader of the 1930s. Having a flare for being creative, he dressed his band in purple blazers, white gloves, and propeller beanies. The band developed into The Arkestra, and over time the costumes and showmanship grew ever more **outlandish**. The musicianship, however, was uniformly excellent, and Sun Ra developed into a serious experimenter, fusing jazz with African music, dance, and acrobatics.

   The word **outlandish** in the passage is closest in meaning to

   Ⓐ prosperous
   Ⓑ bizarre
   Ⓒ relaxing
   Ⓓ melodical

5. Modern descriptions of written languages are in most cases excellent, but they still **omit** an explicit account of a native speaker's competence in his language, by virtue of which one calls him a speaker of English, Japanese, Arabic, or Chinese. Recent studies of language have revealed how more research is needed in order to fully describe linguistic competence.

   The word **omit** in the passage is closest in meaning to

   Ⓐ portray
   Ⓑ contribute
   Ⓒ neglect
   Ⓓ relate

6. All team sports require reactive and proactive players. In soccer, for example, fullbacks, stoppers, sweepers, and midfielders have the job of preventing the opposing team from advancing very far. Goalies are responsible for stopping the ball and keeping their opponents from scoring. By comparison, the center forward has to **take the initiative**, seize the ball, move it down the field, keep it going, and move it forward into the enemy end zone.

   In stating that the center forward has to **take the initiative**, the author means that the center forward's responsibility is to

   Ⓐ play in an offensive way.
   Ⓑ assume a supportive role.
   Ⓒ react to opposing moves.
   Ⓓ wait for others to score.

7. A **disguise** is often used to create an interesting or amusing character. The mask is a type of disguise that is still used in the 21st century during festive occasions. Masks may be outlandish, hideous, or superficially horrible. Festival masks are commonly used during Halloween and Mardi Gras, or at masquerade-themed gatherings.

   The word **disguise** in the passage is closest in meaning to

   Ⓐ elusiveness
   Ⓑ confidant
   Ⓒ omission
   Ⓓ concealment

8. The length, content, and form of folktales vary enormously. Both a short joke and an adventure-filled romance requiring several hours to **narrate** can be characterized as folktales. Folktales may be set in a mythical past, in historic times, or in the present. Storytelling is a basic human need. Therefore folktales, even in technological cultures, remain strong.

   The word **narrate** in the passage is closest in meaning to

   Ⓐ relate
   Ⓑ dictate
   Ⓒ elaborate
   Ⓓ mention

9. Jan Swammerdam was a biologist who studied relatively few organisms, but in great detail. He employed highly **innovative** techniques such as injecting wax into the circulatory system to hold the blood vessels firm. He also dissected fragile structures under water to avoid destroying them.

   The word **innovative** in the passage is closest in meaning to

   Ⓐ intricate
   Ⓑ absurd
   Ⓒ conspicuous
   Ⓓ inventive

10. Contracts between employees and employers state that the worker will do what the employer asks. In return, the employer pays the worker a fee, which the worker can use to purchase goods and services made by other workers who have also entered into a voluntary relationship with another employer. A cooperative spirit and a desire for mutual benefit **accentuate** healthy employer-employee relationships.

    The word **accentuate** in the passage is closest in meaning to

    Ⓐ promote
    Ⓑ determine
    Ⓒ emphasize
    Ⓓ forfeit

Lesson 21

- **affluent**
- **decline**
- **outburst**
- **partisan**
- **pattern**
- **phenomena**
- **philanthropic**
- **placid**
- **plentiful**
- **propensity**
- **reaction**
- **rhythm**
- **run into**
- **scenic**
- **shallow**
- **sheltered**
- **vanishing**

---

affluent *adj.* rich in money or means; prosperous

n. affluence *syn.* wealthy

He is not from an *affluent* family, but he worked hard and was able to attend college.

The *affluent* supporter had a building named in her honor.

decline *v.* to move from good to bad, or from much to little; to refuse

n. decline *syn.* decrease

The old man's health has *declined* since he retired.

Serious communicable diseases are on the *decline* in most parts of the world.

outburst *n.* a sudden and intense release of something

syn. eruption

The joke caused an *outburst* of laughter from the audience.

There was an *outburst* of complaints from the students when the teacher moved the test to Monday.

partisan *adj.* strongly supporting a group or point of view

syn. biased

Partisan political infighting has caused a decline in the efficiency of Congress.

His views reflected his *partisan* bias.

pattern — *n.* a regular, repeated arrangement or action
adj. patterned
v. pattern
syn. habit

The bright *pattern* of the monarch butterfly distracts its predators.
The new stadium was *patterned* after the old traditional ballparks.

phenomena — *n.* natural events or facts; strange or notable happenings
adv. phenomenally
adj. phenomenal
n. phenomenon
syn. events

Rain showers are almost unknown *phenomena* in the Atacama Desert of Chile.
The musician's *phenomenal* performance was applauded by the critics.

philanthropic — *adj.* a feeling of love for people, usually resulting in financial aid to worthy causes
n. philanthropist
n. philanthropy
syn. humanitarian

The *philanthropic* work of the foundation benefits all sectors of society.
His *philanthropy* is recognized around the world.

placid — *adj.* quiet; not easily upset
adv. placidly
syn. calm

The *placid* nature of her personality made her easy to work with.
The waves moved *placidly* toward shore.

plentiful — *adj.* more than sufficient
adv. plentifully
n. plenty
syn. abundant

Examples of Miro's art are *plentiful.*
A balanced diet normally provides *plenty* of the necessary vitamins.

propensity — *n.* a bias toward certain things or actions
syn. tendency

He has a *propensity* to procrastinate.
She has a *propensity* for being extremely friendly to newcomers.

reaction *n.* a reply; a change that occurs when substances are mixed

syn. response

adv. reactively
adj. reactive
v. react
adj. reactionary

When chlorine and ammonia are mixed, the chemical *reaction* causes chlorine gas.

They *reacted* to the report by making some swift changes in management.

rhythm *n.* a regular pattern, usually in music

syn. pulse

adv. rhythmically
adj. rhythmic

The *rhythm* of the rain hitting the roof put him to sleep.

She noticed the *rhythmic* beating of her heart as the moment of truth arrived.

run into *ph. v.* to come into contact with something or someone

syn. encounter

She *ran into* her old roommate at the reunion.

The distracted driver narrowly avoided *running into* the tree.

scenic *adj.* concerning pleasant natural surroundings

syn. picturesque

adv. scenically
n. scenery
n. scene

The *scenic* route to the summit is much more interesting than the fastest route.

The *scenery* in rural Japan is impressive.

shallow *adj.* not far from top to bottom

syn. superficial

adv. shallowly
n. shallowness

Estuaries are typically *shallow* bodies of water.

The results of their research demonstrated the *shallowness* of the hypothesis.

sheltered *adj.* protected from harmful elements; isolated from reality

v. shelter
n. shelter

syn. protected

She has led a *sheltered* life, her parents having done everything for her.

Everyone looked for *shelter* from the blazing sun.

vanishing *adj.* going out of sight

v. vanish

syn. disappearing

The red squirrel is a *vanishing* species that needs a protected habitat to survive.

No one knows with certainty what caused the dinosaurs to *vanish* from the face of the earth.

MATCHING

Choose the synonym.

1. picturesque
   - Ⓐ scenic
   - Ⓑ calm
   - Ⓒ outlandish
   - Ⓓ fertile

2. partisan
   - Ⓐ patterned
   - Ⓑ bizarre
   - Ⓒ abundant
   - Ⓓ biased

3. eruption
   - Ⓐ disguise
   - Ⓑ outburst
   - Ⓒ omission
   - Ⓓ decrease

4. disappear
   - Ⓐ vary
   - Ⓑ vanish
   - Ⓒ reject
   - Ⓓ fabricate

5. shallow
   - Ⓐ swift
   - Ⓑ substantial
   - Ⓒ placid
   - Ⓓ superficial

6. propensity
   - Ⓐ modicum
   - Ⓑ tendency
   - Ⓒ aspect
   - Ⓓ intuition

7. reaction
   - Ⓐ allocation
   - Ⓑ investigation
   - Ⓒ response
   - Ⓓ means

8. rich
   - Ⓐ fertile
   - Ⓑ saturated
   - Ⓒ influential
   - Ⓓ affluent

9. protected
   - Ⓐ plentiful
   - Ⓑ phenomenal
   - Ⓒ sheltered
   - Ⓓ passable

10. rhythm
    - Ⓐ pulse
    - Ⓑ pattern
    - Ⓒ function
    - Ⓓ notion

LESSON 21—MULTIPLE-CHOICE TEST QUESTIONS

1. Until the latter half of the twentieth century, the Chesapeake Bay's sheltered, nutrient-rich waters supported **plentiful** populations of marine life. Commercial fishing and recreational activities abounded. By the 1970s, however, residential and industrial development of the surrounding land had led to significant pollution of the bay. Various projects have been initiated in an effort to reverse the environmental damage that the bay has suffered.

   The word **plentiful** in the passage is closest in meaning to

   Ⓐ vanishing
   Ⓑ abundant
   Ⓒ fascinating
   Ⓓ declining

2. The bee family Apidae, which includes honeybees, no longer uses honeypots that could be damaged by exposure to the elements. Instead, honey and pollen are stored in vertical combs with a layer of cells on each surface. Of the four species of honeybees in this family, only three are found in Asia. Their nests have several combs and are **sheltered** in crevices of rocks or hollows of trees.

   The word **sheltered** in the passage is closest in meaning to

   Ⓐ recovered
   Ⓑ abundant
   Ⓒ discovered
   Ⓓ protected

3. Andrew Carnegie established several independent, **philanthropic** foundations. Among them are funds for the recognition of heroic acts. These include the Carnegie United Kingdom Trust, the Endowment for International Peace, and the Carnegie Foundation for the Advancement of Teaching, which was established in 1905 to provide pensions for college teachers.

   The word **philanthropic** in the passage is closest in meaning to

   Ⓐ partisan
   Ⓑ service
   Ⓒ humanitarian
   Ⓓ financial

4. The world of magic comprises a wide range of **phenomena**, from the intricate ritual beliefs and practices of religious systems, to acts of conjuring and sleight of hand for entertainment. Magic is a social and cultural phenomenon found in all places and in all periods of history, with varying degrees of importance.

   The word **phenomena** in the passage is closest in meaning to

   Ⓐ motions
   Ⓑ patterns
   Ⓒ expectations
   Ⓓ occurrences

5. A person's need for food is determined by age and by average heights and weights. Individual activity levels are also used to determine the level of ideal calorie consumption. For example, a **decrease** in recommended daily calorie consumption with increasing age is consistent with the known reduction in metabolism that occurs with aging and with a normal decrease in physical activity.

   The word **decrease** in the passage is closest in meaning to

   Ⓐ decline
   Ⓑ balance
   Ⓒ resistance
   Ⓓ development

6. Liquids vary in the amount of acid they contain. For example, water contains relatively little acid, while vinegar contains a large quantity. Acidic content is determined by dipping litmus paper into a liquid. This paper is saturated with a colorant obtained from plants called lichens. The colorant **reacts to** the presence of acid by turning different shades of red—the brightness of the shade can be measured on a scale called a pH scale.

   In stating that the colorant **reacts to** the presence of acid in the liquid, the author means that it

   Ⓐ combines chemically with the acid.
   Ⓑ disappears or dissolves in the liquid.
   Ⓒ causes the liquid to lose its redness.
   Ⓓ neutralizes the acid into a base.

7. Gars are long, slender, predatory fish, with a long, tooth-studded jaw and a tough, armored skin. They are a primitive fish that inhabit **placid** fresh waters of the Western Hemisphere. Because of the highly vascular and cellular nature of the gar's swim bladder, it functions as a lung. This makes the gar able to survive in large numbers in the Everglades of the southern United States.

   The word **placid** in the passage is closest in meaning to

   Ⓐ steady
   Ⓑ protected
   Ⓒ calm
   Ⓓ sheltered

8. In the human body, different toxins produce different **reactions**. Irritation of the upper respiratory tract by inhaled formaldehyde gas is rapidly reversible because as soon as inhalation ends, the irritation subsides. In contrast, the response produced by silica dust is irreversible, because once the silicotic nodules are formed, they remain in the lung.

   The word **reactions** in the passage is closest in meaning to

   Ⓐ responses
   Ⓑ narrations
   Ⓒ influences
   Ⓓ harvests

9. Much of the world's unique heritage is endangered by pollution, the advance of human settlements, conflicts over the use of land and resources, and other problems. Thus, many countries are setting aside **scenic** natural areas as rapidly as possible. The tendency of many governments has been to establish as many parks as possible before natural environments are altered by human activities.

   The word **scenic** in the passage is closest in meaning to

   Ⓐ cultivated
   Ⓑ traditional
   Ⓒ delightful
   Ⓓ picturesque

10. A "must carry" rule is designed to ensure that local TV stations do not **vanish** from cable TV offerings. It requires cable systems to carry all local broadcast channels within a certain area of their transmitters. The law was struck down in 1985, although many aspects of that case are still being argued.

    The word **vanish** in the passage is closest in meaning to

    Ⓐ graduate
    Ⓑ pass
    Ⓒ disappear
    Ⓓ elude

LESSON 22

- **account**
- **alleviate**
- **archaic**
- **bring about**
- **enlighten**
- **hasten**
- **hue**
- **influx**
- **intricate**
- **magnitude**
- **oblige**
- **overlook**
- **practical**
- **predominant**
- **prompt**
- **provoke**

---

account *n.* a report of an event; money kept in a bank; a statement of something used or received, usually a financial report

adj. accountable
v. account
n. accounting
n. accountant

syn. story

His *account* of the incident varied from that of the other witnesses.

We need an *accounting* of all the money that was spent.

alleviate *v.* to make something less severe; to improve

syn. lessen

This medicine *alleviates* allergy symptoms.

Regular meditation has been shown to *alleviate* stress.

archaic *adj.* very old; old-fashioned; no longer used

syn. ancient

These *archaic* methods of farming must be brought up-to-date.

His speech was full of *archaic* expressions.

bring about *ph. v.* to cause something to happen

syn. generate

The invention of the cell phone *brought about* an end to the popularity of traditional telephones.

The newly elected president of the club promised to *bring about* positive changes.

enlighten — *v.* to give information or understanding to someone
syn. instruct

n. enlightenment
adj. enlightened

Books often *enlighten* readers to different ways of thinking.

The speaker *enlightened* the audience on how to succeed in college.

hasten — *v.* to cause to go faster; move forward more quickly
syn. accelerate

adj. hastily
adj. hasty
n. hastiness

After notifying the driver's family of the accident, the officer *hastened* to add that their son had not been hurt.

You should not make important decisions *hastily.*

hue — *n.* color
syn. color

The *hue* of the sunset was beautiful.

The *hue* of the room gave it a warm feeling.

influx — *n.* a sudden increase
syn. inflow

Each holiday season, the company experiences an *influx* of customers.

There was an *influx* of Western influence in eastern Asia.

intricate — *adj.* having many parts; finely detailed
syn. complex

adv. intricately
n. intricacy

The *intricate* design of the vase made it a valuable piece for her collection.

I cannot begin to understand all of the *intricacies* of modern automobile motors.

magnitude *n.* of great size or importance

adv. magnificently
adj. magnificent
v. magnify*
n. magnification*

*to increase

syn. dimension

The *magnitude* of shock waves determines the damage that occurs during an earthquake.

The invention of the telephone was a *magnificent* achievement for mankind.

oblige *v.* to have to do something

adv. obligingly
adj. obliging
adj. obligatory
n. obligation

syn. require

She felt *obliged* to choose him as her lab partner.

Payment of the student activity fee was *obligatory*.

overlook *v.* to ignore or neglect

adj. overlooked

syn. disregard

Scientists must not *overlook* any aspect of experimental procedure.

The *overlooked* error raised his score on the test.

practical *adj.* convenient or effective

adv. practically
adj. practicable
n. practicality

syn. functional

Her ambitious plan was not very *practical*.

Space travel to distant planets is not *practicable* at this time.

predominant *adj.* the most noticeable or powerful element

adv. predominantly
n. predominate
n. predominance

syn. principal

The *predominant* export of the Middle East is petroleum.

Many cities in the Southwest are *predominantly* Hispanic.

prompt — *v.* to cause something to happen; do quickly; be on time

adv. promptly
n. promptness

syn. induce

His emotional plea *prompted* the director to give him a second chance.

Promptness is a valued trait in the professional world.

provoke — *v.* to cause or produce negative behavior or result

n. provocation
adj. provocative

syn. trigger

The installation of speed cameras *provoked* an angry response from the public.

The manager did not deliberately *provoke* the argument among his workers.

MATCHING

Choose the synonym.

1. intricate
   - Ⓐ functional
   - Ⓑ complex
   - Ⓒ predominant
   - Ⓓ inordinate

2. disregard
   - Ⓐ overcome
   - Ⓑ disperse
   - Ⓒ decline
   - Ⓓ overlook

3. idle
   - Ⓐ initiated
   - Ⓑ inundated
   - Ⓒ inactive
   - Ⓓ intrinsic

4. archaic
   - Ⓐ plentiful
   - Ⓑ ancient
   - Ⓒ placid
   - Ⓓ absurd

5. bring about
   - Ⓐ generate
   - Ⓑ heighten
   - Ⓒ hasten
   - Ⓓ ignite

6. provoke
   - Ⓐ oblige
   - Ⓑ heighten
   - Ⓒ disregard
   - Ⓓ trigger

7. size
   - Ⓐ allocation
   - Ⓑ magnitude
   - Ⓒ expand
   - Ⓓ advent

8. color
   - Ⓐ hue
   - Ⓑ paint
   - Ⓒ facet
   - Ⓓ scenery

9. require
   - Ⓐ survey
   - Ⓑ induce
   - Ⓒ oblige
   - Ⓓ relinquish

10. account
    - Ⓐ currency
    - Ⓑ poll
    - Ⓒ bank
    - Ⓓ story

LESSON 22—MULTIPLE-CHOICE TEST QUESTIONS

1. Southeast Asian culture has many themes. The most **predominant** of these have been in religion and national history. In religion the main interest was not in actual doctrine but in the life and personalities of the Buddha and the Hindu gods. In national history the interest was in the celebrated heroes of the past. This theme appeared only after the great empires had vanished and the memories of their glory and power endured.

   The word **predominant** in the passage is closest in meaning to

   Ⓐ principal
   Ⓑ active
   Ⓒ archaic
   Ⓓ overlooked

2. The experience of the American frontier fostered raucous politics and rude manners. Conventions were **disregarded** and contempt for intellectual and cultural pursuits flourished. Brazen waste and the exploitation of natural resources abounded. The predominant spirit was to take while the taking was good. Frontier history includes many accounts of men who created empires and acquired great wealth within a short time.

   The word **disregarded** in the passage is closest in meaning to

   Ⓐ hastened
   Ⓑ defied
   Ⓒ overlooked
   Ⓓ induced

3. For religious reasons, the Egyptians considered Canis Major the most important constellation in the sky. Many Egyptian temples were aligned so that at the rising or setting of Sirius, the starlight reached the interior altar. In the Egyptian calendar, the first **practical** calendar created, the advent of Sirius in the morning sky before sunrise marked the beginning of the annual flooding of the Nile.

   The word **practical** in the passage is closest in meaning to

   Ⓐ functional
   Ⓑ accurate
   Ⓒ standard
   Ⓓ celestial

4. Airplanes have extensive agricultural value. They are used to distribute fertilizer, to reseed forest land, and to control forest fires. Many rice growers use planes to seed, fertilize, spray pesticides, and even to **hasten** crop ripening by spraying hormones from the air.

   The word **hasten** in the passage is closest in meaning to

   Ⓐ heighten
   Ⓑ enable
   Ⓒ curtail
   Ⓓ accelerate

5. The development of the audio CD was an improvement over the conventional records and tape recorders of previous decades. The CD created less background noise and was more durable since nothing mechanical has to touch the surface of the disc when it is played. However, it was the digital era of music that sparked an **influx** of new talent in the music industry. The ease with which one can produce music at home, coupled with the power of the Internet, has enabled many amateur musicians to publish their work.

   The word **influx** in the passage is closest in meaning to

   Ⓐ inflow
   Ⓑ excess
   Ⓒ incompletion
   Ⓓ era

6. Scientists are still seeking to **account for** the sudden appearance of precisely patterned circles in grain fields in the north of England. Known as crop circles, they range in size from two to eighty meters in diameter. Their circular geometric pattern is not explained by the way the grain was planted; nor is their flattened appearance easily explained by weather conditions. The farmers who work the land are as mystified as everyone else by these strange phenomena.

   In stating that scientists are seeking to **account for** crop circles, the author means that they are trying to

   Ⓐ measure them in meters.
   Ⓑ describe their geometry.
   Ⓒ explain what causes them.
   Ⓓ grow them in grain fields.

7. Tree buds may be vegetative or reproductive. Vegetative buds produce height growth until the growth process **induces** the formation of flowers. Exactly what is responsible for the formation of a reproductive bud varies, but changes in the number of daylight hours is a common signal in many plants.

   The word **induces** in the passage is closest in meaning to

   Ⓐ obliges
   Ⓑ prompts
   Ⓒ evolves
   Ⓓ creates

8. Some leaders of the Han period in China exerted enormous pressure for the simplification and standardization of writing. The result was a new category of script called clerical script. The **archaic** seal script was often retained for formal titles. It was also adapted to the small seals that have been used as signatures from the Han period to the present. These small red stamps, often present on documents, letters, books, and paintings, signify either authorship or ownership.

   The word **archaic** in the passage is closest in meaning to

   Ⓐ antiquated
   Ⓑ durable
   Ⓒ ancient
   Ⓓ persistent

9. There are six general classes of map symbols: size, lightness and darkness, direction, texture, shape, and color. The mixture of these "visual variables" creates the variety that is found on maps. For example, **hue** is used on urban planning maps to show differences in land use. Different shades may be used to indicate information such as changes in elevation or population density.

   The word **hue** in the passage is closest in meaning to

   Ⓐ color
   Ⓑ dim
   Ⓒ facet
   Ⓓ element

10. Sleep is an intricate form of the resting state. It is observed in animals that have highly developed nervous systems. When they sleep, their nervous systems shift into inactive modes that repair the body and **alleviate** many physical and mental ailments. These inactive modes are no less nuanced than active modes.

    The word **alleviate** in the passage is closest in meaning to

    Ⓐ enhance
    Ⓑ convey
    Ⓒ provoke
    Ⓓ lessen

LESSON 23

- allusion
- analogous
- compel
- compile
- formidable
- intrusive
- periodic
- prone
- prophetic
- proportions
- readily
- reliably
- reluctantly
- renown
- revive
- teeming

---

allusion *n.* a quotation or mention, often of another person's work

v. allude *syn.* reference

J. K. Rowling often *alludes* to Greek and Roman mythology in her character names.

She *alluded* to her Lithuanian heritage in her autobiography.

analogous *adj.* alike in some way

n. analogy *syn.* similar to

The action of light waves is *analogous* to the action of sound waves.

The *analogy* between the behavior of the bacteria in the lab and in the human body is not clear.

compel *v.* to make something happen by necessity or force

adv. compellingly
adj. compelling *syn.* obliged

The representatives were *compelled* to vote in favor of the legislation despite their personal opposition to it.

The lawyer's plea was made in a *compelling* manner.

compile *v.* to collect

n. compilation *syn.* assemble

The film club asked each of its members to *compile* a list of his or her favorite movies.

The book is a *compilation* of Shakespeare's plays.

formidable *adj.* difficult; causing worry or fear
adv. formidably
syn. overwhelming

Their *formidable* opponents gave no sign of weakness.
The man's voice echoed *formidably* throughout the hallway.

intrusive *adj.* the state of being inside when not desired to be there by others
adv. intrusively
v. intrude
n. intrusion
n. intruder
syn. annoying

The *intrusive* bacteria caused his condition to worsen.
The *intrusion* of the hazardous gas made it difficult to live in the house.

periodic *adj.* occurring at specific, determined periods of time
adj. periodical
adv. periodically
syn. regularly

Periodic payments must be made on home loans.
Some people need *periodic* doses of medicine.

prone *adj.* likely to do something
syn. inclined to

Most liquids are *prone* to contract when frozen.
She is *prone* to study hard the night before her tests.

prophetic *adj.* correctly telling about future events
adv. prophetically
v. prophesy
n. prophecy
n. prophet
syn. predictive

His *prophetic* powers were investigated by a team of psychologists.
The brilliant student fulfilled his teacher's *prophecy* that he would be a successful doctor.

proportions *n.* the relationship of size or importance when compared to another object or person
adv. proportionally
adj. proportional
adj. proportionate
adv. proportionately
syn. dimensions

The goal of establishing a space station will take a team effort of major *proportions*.
The pilot's salary is *proportional* to that of pilots of other airlines.

readily *adv.* willingly; easily

adj. ready
v. ready
n. readiness

syn. freely

The workers *readily* complained about the food in the cafeteria.

Her *readiness* to cooperate was an important factor in the investigation.

reliably *adv.* in a trusted way

adj. reliable
adj. reliant
v. rely
n. reliability
n. reliance

syn. dependably

An appliance must perform its task *reliably* to be popular with consumers.

Satellite photos show the smallest details with great *reliability*.

reluctantly *adj.* unwillingly

adj. reluctant
n. reluctance

syn. hesitatingly

Although not completely satisfied with the contract, the officials *reluctantly* agreed to sign it.

The electrician was *reluctant* to estimate the cost of the repair work.

renown *n.* fame

adj. renowned

syn. prominence

This school is of great *renown*.

The *renowned* conductor made a guest appearance at the concert.

revive *v.* to restore to life or bring back into memory

n. revival
adj. revived

syn. renew

The students *revived* the old tradition of having a homecoming dance.

Old plays are sometimes *revived* by applying modern interpretations to their content.

teeming *adj.* to be full of something; crowded

v. teem

syn. overflowing

The pond *teemed* with young fish in the warmer months.

Her essay was *teeming* with convincing arguments.

MATCHING

Choose the synonym.

1. intrusive
   Ⓐ inactive
   Ⓑ intricate
   Ⓒ predictive
   Ⓓ annoying

2. obliged
   Ⓐ distorted
   Ⓑ dependable
   Ⓒ compelled
   Ⓓ settled

3. assemble
   Ⓐ compel
   Ⓑ accelerate
   Ⓒ compile
   Ⓓ renew

4. formidable
   Ⓐ predictive
   Ⓑ overwhelming
   Ⓒ functional
   Ⓓ practical

5. similar to
   Ⓐ unlike
   Ⓑ analogous
   Ⓒ archaic
   Ⓓ prone

6. teeming
   Ⓐ cooperating
   Ⓑ precipitating
   Ⓒ grouping
   Ⓓ overflowing

7. hesitatingly
   Ⓐ reluctantly
   Ⓑ readily
   Ⓒ compellingly
   Ⓓ practically

8. allusion
   Ⓐ reference
   Ⓑ account
   Ⓒ negotiation
   Ⓓ summary

9. regularly
   Ⓐ routinely
   Ⓑ actually
   Ⓒ periodically
   Ⓓ gradually

10. renown
    Ⓐ domination
    Ⓑ prophecy
    Ⓒ prominence
    Ⓓ position

LESSON 23—MULTIPLE-CHOICE TEST QUESTIONS

1. New annual growth of trees produces growth rings. In most instances, the age of a tree can be **reliably** determined by counting the rings of a trunk's cross section. Most of the growth ring wood cells are dead. Only young xylem cells, those that grow during the current growing season, are alive. As a result, the ratio of dead to living wood cells increases as the girth of the tree increases.

   The word **reliably** in the passage is closest in meaning to

   Ⓐ periodically
   Ⓑ dependably
   Ⓒ approximately
   Ⓓ ordinarily

2. Lightships and buoys have an important function in coastal waters. They mark channels and thereby safely guide passing ships around hazards or shallow waters. Their great advantage is mobility, making them **readily** redeployable to meet changing conditions. For example, submerged hazards such as sandbars can change location rapidly under the influence of the sea. The use of buoys makes it possible to efficiently mark safe channels at all times.

   The word **readily** in the passage is closest in meaning to

   Ⓐ freely
   Ⓑ reluctantly
   Ⓒ repeatedly
   Ⓓ occasionally

3. The construction of the Saint Lawrence Seaway was an undertaking of great **proportions**. Constructing a link between the Great Lakes and the Atlantic seaboard had been proposed since 1535. Locks built in the 1800s by Canada became operational in 1901 on the upper Saint Lawrence River. But this original seaway was not deep or wide enough for modern ships. Canada and the United States constructed the new seaway, which became operational in 1959.

   The word **proportions** in the passage is closest in meaning to

   Ⓐ triumphs
   Ⓑ renown
   Ⓒ dimensions
   Ⓓ strength

4. In European folklore, mermaids are mythical beings who, like sprites, have magical and **prophetic** powers. They love music and song. Though very long-lived, they are mortal and have no souls. Although sometimes kindly, mermaids are generally dangerous to man. Their gifts have typically brought misfortune, and, if offended, they have caused floods or other disasters. To see one on a voyage is an omen of shipwreck.

   The word **prophetic** in the passage is closest in meaning to

   Ⓐ formidable
   Ⓑ intrusive
   Ⓒ predictive
   Ⓓ renowned

5. In Western cultures, the absence of a formal definition of responsibilities has produced an ambiguous and often conflicting set of expectations for young people. At the same time, young people are **prone** to experience peer pressure. They are told to behave maturely, while being denied access to the rights and privileges of adults.

   The word **prone** in the passage is closest in meaning to

   Ⓐ obliged
   Ⓑ positioned
   Ⓒ cautioned
   Ⓓ inclined

6. Among the great orchestras of the world, the Philadelphia Orchestra stands out for several reasons. One is the overall quality of its musicians, although it is especially **renowned for** its violin players. Another is the orchestra's famous recordings of nineteenth-century music, including the nine symphonies of Ludwig von Beethoven. A third is the orchestra's many international concert tours. For example, it was the first U.S. orchestra to visit China.

   In saying that this orchestra is especially **renowned for** its violinists, the author means that it

   Ⓐ has an unusual violin section.
   Ⓑ is famous for the violin players.
   Ⓒ has made a lot of recordings.
   Ⓓ pays the violinists more money.

7. The body of scales or bracts of a cone contains the reproductive organs of certain flowerless plants. The cone, a distinguishing feature of pines and other evergreens, is crudely **analogous** to the flowers of other plants.

   The word **analogous** in the passage is closest in meaning to

   Ⓐ apparent
   Ⓑ constant
   Ⓒ speculative
   Ⓓ similar

8. Most physicians participate in continuing education to keep up with the massive amount of information being discovered each year in their fields. Many states require that physicians **periodically** prove that they have actively participated in continuing medical education in order to maintain their certification to practice medicine.

   The word **periodically** in the passage is closest in meaning to

   Ⓐ nominally
   Ⓑ partially
   Ⓒ persistently
   Ⓓ regularly

9. Peace pipes are the large, ornately decorated tobacco pipes of the Indians of eastern North America. They functioned as symbols of truce and were ceremonially smoked for purposes of binding or renewing alliances. Peace pipes attained so much symbolic importance that it was thought that smoking the pipe with others **compelled** everyone present to be united in friendship.

   The word **compelled** in the passage is closest in meaning to

   Ⓐ obliged
   Ⓑ sheltered
   Ⓒ shifted
   Ⓓ dependable

10. The Spanish conquerors attempted to replace Aztec medicine with their own. When Aztec medical personnel resisted they were killed and Spanish medicine **intruded** into Aztec culture. However, some elements of Spanish medicine were compatible with the folk medical practices and became part of a new folk system. Mexican folk medicine thrived, yet there were many regional differences.

    The word **intruded** in the passage is closest in meaning to

    Ⓐ enacted
    Ⓑ imported
    Ⓒ emphasized
    Ⓓ imposed

Lesson 24

- **affordable**
- **contaminated**
- **discernible**
- **flourishing**
- **insufficient**
- **maintain**
- **mediocre**
- **negligible**
- **parallel**
- **potent**
- **reciprocate**
- **remarkable**
- **scattered**
- **somewhat**
- **stem from**
- **tedious**

---

affordable — *adj.* able to be done, usually referring to something you can do without damage or loss

adv. affordably
v. afford

syn. economical

The new dictionary is quite *affordable*.

He could *afford* the house because of current low interest rates.

contaminated — *adj.* to make something impure by adding something dirty or a poisonous substance

v. contaminate
n. contamination

syn. pollute

This *contaminated* water supply must be closed off to the public.

Bacteria and insects are frequently agents of food *contamination*.

discernible — *adj.* noticeable; easily seen

adv. discernibly
v. discern
n. discernment

syn. detectable

A feeling of anxiety was *discernible* among the members of the team.

The new student was unable to *discern* the humor of the teacher's joke.

flourishing — *adj.* active and growing; healthy

v. flourish

syn. thriving

Small *flourishing* companies would be harmed by an increase in the minimum wage.

A young mind will *flourish* with the proper guidance.

insufficient *adj.* not enough; unsatisfactory
syn. inadequate

He had *insufficient* materials to build his construction project.
A small breakfast is usually *insufficient* to have a good start to the day.

maintain *v.* to support; to keep in good condition
n. maintenance
syn. preserve

The building had to be renovated because it was not well *maintained.*
Proper *maintenance* of a car's engine will preserve its performance and value.

mediocre *adj.* of average quality; not good or bad
n. mediocrity
syn. average

This is a *mediocre* research report.
The *mediocrity* of his work was disappointing.

negligible *adj.* hardly noticeable; scarcely detectable
v. to ignore; to give little attention
syn. insignificant
adv. negligibly
adj. neglected
adj. neglectful
adj. negligent
n. neglect
n. negligence
v. neglect

The amount of bacteria in the culture was *negligible.*
His *negligence* caused him to lose all of the work he had done on the computer.

parallel *adj.* being almost of the same type or time; comparable
v. parallel
syn. similar

There were many *parallels* between his life and mine.
Her background *parallels* mine.

potent *adj.* very strong
syn. powerful

He gave a *potent* speech at the convention.
The venom of the coral snake is extremely *potent.*

reciprocate *v.* to give something or express a feeling in return
syn. respond

After he fixed her car, she *reciprocated* by buying him lunch.
He is very polite, and I *reciprocate* by showing him the same politeness.

remarkable *adj.* worthy of mention; uncommon
adv. remarkably
syn. exceptional

The invention of the radio was a *remarkable* achievement.
The actor was *remarkably* calm before his performance.

scattered *adj.* spread out or separated widely
v. scatter
syn. dispersed

Hurricane Andrew left debris *scattered* throughout Miami.
The crowd *scattered* when it began to rain heavily.

somewhat *adj.* a little
syn. slight

They feel *somewhat* tired after the mile run.
Buying food at a convenience store can be *somewhat* expensive.

stem from *ph. v.* to emerge or develop from something
syn. originate

The author's talent in writing *stems from* his love of reading books.
Many opportunities have *stemmed from* his decision to attend the university.

tedious *adj.* long and tiring
adv. tediously
n. tedium
syn. monotonous

The *tedious* lecture bored most of the audience.
Some people become frustrated by the *tedium* of daily living.

MATCHING

Choose the synonym.

1. discernible
   - Ⓐ exceptional
   - Ⓑ detectable
   - Ⓒ solid
   - Ⓓ negligent

2. average
   - Ⓐ ample
   - Ⓑ approximate
   - Ⓒ slight
   - Ⓓ mediocre

3. originate
   - Ⓐ stem from
   - Ⓑ preserve
   - Ⓒ maintain
   - Ⓓ disperse

4. potent
   - Ⓐ powerful
   - Ⓑ reliable
   - Ⓒ firm
   - Ⓓ durable

5. affordable
   - Ⓐ remarkable
   - Ⓑ formidable
   - Ⓒ economical
   - Ⓓ proportional

6. similar
   - Ⓐ prophetic
   - Ⓑ substantial
   - Ⓒ parallel
   - Ⓓ varied

7. insufficient
   - Ⓐ inadequate
   - Ⓑ satisfactory
   - Ⓒ acute
   - Ⓓ abysmal

8. negligible
   - Ⓐ exceptional
   - Ⓑ intricate
   - Ⓒ insignificant
   - Ⓓ scattered

9. thriving
   - Ⓐ flourishing
   - Ⓑ vanishing
   - Ⓒ polluting
   - Ⓓ astounding

10. monotonous
    - Ⓐ ambiguous
    - Ⓑ hazardous
    - Ⓒ prosperous
    - Ⓓ tedious

LESSON 24—MULTIPLE-CHOICE TEST QUESTIONS

1. The *Ceratosaurus*, a genus of large carnivorous dinosaurs found as fossils in Late Jurassic rocks of North America, was similar to, and possibly closely related to, the *Allosaurus*. *Ceratosaurus* weighed up to 2 tons. This dinosaur was **somewhat** smaller than *Allosaurus*. It had a distinctive horn on its snout, a row of bony plates down the middle of its back, and four clawed fingers rather than three.

   The word **somewhat** in the passage is closest in meaning to

   Ⓐ potently
   Ⓑ uniquely
   Ⓒ slightly
   Ⓓ peculiarly

2. The countries of Scandinavia were influenced by the spirit of improvement prevalent throughout Europe during the eighteenth century, but showed less advanced agriculture than others. Danish farmers were somewhat slowed in using new methods because of political restrictions. At the end of the nineteenth century, however, these political restrictions lessened, and the agriculture industry **reciprocated** by developing solid advances in farming techniques.

   The word **reciprocated** in the passage is closest in meaning to

   Ⓐ repelled
   Ⓑ emulated
   Ⓒ stagnated
   Ⓓ responded

3. Tourists throng to Baltimore's Inner Harbor year-round. The Inner Harbor was built in an area that was once a **contaminated** industrial port. This area underwent rapid development in the 1980s. It is now a waterside array of high-fashion stores, new hotels, outdoor performances, moving boats, docked ships, and locales for eating and drinking.

   The word **contaminated** in the passage is closest in meaning to

   Ⓐ deserted
   Ⓑ polluted
   Ⓒ dangerous
   Ⓓ flourishing

4. The Northwest Territories are Canada's most sparsely settled area. Most settlements consist of only a few hundred people. About two-thirds of Canada's Inuit Eskimos live there, **scattered** throughout the Arctic sector. Most Europeans who live in this territory live in the Mackenzie Valley.

   The word **scattered** in the passage is closest in meaning to

   Ⓐ maintained
   Ⓑ sheltered
   Ⓒ organized
   Ⓓ distributed

5. Plastics are a vast group of synthetic materials whose structures are based on the chemistry of carbon. They are also called polymers because they are made of extremely long chains of carbon atoms. An important characteristic of plastics is that they can be readily molded into finished products by the application of heat. As a finished product, one of its well-known properties includes **remarkable** resistance to heat.

   The word **remarkable** in the passage is closest in meaning to

   Ⓐ periodic
   Ⓑ proportional
   Ⓒ exceptional
   Ⓓ practical

6. Extensive water storage is common to a class of animals called ruminants. The class includes sheep and cattle, but the class member best known for storing water is the camel. There are two types of camel, the single-humped dromedary and the double-humped Bactrian camel found in the dry steppes of central Asia, where there is **insufficient** water for other animals to survive long-term. The ability of these animals to store water makes them the ideal beasts of burden on long treks across the desert.

   The word **insufficient** in the passage is closest in meaning to

   Ⓐ inadequate
   Ⓑ abysmal
   Ⓒ endemic
   Ⓓ intrinsic

7. As computer systems improve, databases will play an increasingly important role as sources of information for the general public. As databases become more refined, the need for awareness of a particular database will become more important. Users will need to be able to **discern** how reliable information coming from a database is.

   The word **discern** in the passage is closest in meaning to

   Ⓐ maintain
   Ⓑ account
   Ⓒ determine
   Ⓓ classify

8. The late 1970s and 1980s were years of delirious skyscraper construction. This was found in the cities that experienced economic progress, such as Dallas, Houston, and Atlanta in the southern United States, and also Hong Kong, Bangkok, and Singapore. Although New Yorkers, in particular, had reason to complain that the building of **mediocre** skyscrapers was choking Manhattan, few distinguished profiles were added to the skylines of modern cities.

   The word **mediocre** in the passage is closest in meaning to

   Ⓐ average
   Ⓑ renowned
   Ⓒ functional
   Ⓓ contemporary

9. The deserts of the world are distributed in a pair of **parallel** belts lying approximately 25 degrees north and south of the equator. Of these, the world's largest desert is found in the Northern Hemisphere. The Sahara and smaller deserts, forming much of the arid portion of the Middle East, are located in high-pressure regions directly influenced by global circulation of the atmosphere.

   The word **parallel** in the passage is closest in meaning to

   Ⓐ proportional
   Ⓑ noticeable
   Ⓒ broad
   Ⓓ similar

10. The life of the Atlantic salmon is typical of all salmon. The young fish leave the streams of their origin and spread into the feeding water of the cold seas. When they are sexually mature, they return to their home streams. In early summer, vast numbers of fish can be observed in their run upstream. **Potent** river currents and swift rapids are insufficient to stop the salmon's journey. It is not known how the fish identify the right river system and the specific nesting sites, but research indicates that the fish sense a chemical code specific to their home stream.

    The word **potent** in the passage is closest in meaning to

    Ⓐ deep
    Ⓑ powerful
    Ⓒ stagnant
    Ⓓ quick

LESSON 25

- **briefly**
- **circulate**
- **consistently**
- **exhibit**
- **found**
- **improperly**
- **impulsively**
- **infrequently**
- **isolated**
- **overtly**
- **profoundly**
- **sharply**
- **situated**
- **subsequently**
- **unmistakable**
- **upstanding**

---

briefly — *adv.* short, usually in time
syn. concisely

adj. brief
n. brevity

The visiting professor spoke *briefly* at the faculty meeting.

Solar eclipses are *brief* moments when the Earth and Moon cross the Sun's fixed position in the solar system.

circulate — *v.* to cause to move along a fixed path; move freely
syn. distribute

adj. circulatory
n. circulation

The news of the president's visit *circulated* quickly throughout the city.

A dollar bill remains in *circulation* for approximately one and a half years.

consistently — *adv.* without changing; keeping the same principles, ideas, or quality
syn. dependably

adj. consistent
v. consist
n. consistency

The temperature must be maintained *consistently* at 75° centigrade.

The policy of the government concerning unemployment has been *consistent.*

exhibit — *v.* to show or demonstrate
syn. display

n. exhibit
n. exhibition
n. exhibitor

The compound *exhibits* the qualities of an acid.

It was the best *exhibition* of talent that I have ever seen.

found *v.* to establish; start up;
n. foundation* — *a philanthropic organization
n. founder
syn. establish

The wealthy woman *founded* a hospital in her hometown.
The *foundation* maintained a number of philanthropic activities.

improperly *adv.* not following established rules; not desirable
adj. improper
n. impropriety
syn. inappropriately

The disappointing outcome was a result of an *improperly* prepared petri dish.
There was an *impropriety* with the way the funds were spent.

impulsively *adv.* acting without thinking
adj. impulsive
n. impulse
n. impulsiveness
syn. capriciously

She reacted *impulsively* to the loud noise.
Many shoppers buy items on *impulse.*

infrequently *adv.* almost never
adj. infrequent
n. infrequency
syn. rarely

Tornadoes occur *infrequently* in the eastern part of the United States.
Deserts are characterized by their *infrequent* rainfall.

isolated *adj.* to keep separated from others
v. isolate
n. isolation
syn. secluded

The failure of the communications system left the towns *isolated.*
The doctors were unable to *isolate* the cause of the epidemic.

overtly *adv.* in a way clearly seen; not done secretly
adj. overt
syn. openly

He *overtly* disregarded the regulations.
Her *overt* attempt to take control of the discussion failed.

profoundly *adv.* in a deep way; showing deep knowledge of a subject

adj. profound
n. profundity

syn. significantly

Everyone was *profoundly* impressed by the news reports.

The Nobel Prize is a *profound* recognition of outstanding achievement.

sharply *adv.* showing sensitivity or quick thinking; showing a quick change in direction

adj. sharp
v. sharpen
n. sharpness

syn. quickly

Car prices rose *sharply* over the past year.

There was a *sharp* change in the humidity after the storm.

situated *adj.* being found in a certain place

n. situation*
v. situate

*a current condition

syn. located

The resort town of Cancun is *situated* in the northern part of the Yucatan peninsula.

They found themselves in a very difficult *situation*.

subsequently *adv.* following; coming after something

adj. subsequent

syn. afterward

The public applauded the president's actions and *subsequently* his ratings in the polls improved.

This report, and all *subsequent* reports, must be written in the appropriate style.

unmistakable *adj.* clearly able to be determined

adj. unmistakably

syn. indisputable

The markings of the insect provided for an *unmistakable* identification of the species.

It is *unmistakably* clear that the report must be finished by noon.

upstanding *adj.* marked by integrity; good, honest

n. upstandingness

syn. moral

The school only accepts *upstanding* young adults.

The neighborhood has been kept clean and beautiful thanks to its *upstanding* residents.

MATCHING

Choose the synonym.

1. consistently
   - Ⓐ dependably
   - Ⓑ significantly
   - Ⓒ readily
   - Ⓓ diligently

2. capriciously
   - Ⓐ impulsively
   - Ⓑ profoundly
   - Ⓒ reluctantly
   - Ⓓ scarcely

3. moral
   - Ⓐ diligent
   - Ⓑ outstanding
   - Ⓒ generic
   - Ⓓ upstanding

4. circulated
   - Ⓐ sharpened
   - Ⓑ distributed
   - Ⓒ maintained
   - Ⓓ encircled

5. briefly
   - Ⓐ rarely
   - Ⓑ reliably
   - Ⓒ concisely
   - Ⓓ severely

6. exhibited
   - Ⓐ displayed
   - Ⓑ founded
   - Ⓒ located
   - Ⓓ highlighted

7. overtly
   - Ⓐ entirely
   - Ⓑ openly
   - Ⓒ evenly
   - Ⓓ actually

8. inappropriately
   - Ⓐ disapprovingly
   - Ⓑ approximately
   - Ⓒ improperly
   - Ⓓ unintentionally

9. secluded
   - Ⓐ situated
   - Ⓑ isolated
   - Ⓒ established
   - Ⓓ shifted

10. indisputably
    - Ⓐ severely
    - Ⓑ infrequently
    - Ⓒ significantly
    - Ⓓ unmistakably

LESSON 25—MULTIPLE-CHOICE TEST QUESTIONS

1. The colossal Statue of Liberty is **situated** in New York harbor on a small island park near Ellis Island. Standing 302 feet high including its base, it shows a woman holding a torch in her raised right hand. In her left, there is a tablet proclaiming liberty, bearing the date July 4, 1776. An elevator rises to the balcony level, and a spiral staircase leads to an observation platform in the statue's crown.

   The word **situated** in the passage is closest in meaning to

   Ⓐ visited
   Ⓑ exhibited
   Ⓒ isolated
   Ⓓ located

2. In its earliest forms, astrology consisted of simple omens that astrologers interpreted from the celestial bodies in the sky. In its developed form, astrology analyzes the presumed effects of the Sun, Moon, planets, and stars on the Earth for a specific time and place. Astrologists also contend that the position of constellations at the moment of your birth **profoundly** influences your future.

   The word **profoundly** in the passage is closest in meaning to

   Ⓐ subsequently
   Ⓑ significantly
   Ⓒ unmistakably
   Ⓓ consistently

3. When a language is devised as a means of communication between persons having no language in common, it is called a lingua franca. This lingua franca is native to none of those using it. A lingua franca with a **sharply** reduced grammar and vocabulary is called a pidgin. When a whole speech community gives up its former language or languages and takes a pidgin as its native tongue, the pidgin becomes a creole.

   The word **sharply** in the passage is closest in meaning to

   Ⓐ severely
   Ⓑ overtly
   Ⓒ impulsively
   Ⓓ improperly

4. Cedarwood is a light, soft, resinous, and durable wood, even when it makes contact with soil or moisture. It is an important timber used in construction in regions where it is found, but is **infrequently** used elsewhere. Many varieties of the Atlas cedar are popular ornamental trees in North America, especially along the Pacific and Gulf coasts.

   The word **infrequently** in the passage is closest in meaning to

   Ⓐ rarely
   Ⓑ briefly
   Ⓒ selectively
   Ⓓ continually

5. In 1876 the Johns Hopkins University was **founded** in Baltimore as the first U.S. institution to incorporate the German ideal of university education. Since that time, graduate education has become an important aspect of many institutions. Older universities, such as Harvard and Yale, and newer ones, such as Stanford and Chicago, have embraced the aims of advanced learning conducted in a spirit of freedom and autonomy.

   The word **founded** in the passage is closest in meaning to

   Ⓐ erected
   Ⓑ distinguished
   Ⓒ criticized
   Ⓓ established

6. Recent studies in psychology have explored the reasons why some purchases are made **on impulse** while others are given a significant amount of forethought. One finding is that shoppers are more likely to impulsively buy clothes than garden tools. It suggests that buying on impulse is strongly related to shoppers' attitudes about themselves and to their "self-images." Useful objects such as garden tools engage shoppers less personally than items that enhance their appearance.

   In discussing purchases made **on impulse**, the author is referring to purchases that shoppers make

   Ⓐ after weighing all the pluses and minuses.
   Ⓑ on a moment's notice and without thinking.
   Ⓒ in boutiques rather than department stores.
   Ⓓ to alter the feelings of people around them.

7. *The Adventures of Huckleberry Finn* by Mark Twain can be interpreted on several levels. On the surface, it is a picturesque novel in which young Huck Finn relates his adventures as he travels down the Mississippi River with a runaway slave named Jim. On another level, it is a societal satire on the constraints of civilization. Huckleberry Finn becomes a study of nature's indifference; the river, like society, is sometimes benevolent, sometimes malicious, and always **impulsive**.

   The word **impulsive** in the passage is closest in meaning to

   Ⓐ abundant
   Ⓑ baffling
   Ⓒ capricious
   Ⓓ philanthropic

8. Because of New Zealand's location, there was no higher animal life in the country when the Maori arrived. There were two species of lizard: the gecko, and the tuatara, a reptile that was extinct everywhere else for 100,000,000 years. There were also a few primitive species of frogs and two species of bats. These are all living today, but are confined to outlying islands and **isolated** parts of the country.

   The word **isolated** in the passage is closest in meaning to

   Ⓐ secluded
   Ⓑ negligible
   Ⓒ protected
   Ⓓ unlikely

9. The American painter Frank Duveneck was an important influence on other American artists of his generation. In 1870, he went to Munich to study at the Royal Academy, where he had a **brief** acquaintance with William Merritt Chase. Duveneck was an admirer of the realism of Gustave Courbet, but his Munich work also shows how well he had assimilated the masterful brushwork and the skill in capturing expressions of the Dutch portraitist Frans Hals.

   The word **brief** in the passage is closest in meaning to

   Ⓐ thriving
   Ⓑ fleeting
   Ⓒ superficial
   Ⓓ fertile

10. A dramatic monologue is a speech of long duration made by a character to a second person. In fiction, an interior monologue is a type of monologue that **exhibits** the thoughts, feelings, and associations passing through a character's mind.

    The word **exhibits** in the passage is closest in meaning to

    Ⓐ clarifies
    Ⓑ examines
    Ⓒ displays
    Ⓓ answers

LESSON 26

- **abolish**
- **chaotic**
- **controversial**
- **exemplify**
- **factor in**
- **falter**
- **gratifying**
- **launch**
- **legitimate**
- **lethargy**
- **particular**
- **radiant**
- **span**
- **spontaneous**
- **stream**
- **striking**

---

abolish *v.* to put an end to something
syn. eliminate

Many states have *abolished* the use of cell phones while driving.
Activists have been attempting to *abolish* animal testing for decades.

chaotic *adj.* being in complete disorder and confusion
n. chaos *syn.* disorganized

The traffic in Seoul is often *chaotic.*
There was complete *chaos* when the world champions arrived at the airport.

controversial *adj.* causing disagreement or argument
adv. controversially *syn.* divisive
n. controversy

The governor made a *controversial* decision to raise taxes.
The *controversy* was caused by the proposal to build an airport in the area.

exemplify *v.* to give an example
adj. exemplary *syn.* symbolize

The recent downturn in the housing industry *exemplifies* the poor economic conditions.
Her *exemplary* academic achievement is representative of most students at this institution.

factor in *ph. v.* to account for something while making a decision or analysis

syn. consider

The family had to *factor in* the price of gasoline as they planned their road trip.

The architect did not *factor in* the required distance from the sidewalk in his design.

falter *v.* to hesitate or waver

syn. weaken

In 2008, the United States economy began to *falter* dramatically.

He *faltered* under peer pressure and agreed to dance with the girl.

gratifying *adj.* giving pleasure or a feeling of accomplishment; showing thanks

syn. satisfying

adv. gratefully
adj. grateful
v. gratify
n. gratification
n. gratefulness

Studying abroad can be a very *gratifying* experience.

She was *grateful* for all the work he had done for her.

launch *v.* to cause something to begin

syn. initiate

n. launch
n. launching

The company *launched* a new program to attract more clients.

The *launching* of the first Soviet *Sputnik* created concern among the American public.

legitimate *adj.* reasonable; lawful

syn. authentic

adv. legitimately
n. legitimacy

The engineer had a *legitimate* reason for changing the design of the building.

The *legitimacy* of the theory has yet to be determined.

lethargy — *n.* a lack of energy or commitment; lazy; indifferent

adj. lethargic
adv. lethargically

syn. sluggishness

The hippopotamus basking in the sun displayed almost total *lethargy*.

When it is time to do homework assignments, many students become *lethargic*.

particular — *adj.* a certain way or thing; unusual; hard to please;
*especially

adv. particularly*

syn. specific

The speaker has a *particular* way of persuading his audience.

Some customers are *particularly* difficult to satisfy.

radiant — *adj.* sending out in all directions, especially heat or light

adv. radiantly
n. radiance
n. radiation
n. radiator

syn. bright

The actor's *radiant* smile captivated the audience.

The *radiance* of the fire prevented the firefighters from entering the house.

span — *v.* the length of time or distance from one limit to the other; to cross

n. span

syn. cover

The old man's life *spanned* two centuries.

The *span* of the bridge is three miles.

spontaneous — *adj.* unplanned; uncontrolled

adv. spontaneously
n. spontaneity

syn. instinctive

The *spontaneous* combustion inside the cylinder creates the power of the motor.

The crowd reacted *spontaneously* to the danger.

stream *n.* a natural flow of something; a pouring out
v. stream *syn.* river

There was a constant *stream* of information coming from the White House.

Water *streamed* from the dam as workers attempted to make the repairs.

striking *adj.* drawing special attention to
adv. strikingly *syn.* remarkable

His *striking* proposal saved the company from bankruptcy.

That was a *strikingly* convincing argument that the speaker delivered.

MATCHING

Choose the synonym.

1. gratifying
   - Ⓐ spontaneous
   - Ⓑ thriving
   - Ⓒ satisfying
   - Ⓓ analogous

2. disorganized
   - Ⓐ disrupted
   - Ⓑ chaotic
   - Ⓒ instinctive
   - Ⓓ discernible

3. factor in
   - Ⓐ compile
   - Ⓑ tolerate
   - Ⓒ consist
   - Ⓓ consider

4. launch
   - Ⓐ initiate
   - Ⓑ isolate
   - Ⓒ compel
   - Ⓓ stream

5. lethargic
   - Ⓐ spontaneous
   - Ⓑ analogous
   - Ⓒ sluggish
   - Ⓓ conscientious

6. symbolize
   - Ⓐ radiate
   - Ⓑ exemplify
   - Ⓒ span
   - Ⓓ synthesize

7. legitimate
   - Ⓐ peculiar
   - Ⓑ authentic
   - Ⓒ sharp
   - Ⓓ subsequent

8. abolish
   - Ⓐ eliminate
   - Ⓑ falter
   - Ⓒ influx
   - Ⓓ allude

9. falter
   - Ⓐ underscore
   - Ⓑ transport
   - Ⓒ weaken
   - Ⓓ withdraw

10. radiant
    - Ⓐ covered
    - Ⓑ bright
    - Ⓒ potent
    - Ⓓ tedious

LESSON 26—MULTIPLE-CHOICE TEST QUESTIONS

1. In the communications and computer fields, research in optical switching is motivated by the need to transmit data **streams** at constantly higher speeds more efficiently. At the same time, customers demand transmission and switching rates far higher than can be provided by a purely electronic system. Due to developments in semiconductor lasers and in fiber optics, transmission at higher speeds is now possible.

   The word **streams** in the passage is closest in meaning to

   Ⓐ flows
   Ⓑ pieces
   Ⓒ files
   Ⓓ particles

2. A **striking** example of a successful multiethnic country is Switzerland, where French, German, and Italian speakers from diverse religious groups live and work in harmony and prosperity. Ethnic diversity in Switzerland appears to have stimulated rather than divided the Swiss population. Studies of conditions in Switzerland demonstrate that harmony can coexist with diversity when certain characteristics are shared.

   The word **striking** in the passage is closest in meaning to

   Ⓐ spontaneous
   Ⓑ characteristic
   Ⓒ legitimate
   Ⓓ remarkable

3. In one of the most influential books on education ever written, Émile Rousseau argued that society should protect children from the corrupt nature of civilization and cautiously nurture their natural, **spontaneous** impulses, which, in Rousseau's mind, were always healthy. He further maintained that it was important to avoid premature intellectualization of emotion so that the child's intellect could develop without distortion.

   The word **spontaneous** in the passage is closest in meaning to

   Ⓐ chaotic
   Ⓑ gratifying
   Ⓒ instinctive
   Ⓓ uninterrupted

4. The water available to fulfill a **particular** need is known as the water supply. When the need is domestic, industrial, or agricultural, the water must fulfill both quality and quantity requirements. Water supplies can be acquired by several types of water resources projects, such as dams, reservoirs, or wells.

   The word **particular** in the passage is closest in meaning to

   Ⓐ critical
   Ⓑ common
   Ⓒ gratifying
   Ⓓ specific

5. Joseph Haydn was undoubtedly the most prolific of all symphony writers; his works **spanned** what has been called the Classical Era. He is most celebrated for taking the established forms of the symphony and shaping them into the forceful media for musical expression through invention and experimentation. These were recognized as innovations by composers who followed.

   The word **spanned** in the passage is closest in meaning to

   Ⓐ exemplified
   Ⓑ covered
   Ⓒ launched
   Ⓓ interpreted

6. Egyptomania, a term for the renewed interest in Egyptian culture that took place in Europe in the early 1800s, was inspired by Napoleon's Egyptian Campaign. During this era, a special interest arose for mummies. In fact, mummy unwrapping parties were a popular pastime among affluent people. Until they were later **abolished**, these parties, in which the mummies were unwrapped for entertainment, led to the destruction of an incalculable number of ancient Egyptian mummies.

   The word **abolished** in the passage is closest in meaning to

   Ⓐ weakened
   Ⓑ eliminated
   Ⓒ funded
   Ⓓ lessened

7. An intaglio is an engraved gem that, when pressed into softened wax, produces an image in relief. This wax seal was once used as a means to identify **legitimate** letters and documents. The first engraving of hard stones existed as early as about 4000 B.C. in Mesopotamia, but the style of typical intaglios, which were usually mounted on rings, was developed by the ancient Greeks.

   The word **legitimate** in the passage is closest in meaning to

   Ⓐ normal
   Ⓑ authentic
   Ⓒ robust
   Ⓓ secure

8. In the late 1920s and early 1930s, the trucking industry was quite **chaotic**. It was dominated by large numbers of itinerant owner-operators. The industry was considered to be unstable and in need of regulation. The National Industrial Recovery Act of 1933 brought together two organized groups of trucking officials to develop standards of fair competition. This action led to the formation of the American Trucking Associations.

   The word **chaotic** in the passage is closest in meaning to

   Ⓐ disorganized
   Ⓑ inordinate
   Ⓒ formidable
   Ⓓ imposing

9. Singapore is the only nation outside of mainland China and Taiwan where the majority of the population is ethnic Chinese. Its culture **exemplifies** this Chinese heritage, coupled with various diverse cultural influences. Its British colonial architecture and Chinese, Hindu, and Muslim shrines reflect the cultural diversity found in this international setting.

   The word **exemplifies** in the passage is closest in meaning to

   Ⓐ symbolizes
   Ⓑ radiates
   Ⓒ shelters
   Ⓓ cultivates

10. The field of opera once belonged exclusively to the Europeans. Successful American opera seemed to be confined to Gershwin's *Porgy and Bess* and other obscure operatic works. More recently the opera world has witnessed growth in successful operatic works by Americans. In addition, new opera companies and small opera groups have been established. These developments are particularly **gratifying** to those who favor bringing a more American flavor to the opera stage.

    The word **gratifying** in the passage is closest in meaning to

    Ⓐ prophetic
    Ⓑ remarkable
    Ⓒ bizarre
    Ⓓ satisfying

LESSON 27

- **aptly**
- **demonstration**
- **deviate**
- **ingredients**
- **involuntarily**
- **marvel**
- **moderate**
- **motivate**
- **odd**
- **profuse**
- **reflection**
- **succinct**
- **supposedly**
- **sustained**
- **synthesis**
- **tangible**

---

aptly — *adv.* having a tendency to do something; likely

adj. apt
n. aptness

syn. appropriately

It was an *aptly* timed remark.

Emotional problems are *apt* to damage personal relationships.

demonstration — *n.* a show or exhibit

*overtly showing emotion

adv. demonstrably
v. demonstrate
adj. demonstrative*
adj. demonstrable

syn. display

The *demonstration* clarified the procedure for everyone.

I have never seen the politicians so *demonstrative* of their feelings.

deviate — *v.* to break away from what is normal or average

n. deviation

syn. differ

She *deviated* from the typical study path and graduated early.

He enjoys *deviating* from the main trail when he goes hiking.

ingredients — *n.* things combined to make something; the contents of something

syn. elements

The *ingredients* of the product are kept secret.

Good style, punctuation, and grammar are the important *ingredients* of a good essay.

involuntarily *adv.* in an unthinking manner; not chosen
adj. involuntary *syn.* automatically

He *involuntarily* worked overtime.

Reflexes are *involuntary* reactions to external stimuli.

marvel *n.* something that surprises or impresses
adv. marvelously *syn.* wonder
adj. marvelous

The Great Wall of China is one of the world's *marvels.*

The weather was *marvelous* for an afternoon get-together in the park.

moderate *adj.* not too much, not too little; *to reduce
adv. moderately
v. moderate*
n. moderation *syn.* medium

She made the best of her *moderate* dancing ability.

The Broadway play was *moderately* successful.

motivate *v.* to provide a reason or purpose for doing something
n. motivation
adj. motivated *syn.* encourage

Grades *motivate* most students to do well in their studies.

The speaker gave a *motivational* speech that inspired everyone in the audience.

odd *adj.* unusual
adv. oddly *syn.* strange
n. oddity

It is *odd* to find a person who speaks many languages.

The moon rock is an *oddity* available at the museum for all to view.

profuse *adj.* to be very generous, often in excess
n. profuseness *syn.* abundant
adv. profusely

The company apologized *profusely* for the defects in its product.

She deserved the *profuse* praise from her teacher.

reflection — *n.* a picture or element thrown back

adj. reflected
v. reflect

syn. image

His bright smile was a *reflection* of his satisfaction.

In order for us to perceive something visually, light must be *reflected* from the object's surface.

succinct — *adj.* short and to the point

adv. succinctly

syn. concise

Since she had little time to speak, the biologist made her presentation *succinct.*

The class assignment is to summarize the book's plot as *succinctly* as possible.

supposedly — *adv.* according to reports or hearsay; widely believed or accepted

adj. supposed
v. suppose
n. supposition

syn. presumably

The new trains are *supposedly* able to reach speeds of 150 miles per hour.

The stockbroker's *supposition* is that the economy will improve.

sustained — *adj.* continuing in a constant way; remaining strong

v. sustain
adj. sustenance

syn. consistent

Sustained rainfall is the only hope they have for relief from the drought.

Luckily, the trees did not *sustain* any damage from the attack of the locusts.

synthesis — *n.* the mixing of separate things to form a whole;
*not made by nature

adv. synthetically*
adj. synthetic*
v. synthesize

syn. combination

The language of Papiamento is a *synthesis* of Dutch and native Indian languages of Curaçao.

Vitamins are *synthetically* produced.

tangible *adj.* real; that which can be felt

adv. tangibly
n. tangibility

syn. concrete

The work of a teacher seldom produces *tangible* results until years after a student has graduated.

The solution to this problem can be *tangibly* demonstrated.

MATCHING

Choose the synonym.

1. marvel
   - Ⓐ ridge
   - Ⓑ chaos
   - Ⓒ wonder
   - Ⓓ combination

2. display
   - Ⓐ disperse
   - Ⓑ decline
   - Ⓒ disguise
   - Ⓓ demonstration

3. succinct
   - Ⓐ odd
   - Ⓑ moderate
   - Ⓒ strange
   - Ⓓ concise

4. appropriately
   - Ⓐ supposedly
   - Ⓑ aptly
   - Ⓒ tangibly
   - Ⓓ durably

5. moderate
   - Ⓐ sustained
   - Ⓑ medium
   - Ⓒ sharp
   - Ⓓ periodic

6. involuntary
   - Ⓐ infrequent
   - Ⓑ substantial
   - Ⓒ automatic
   - Ⓓ immeasurable

7. elements
   - Ⓐ ingredients
   - Ⓑ measurements
   - Ⓒ marks
   - Ⓓ spans

8. motivate
   - Ⓐ travel
   - Ⓑ isolate
   - Ⓒ sustain
   - Ⓓ encourage

9. reflection
   - Ⓐ image
   - Ⓑ synthesis
   - Ⓒ solid
   - Ⓓ tightness

10. tangible
    - Ⓐ firm
    - Ⓑ consistent
    - Ⓒ concrete
    - Ⓓ tedious

LESSON 27—MULTIPLE-CHOICE TEST QUESTIONS

1. The mechanical traps of various carnivorous plants can be observed in many varieties. However, the snap trap, such as that found on the Venus Flytrap, is found only in the sundew family of plants. When an animal touches its sensory hairs, the prey is trapped by a rapid **automatic** closure of a set of lobes that surround the animal. After that, the digestion process starts. Any insect that lands on the Venus Flytrap will become a meal for the plant.

   The word **automatic** in the passage is closest in meaning to

   Ⓐ temporary
   Ⓑ incessant
   Ⓒ involuntary
   Ⓓ impartial

2. In the Western world, contemplation on art began with the philosophers of ancient Greece. Plato discussed proportion as the source of beauty, and imitation as the primary mode of art. Aristotle identified different kinds of imitation, and Xenocrates wrote technical dissertations on painting and sculpture that examined the ideal **synthesis** of proportion and imitation in terms of the lives of classical Greek artists.

   The word **synthesis** in the passage is closest in meaning to

   Ⓐ image
   Ⓑ symbolism
   Ⓒ display
   Ⓓ combination

3. Anthropologists who study human communication tend to focus on its central role in the survival of a society. Communication serves to preserve and transmit all aspects of a culture. A society communicates its culture through language. The concepts of honor, bravery, love, cooperation, and honesty are embedded in all languages. There is no human culture that has **deviated** from the development of the expression of these traits.

   The word **deviated** in the passage is closest in meaning to

   Ⓐ dispersed
   Ⓑ differed
   Ⓒ thrived
   Ⓓ eroded

4. Based on the inscriptions called codices, linguists believe that the Maya spoke a language closely related to modern Native American groups. During the classical period, the Maya also had **sustained** contact with warriors and traders from Teotihuacan in central Mexico, the largest and most powerful state of the era. There is no proof of a conquest, but the Maya embraced some foreign deities, symbols, and styles of clothing of other groups.

   The word **sustained** in the passage is closest in meaning to

   Ⓐ tangible
   Ⓑ consistent
   Ⓒ moderate
   Ⓓ measurable

5. The Oregon Trail followed the Sweetwater River westward from the vicinity of Casper to South Pass. Independence Rock, a granite monolith on the north bank of the river near a reservoir, was a significant trail landmark. The river was **supposedly** named by General William Ashley in 1823 because its water tasted sweet to his trappers.

   The word **supposedly** in the passage is closest in meaning to

   Ⓐ presumably
   Ⓑ oddly
   Ⓒ aptly
   Ⓓ predictably

6. At 46,000 gross tons, the *Titanic* was the largest floating object ever built. It was 853 feet long, 93 feet wide, and 61 feet high. As many people said, it was **aptly named** the *Titanic*—in ancient Greek mythology, the Titans ruled the universe until Zeus defeated and replaced them. The mighty *Titanic* was also overthrown: while carrying over 2,200 passengers, it crashed into an iceberg off Newfoundland and sank on April 14, 1912.

   In stating that the *Titanic* was **aptly named**, the author means that

   Ⓐ the ship's captain was criminally negligent.
   Ⓑ there were too many passengers on board.
   Ⓒ the ship's name, *Titanic*, was appropriate.
   Ⓓ the word Titanic comes from Greek history.

7. The date of the earliest UFO sighting in history is unknown and the evidence for such sightings is scanty and purely speculative. The beginning of the UFO phenomenon began with the sighting of dirigiblelike "mystery ships" over the United States in 1896–1897. In 1946, people in Scandinavia reported large-scale sightings of "ghost rockets," **odd**-looking "rockets" that made no noise. None of these phenomena has been satisfactorily explained.

   The word **odd** in the passage is closest in meaning to

   Ⓐ strange
   Ⓑ ample
   Ⓒ intriguing
   Ⓓ elusive

8. A living cell is a **marvel** of detailed and complex structure. When examined with a microscope, it gives the appearance of almost chaotic activity. On a deeper level, it is known that molecules are being synthesized at a tremendous rate. Almost any enzyme causes the synthesis of more than 100 other molecules per second. In 10 minutes, a large percentage of the total mass of a metabolizing bacterial cell has been synthesized.

   The word **marvel** in the passage is closest in meaning to

   Ⓐ invention
   Ⓑ wonder
   Ⓒ magnification
   Ⓓ swiftness

9. In the 1790s, a variety of agricultural machinery was developed. At that time, an efficient seed drill had been designed but still required **demonstrations** in the 1830s to convince farmers of its value. A few threshing machines were in use before 1800, and gradually increased in popularity. However, in the 1830s, farm laborers in England rebelled because the machines deprived them of winter employment.

   The word **demonstrations** in the passage is closest in meaning to

   Ⓐ illustrations
   Ⓑ circulations
   Ⓒ displays
   Ⓓ preconceptions

10. The oxygen supply in the Earth's atmosphere is a result of photosynthesis by green plants. Plants require all the essential **ingredients** of photosynthesis to build the vital compounds and structures. Water is required, because cell enlargement is a result of internal water pressure extending the walls. This explains why in periods of drought, plants tend to have smaller leaves.

    The word **ingredients** in the passage is closest in meaning to

    Ⓐ characteristics
    Ⓑ parts
    Ⓒ basics
    Ⓓ elements

LESSON 28

- aggravating
- amusement
- conceivably
- convert
- curative
- debilitating
- deplete
- finite
- perceive
- security
- singular
- toxic
- tranquility
- trite
- undeniably
- underestimated

---

aggravating *adj.* making worse; annoying

n. aggravation
v. aggravate

syn. irritating

The *aggravating* delay was caused by road repairs.

The shortage of work *aggravated* the crisis in the small town.

amusement *n.* something that holds interest and is enjoyable

adv. amusingly
adj. amusing
v. amuse

syn. diversion

We listened in *amusement* as he tried to convince his friend to lend him $50.

His *amusing* comment made everyone laugh.

conceivably *adv.* feasibly; believably

adj. conceivable
v. conceive

syn. possibly

They could *conceivably* earn first place with their science project.

It is *conceivable* that humans will travel to distant planets one day.

convert *v.* to change from one form or state to another

adj. convertible
n. conversion

syn. alter

When boiled, liquids *convert* into gases.

The *conversion* from Fahrenheit to centigrade can be easily made.

curative *adj.* being able to restore to good condition

n. cure *syn.* healing

The *curative* properties of certain plants have been well documented.

There is no simple *cure* for the ills of society.

debilitating *adj.* weakening

v. debilitate *syn.* weakening
n. debility

The lack of investment savings has a *debilitating* effect on the economy.

The patient's *debility* limited his mobility.

deplete *v.* to use up; reduce greatly

adj. depleted *syn.* consume
n. depletion

She *depleted* all of her savings to buy the new bicycle.

The *depletion* of the Earth's oil reserves poses a threat to our current way of life.

finite *adj.* of a certain amount; having an end; not infinite

syn. limited

There are a *finite* number of explanations for the unusual results.

Is there a *finite* number of stars in the universe?

perceive *v.* to sense; become aware of

adv. perceptibly *syn.* observe
adj. perceivable
adj. perceptive
adv. perceptively
n. perception

We *perceive* major differences between the two political parties.

Porpoises are very *perceptive* mammals.

security *n.* the feeling of freedom from danger, doubt, or worry

adv. securely *syn.* safety
adj. secure
v. secure

Her sense of *security* increased as her grades improved.

We *secured* all of the doors of the lab before leaving.

singular *adj.* the only one of its kind; extraordinary
syn. unique

The platypus is a *singular* example of a mammal that lays eggs.
Her scientific experiment was a *singular* success!

toxic *adj.* harmful; capable of being fatal
n. toxicity *syn.* poisonous

Disposal of *toxic* wastes is an ongoing environmental issue.
This product has the highest *toxicity* of any known to science.

tranquility *n.* calm; quietness
adv. tranquilly *syn.* peacefulness
adj. tranquil
v. tranquilize

The *tranquility* of the lake at sunrise inspired a profound sense of well-being.
His *tranquil* manner of expression made us all feel more secure.

trite *adj.* overused or lacking originality; commonplace
syn. cliché

He finds the expression "fit as a fiddle" to be quite *trite*.
She tries to avoid using *trite* examples and vocabulary in her writing.

undeniably *adv.* clearly true
adj. undeniable *syn.* absolutely

Of all the planets in our solar system, the Earth is *undeniably* the most conducive to supporting life.
It is *undeniable* that he has skill, but he needs to show more initiative.

underestimated *adj.* guessed lower than the actual quantity
v. underestimate *syn.* miscalculated

The *underestimated* demand for tickets made the theater manager plan better for the next performance.
The treasurer *underestimated* the cost of the new furniture.

MATCHING

Choose the synonym.

1. curative
   - Ⓐ healing
   - Ⓑ gratifying
   - Ⓒ toxic
   - Ⓓ conceivable

2. limited
   - Ⓐ sustained
   - Ⓑ ample
   - Ⓒ finite
   - Ⓓ approximate

3. amusement
   - Ⓐ peacefulness
   - Ⓑ demonstration
   - Ⓒ diversion
   - Ⓓ marvel

4. security
   - Ⓐ power
   - Ⓑ safety
   - Ⓒ trap
   - Ⓓ cure

5. debilitating
   - Ⓐ convincing
   - Ⓑ formidable
   - Ⓒ accelerating
   - Ⓓ weakening

6. singular
   - Ⓐ unique
   - Ⓑ solid
   - Ⓒ available
   - Ⓓ resilient

7. conceivably
   - Ⓐ absolutely
   - Ⓑ aptly
   - Ⓒ possibly
   - Ⓓ tranquilly

8. alter
   - Ⓐ sustain
   - Ⓑ launch
   - Ⓒ foster
   - Ⓓ convert

9. depleted
   - Ⓐ retained
   - Ⓑ consumed
   - Ⓒ polluted
   - Ⓓ inundated

10. perceive
    - Ⓐ deny
    - Ⓑ miscalculate
    - Ⓒ observe
    - Ⓓ estimate

LESSON 28—MULTIPLE-CHOICE TEST QUESTIONS

1. Less than one percent of all freight cargo is carried by air, most being carried by surface methods. Nevertheless, this curious fact significantly **underestimates** the importance of air freight. In terms of value of cargo carried, air transport is greater than all other modes. By the early 1990s Tokyo's Narita Airport and New York's John F. Kennedy Airport were handling in excess of one million tons of cargo per year.

   The word **underestimates** in the passage is closest in meaning to

   Ⓐ understands
   Ⓑ assesses
   Ⓒ highlights
   Ⓓ miscalculates

2. Margaret Mead, a well-known cultural anthropologist, was associated with the American Museum of Natural History in New York City from 1926 until her death. In the 1980s, her work, in particular her famous study of Samoa, became a subject of controversy. Her critics alleged that her belief in the predominate influence of culture in shaping personality led her to misread evidence and overgeneralize. Her defenders endorsed her **undeniably** keen observations.

   The word **undeniably** in the passage is closest in meaning to

   Ⓐ absolutely
   Ⓑ inconsistently
   Ⓒ presumably
   Ⓓ unexpectedly

3. While many people refer to the Arctic as being covered in a "solid sheet of ice," this **trite** expression is also incorrect. Ice, a nearly pure solid, contains few foreign ions in its structure. It contains particles of matter and gases, which are trapped in bubbles within the ice. A change in makeup of these materials over time is recorded in the successive layers of ice. This has been used to interpret the history of the environment of Earth's surface and the influence of human activities on the environment.

   The word **trite** in the passage is closest in meaning to

   Ⓐ complex
   Ⓑ ambiguous
   Ⓒ cliché
   Ⓓ important

4. Wang Wei was a Chinese poet, painter, and scholar of the Tang dynasty. He left behind both a significant body of lyrical poetry and delicately depicted landscape paintings. These paintings reflected a love of nature and an inner **tranquility** derived from Buddhism and meditation. He is traditionally credited with founding the Southern School of Chinese landscape painting.

   The word **tranquility** in the passage is closest in meaning to

   Ⓐ peacefulness
   Ⓑ amusement
   Ⓒ fulfillment
   Ⓓ security

5. The problem of ocean pollution has been acknowledged at national and international levels. The U.S. Congress passed an act in 1988 that phased in a complete prohibition of ocean dumping by 1991. Also in 1988, 65 nations agreed to stop burning **toxic** waste at sea by 1994. The legality of the latter measure remains debatable and may be proven unenforceable, mirroring the experience of a 1977 law that attempted the same prohibition.

   The word **toxic** in the passage is closest in meaning to

   Ⓐ inordinate
   Ⓑ debilitating
   Ⓒ poisonous
   Ⓓ dispersed

6. Before Alexander Fleming made his great discovery, he had been studying losozyme, an enzyme found in tears that prevents infection. However, he wanted to find a substance with **curative powers**, something that would keep bacteria from growing and multiplying altogether. By accident, he noticed a mold growing in one of his laboratory dishes that had this effect. It turned out to be penicillin, one of the most widely used antibiotics today.

   In stating that Fleming wanted to find a substance with **curative powers**, the author means that he was looking for a medicine that would

   Ⓐ regulate a patient's exposure to germs.
   Ⓑ combat disease-causing bacteria.
   Ⓒ control a patient's body temperature.
   Ⓓ increase a patient's level of infection.

7. So-called prophetic dreams in ancient Middle Eastern cultures were often used to help the sick. In classical Greece, ailing people came to dream in special temples where priests and priestesses advised them about their dreams' **curative** benefits. A similar practice known as dream incubation is known to have existed in the ancient cultures of Babylon and Egypt.

   The word **curative** in the passage is closest in meaning to

   Ⓐ corrective
   Ⓑ fertile
   Ⓒ healing
   Ⓓ ample

8. Chronic fatigue syndrome is a disorder characterized by at least six months of **debilitating** fatigue that begins abruptly and is usually accompanied by mild fever, sore throat, tender muscles, joint pain, headache, sleep disorders, confusion, memory loss, and vision problems. Once considered an imagined rather than a specific physical condition, chronic fatigue syndrome remains controversial.

   The word **debilitating** in the passage is closest in meaning to

   Ⓐ weakening
   Ⓑ disruptive
   Ⓒ tangible
   Ⓓ persistent

9. Fireworms are marine worms that inhabit warm tropical waters. They produce an **aggravating** stinging sensation if touched. One particular species, *H. carunculata*, found in the coral reefs of the Caribbean Sea, has a body covered with fine, white, brittle bristles that embed themselves in human skin if touched.

   The word **aggravating** in the passage is closest in meaning to

   Ⓐ disruptive
   Ⓑ annoying
   Ⓒ irritating
   Ⓓ formidable

10. Scientists have tried to find a way to make hurricanes less dangerous by analyzing their component parts and neutralizing them. A hurricane contains huge quantities of supercooled water and silver iodide. Seeding the hurricane could **conceivably** produce some changes in storm behavior. Aircraft seeding experiments have obtained some minor, short-lived changes resulting in decreased wind speeds for a few hours.

    The word **conceivably** in the passage is closest in meaning to

    Ⓐ presumably
    Ⓑ consistently
    Ⓒ possibly
    Ⓓ noticeably

LESSON 29

- **acknowledge**
- **acquire**
- **adage**
- **assimilate**
- **assortment**
- **caliber**
- **condensed**
- **contradictory**
- **disregard**
- **precious**
- **prominent**
- **requisite**
- **stable**
- **unravel**
- **vague**
- **vast**

---

acknowledge — *v.* to know, remember, and accept the existence of something

n. acknowledgment
adj. acknowledged

syn. recognize

The foreman *acknowledged* the fact that there had been a mistake in the design of the house.

The promotion he received was an *acknowledgment* of his excellent work.

acquire — *v.* to gain or come to possess

adj. acquisitive
n. acquisition

syn. obtain

He *acquired* two beautiful paintings during his visit to Taipei.

The office's most recent *acquisition* was a new photocopier.

adage — *n.* a traditional saying

syn. proverb

There is an old *adage* that states, "Slow and steady wins the race."

Over the years, the author's sayings became popular *adages* in his town.

assimilate — *v.* to become a part of

n. assimilation

syn. incorporate

The United States of America has *assimilated* people from all parts of the world.

Assimilation of a new cultural environment can be difficult.

assortment — *n.* a variety
adj. assorted — *syn.* selection

You have an *assortment* of elective courses from which to choose.
He bought a box of *assorted* books at the book fair.

caliber — *n.* the standard of; the degree of goodness
syn. quality

The high *caliber* of her work earned her a raise in pay.
Only parts of the highest *caliber* can be used to make repairs on the spacecraft.

condensed — *adj.* made smaller; shortened; merge
v. condense — *syn.* summarize

This is a *condensed* version of the original research report.
Try to *condense* the two chapters into one.

contradictory — *adj.* not agreeing with the facts or previous statements made on the subject; declared wrong
v. contradict
n. contradiction
syn. inconsistent

It is *contradictory* to say that you know French after studying it for only three months.
The expert *contradicted* himself during his presentation.

disregard — *v.* to pay no attention
n. disregard — *syn.* ignore

They *disregarded* the no parking signs and were ticketed by the police.
His *disregard* of the lab instructions caused him to make many errors.

precious — *adj.* having much monetary or sentimental value; beautiful
syn. cherished

This golden ring is my most *precious* possession.
The *precious* stone was one of a kind.

prominent *adj.* famous; having a high position

adv. prominently *syn.* renowned
n. prominence

Their talent for locating oil deposits made them *prominent* geologists in the corporation.

He gained *prominence* through his television appearances.

requisite *adj.* needed for a specific purpose; *a formal request

v. require
n. requirement *syn.* demanded
n. requisition*
v. requisition*

Here is the list of *requisite* courses for the master's degree in biology.

The project team made a *requisition* for a new set of reference books.

stable *adj.* experiencing few or no changes; not moving

adv. stably *syn.* steady
n. stability

Be sure the ladder is *stable* before climbing it.

Most people believe that maintaining economic *stability* is an important goal of every government.

unravel *v.* to organize; make clear

n. unraveling *syn.* separate

The detective was not able to *unravel* the mystery of the missing money.

The *unraveling* of the Soviet Union took place in the span of a few months.

vague *adj.* not clear; ambiguous

adv. vaguely *syn.* unclear
n. vagueness

She has only *vague* memories of her childhood.

The *vagueness* of his directions caused us to get lost.

vast *adj.* very much; very large

adv. vastly *syn.* huge

I have noticed a *vast* improvement in your English vocabulary.

Unfortunately, the water quality has deteriorated *vastly* since my last visit here.

MATCHING

Choose the synonym.

1. caliber
   - Ⓐ volume
   - Ⓑ marvel
   - Ⓒ quality
   - Ⓓ acclaim

2. ignore
   - Ⓐ disregard
   - Ⓑ separate
   - Ⓒ deplete
   - Ⓓ withstand

3. acknowledged
   - Ⓐ exaggerated
   - Ⓑ recognized
   - Ⓒ exemplified
   - Ⓓ accentuated

4. assortment
   - Ⓐ assertion
   - Ⓑ selection
   - Ⓒ pattern
   - Ⓓ ingredient

5. obtain
   - Ⓐ acquire
   - Ⓑ unravel
   - Ⓒ relinquish
   - Ⓓ perceive

6. steady
   - Ⓐ stable
   - Ⓑ precious
   - Ⓒ staple
   - Ⓓ tangible

7. condensed
   - Ⓐ summarized
   - Ⓑ emphasized
   - Ⓒ legitimized
   - Ⓓ conformed

8. assimilate
   - Ⓐ illustrate
   - Ⓑ incorporate
   - Ⓒ investigate
   - Ⓓ isolate

9. renown
   - Ⓐ reaction
   - Ⓑ vast
   - Ⓒ prominent
   - Ⓓ requisite

10. contradictory
    - Ⓐ ambiguous
    - Ⓑ requisite
    - Ⓒ inconsistent
    - Ⓓ disregarded

LESSON 29—MULTIPLE-CHOICE TEST QUESTIONS

1. By the end of 1998, the Internet's World Wide Web had become so commonplace in the public consciousness that even nontechnical adults were likely to **acknowledge** having heard of the "Net" and the "Web." Companies large and small began including a website address in their advertising. Furthermore, large telecommunications firms began offering their customers Internet access services.

   The word **acknowledge** in the passage is closest in meaning to

   Ⓐ deny
   Ⓑ remember
   Ⓒ concede
   Ⓓ cherish

2. Traditionally, the South Pacific Melanesians completed the **requisite** destruction of their art objects once their ceremonial purposes were achieved. Part of the artistic tradition included the need to destroy and then recreate art objects as ritualistic or social needs arose. As a result of this behavior, the Melanesian artistic tradition existed solely as an artistic concept in the mind of the artist who often worked without models of previous works.

   The word **requisite** in the passage is closest in meaning to

   Ⓐ required
   Ⓑ renowned
   Ⓒ reluctant
   Ⓓ reliable

3. Nuclear families of the preindustrial era were bound to a set of social obligations that made the nuclear family subordinate to the wishes of the larger family. This extended family system began to **unravel** with the advent of the Industrial Revolution. Aspirations for greater personal freedom and changing economic conditions produced a slow movement toward more independent nuclear families.

   The word **unravel** in the passage is closest in meaning to

   Ⓐ form
   Ⓑ condense
   Ⓒ assimilate
   Ⓓ separate

4. In 1941 President Franklin D. Roosevelt drafted The Four Freedoms. It was a list of basic human rights: freedom of speech and expression, freedom of worship, freedom from want, and freedom from fear. Later in the same year, these were incorporated into the Atlantic Charter, a British and American statement of goals for a peaceful world. Some leaders criticized The Four Freedoms for being too **vague** to serve as a guide for prudent statesmanship.

   The word **vague** in the passage is closest in meaning to

   Ⓐ contradictory
   Ⓑ prominent
   Ⓒ specific
   Ⓓ unclear

5. The earliest-known handcrafted carpet, about 2,500 years old, was discovered in ice in a tomb at Pazyryk, Siberia. Rugs were also made in Persia approximately 200 years later during the reign of Cyrus, whose tomb was covered with **precious** carpets. By the sixteenth century, rug making was a highly developed craft in Persia and Turkey.

   The word **precious** in the passage is closest in meaning to

   Ⓐ fine
   Ⓑ marvelous
   Ⓒ intricate
   Ⓓ astounding

6. A bar code is a tiny cluster of vertical lines and horizontal numbers against a white field found on many products today. This electronic code is not **prominently displayed**; rather, it is usually tucked away somewhere on the backside of the packaging. The digits in the code indicate the name and price of the product; more importantly, they help merchants maintain their stock by subtracting each purchase from the store's inventory.

   In saying that bar codes are not **prominently displayed**, the author means that they

   Ⓐ cover most of the packaging.
   Ⓑ can be scanned by a computer.
   Ⓒ are invisible to the naked eye.
   Ⓓ may be somewhat difficult to find.

7. Scientists believe that the volume of water in the oceans has not changed dramatically during the last few hundred million years. This conclusion is drawn from evidence indicating that the interiors of the continents have never been covered by the oceans. However, in recent decades, the oceans have noticeably increased in volume due to global warming, although some scientists **disregard** this evidence and maintain that global warming is not a real phenomenon.

   The word **disregard** in the passage is closest in meaning to

   Ⓐ ignore
   Ⓑ deny
   Ⓒ dispute
   Ⓓ conceal

8. The dynamic growth of communications networks after 1995, especially in the scholarly world, has accelerated the establishment of the "virtual library." At the core of this development is public-domain information. Residing in databases distributed worldwide, a growing portion of this **vast** resource is now accessible almost immediately through the Internet.

   The word **vast** in the passage is closest in meaning to

   Ⓐ dense
   Ⓑ huge
   Ⓒ extensive
   Ⓓ core

9. Discount stores sell products at prices lower than those found in conventional retail outlets. Some, such as department stores, offer wide **assortments** of goods. Other discount chains specialize, offering special types of merchandise such as jewelry, electronic equipment, or electrical appliances. Discount stores have become international phenomena. They have spread to Western Europe, Latin America, Australia, and Japan.

   The word **assortments** in the passage is closest in meaning to

   Ⓐ amusements
   Ⓑ patterns
   Ⓒ proportions
   Ⓓ selections

10. The major reasons for establishing a wildlife refuge are to **acquire** protection for a group of animals that have become significantly reduced in number and to suitably improve the habitat so that animals will breed and flourish. Often, restrictions or prohibitions are placed on development, hunting, trapping, trespassing, or fishing.

    The word **acquire** in the passage is closest in meaning to

    Ⓐ obtain
    Ⓑ endorse
    Ⓒ receive
    Ⓓ access

LESSON 30

- **charisma**
- **clever**
- **convince**
- **endure**
- **forfeit**
- **precarious**
- **severe**
- **sporadic**
- **stumble upon**
- **superior**
- **truncate**
- **wanton**
- **widespread**
- **wisdom**
- **witticism**
- **woo**

---

charisma — *n.* a special quality that endears other people to the person who has this quality

adj. charismatic

syn. appeal

She has *charisma* that no other candidate possesses.

John F. Kennedy was known for his *charismatic* personality.

clever — *adj.* intelligent; resourceful

adv. cleverly
n. cleverness

syn. astute

Everyone appreciated their *clever* idea.

His *cleverness* enabled him to rise quickly in the organization.

convince — *v.* to make someone see things your way

adv. convincingly
adj. convincing

syn. persuade

They could not *convince* the girls to go to the dance with them.

The video made a *convincing* argument for the recycling of paper and plastic materials.

endure — *v.* to last; suffer pain

adj. endurable
adj. enduring
n. endurance

syn. persevere

How he is able to *endure* living next to the airport is beyond my comprehension.

The *endurance* displayed by the athlete gave evidence of his rigorous training.

forfeit *v.* to give up; have something taken away, usually by rule or regulation

n. forfeit

syn. relinquish

You may have to *forfeit* your home country's citizenship to become a citizen of another country.

The *forfeit* occurred because not enough players showed up.

precarious *adj.* not safe, firm, or steady

adv. precariously

syn. hazardous

The diver put himself in a *precarious* situation among the sharks.

The cup was positioned *precariously* on the edge of the table.

severe *adj.* extreme; harmful

adv. severely
n. severity

syn. intense

The weather service issued a *severe* storm warning for most of Michigan.

The *severity* of his condition will not be known until the test results are studied.

sporadic *adj.* not consistent; irregular

adv. sporadically

syn. erratic

The radio communications were subject to *sporadic* sunspot interference.

Violent storms occur *sporadically* in the Southwest.

stumble upon *ph. v.* to discover or run into a person or thing accidentally

syn. come across

She *stumbled upon* a lot of interesting information about her research topic.

We might *stumble upon* deer while hiking in the woods.

superior *adj.* excellent quality; above all the rest

n. superiority

syn. exceptional

This is a *superior* fossil of a trilobite.

The restaurant's *superiority* was established shortly after it opened.

truncate *v.* to shorten; to end something suddenly

adj. truncated *syn.* cut

The television program was *truncated* because the soccer match went into extra time.

The publishers of the newspaper asked the writer to *truncate* her report.

wanton *adj.* done without thought or consideration; grossly negligent

adv. wantonly *syn.* senseless

Her *wanton* disregard of the rules was unexplainable.

The jealous man was *wantonly* impolite to the winner.

widespread *adj.* found everywhere

syn. extensive

There is a *widespread* rumor that there will be no class next Thursday.

The political influence of the developed countries of the world is *widespread.*

wisdom *n.* knowledge and understanding

adv. wisely *syn.* insight
adj. wise

It is often said that *wisdom* is the product of experience.

It was a *wise* decision for you to buy a car.

witticism *n.* a joke; a funny story

adv. wittily *syn.* humor
adj. witty
n. wit
n. wittiness

His *witticisms* captivated the audience.

Mark Twain was famous for his sharp *wit.*

woo *v.* to make efforts to attain or gain something

syn. attract

The directors tried to *woo* the support of the union.

The opponents of the proposed highway *wooed* nearby residents to defend their position.

MATCHING

Choose the synonym.

1. astute
   Ⓐ acknowledge
   Ⓑ extensive
   Ⓒ clever
   Ⓓ weak

2. sporadic
   Ⓐ prophetic
   Ⓑ intrinsic
   Ⓒ erratic
   Ⓓ archaic

3. relinquish
   Ⓐ recover
   Ⓑ disperse
   Ⓒ forfeit
   Ⓓ deplete

4. persevering
   Ⓐ enduring
   Ⓑ ineffective
   Ⓒ secure
   Ⓓ sincere

5. superior
   Ⓐ prosperous
   Ⓑ sustained
   Ⓒ superficial
   Ⓓ exceptional

6. truncate
   Ⓐ impress
   Ⓑ cut
   Ⓒ uphold
   Ⓓ postpone

7. precarious
   Ⓐ peculiar
   Ⓑ dangerous
   Ⓒ widespread
   Ⓓ aggravating

8. persuade
   Ⓐ convince
   Ⓑ conform
   Ⓒ confirm
   Ⓓ conceal

9. wisdom
   Ⓐ acceleration
   Ⓑ insight
   Ⓒ caution
   Ⓓ marvel

10. intense
    Ⓐ instant
    Ⓑ hazardous
    Ⓒ severe
    Ⓓ robust

LESSON 30—MULTIPLE-CHOICE TEST QUESTIONS

1. The circulation war of the tabloids that took place in New York City in the 1920s was copied in Britain in the 1930s. This brought numerous circulation-boosting schemes. Prizes for readers were introduced in the 1890s and had become popular measures to **woo** new subscribers by the 1900s. Although the practice was condemned by the Newspaper Proprietors' Association, gift schemes grew along with the number of newspapers for many years. They continue today.

   The word **woo** in the passage is closest in meaning to

   Ⓐ forfeit
   Ⓑ attract
   Ⓒ convince
   Ⓓ deceive

2. Intensity, intimacy, and omnipresence have been identified as the distinctive characteristics of the motion-picture image. Its intensity stems from its power to capture the complete attention of the theatergoer. Outside the theater, a person's attention is usually divided among the elements of the limitless reality around him or her, except for **sporadic** moments of concentration on what is selected for closer examination.

   The word **sporadic** in the passage is closest in meaning to

   Ⓐ occasional
   Ⓑ charismatic
   Ⓒ recurrent
   Ⓓ splendid

3. Established in 1942, the Voice of America is the international radio network of the U.S. Information Agency. Its charge is the **widespread** decree of a favorable understanding of the United States abroad. It achieves this task with a wide range of programs, including news, editorials, features, and music. The VOA has established a long-term modernization plan to increase its number of broadcasting languages from 42 to 60.

   The word **widespread** in the passage is closest in meaning to

   Ⓐ unlimited
   Ⓑ discernible
   Ⓒ extensive
   Ⓓ alluring

4. Jellyfish capture their prey by using nematocysts, small stinging organs found on their tentacles. They feed on organisms such as plankton, fish, and other jellyfish they may **stumble upon** while propelling themselves through the ocean. Their movement is produced through rhythmic contractions of the bell's perimeter surface, which discharges water. This causes water to move the animal forward by jet propulsion. Some varieties of jellyfish are able to swim well, but most are weak swimmers that drift with sea currents.

   The phrasal verb **stumble upon** in the passage is closest in meaning to

   Ⓐ encounter
   Ⓑ ingest
   Ⓒ engender
   Ⓓ attack

5. During his administration, Thomas Jefferson pursued a policy of expansion. He seized an opportunity when Napoleon Bonaparte decided to **forfeit** French ambitions in North America by offering the Louisiana Territory for sale. This remarkable acquisition, purchased for a few cents per acre, more than doubled the area of the United States. Jefferson had no constitutional right to complete the transaction. Nevertheless, he made up the rules as he went along, broadly interpreting the Constitution.

   The word **forfeit** in the passage is closest in meaning to

   Ⓐ accelerate
   Ⓑ restrain
   Ⓒ relinquish
   Ⓓ disrupt

6. In some countries, high-speed driving is **severely punished**, while in others speed is ignored, tolerated, or encouraged. For example, French police fine drivers as much as 380 euros on the spot for driving more than 110 kilometers per hour, while the famous German expressway known as the "Autobahn" has no speed limit, although sections of it may have recommended limits. The lack of a speed limit and lighter police surveillance turn many drivers into skillful competitors.

   In stating that high-speed driving is **severely punished**, the author means that

   Ⓐ offenders are sure to be arrested at once.
   Ⓑ exceeding the limit carries the death penalty.
   Ⓒ authorities impose a large fine.
   Ⓓ speeding is officially encouraged.

7. As a U.S. congressman, Davy Crockett won a reputation as a **witty**, shrewd, and outspoken backwoodsman. It was in Washington that the legend of this man as a coonskin-hatted bear hunter and tall-tale teller was created. There, his political allies promoted this image so he could compete with President Jackson's image as a democrat.

   The word **witty** in the passage is closest in meaning to

   Ⓐ robust
   Ⓑ scattered
   Ⓒ humorous
   Ⓓ instinctive

8. The volcanic areas of southern Guatemala contain some of the nation's most richest soils. However, the northern parts of this region are particularly subject to erosion encouraged by steep slopes and deforestation. Within the Sierra region, heavier rainfall combined with thinner soils on the steep slopes and the **wanton** destruction of forests have led to widespread erosion.

   The word **wanton** in the passage is closest in meaning to

   Ⓐ senseless
   Ⓑ sustained
   Ⓒ proportional
   Ⓓ outlandish

9. In all the Apache groups, the family structure was matrilocal. The women cared for the children, gathered plant food, and collected firewood and water. The men of the family hunted, fought, raided, and made weapons and shields. The most persuasive, tenacious, and successful family heads became Apache leaders. Those in authority were chosen because they had personal **charisma** and success in warfare.

   The word **charisma** in the passage is closest in meaning to

   Ⓐ obligations
   Ⓑ fallacies
   Ⓒ appeal
   Ⓓ capriciousness

10. Bishop Wright profoundly influenced the lives of his children. Wilbur and Orville, like their father, were independent thinkers. They had deep confidence in their own talents, and an unwavering faith in the soundness of their judgment. They were taught to **endure** difficulties and continue in the face of disappointment. Those qualities, when combined with their unique talents, help to explain the accomplishments of the Wright brothers as inventors.

    The word **endure** in the passage is closest in meaning to

    Ⓐ disguise
    Ⓑ endorse
    Ⓒ reject
    Ⓓ persevere

ANSWERS TO EXERCISES

MATCHING / **MULTIPLE-CHOICE TEST QUESTIONS**

LESSON 1

Matching		Multiple-Choice	
1. **A**	6. **C**	1. **D** autonomous—independent	6. **B** condemn or oppose their use
2. **A**	7. **D**	2. **C** persistent—constant	7. **C** to intervene—to get involved
3. **C**	8. **B**	3. **A** haphazardly—carelessly	8. **A** abrupt—sudden
4. **A**	9. **D**	4. **A** disrupt—disturb	9. **D** acceptable—permissible
5. **C**	10. **B**	5. **D** adverse—unfavorable	10. **B** acclaim—praise

LESSON 2

Matching		Multiple-Choice	
1. **C**	6. **B**	1. **C** celebrated—renowned	6. **D** view city life as advantageous
2. **A**	7. **A**	2. **A** energetic—vigorous	7. **D** advent—arrival
3. **D**	8. **C**	3. **C** distribution—dispensing	8. **A** agile—nimble
4. **B**	9. **C**	4. **A** contemporary—current	9. **C** encouraged—stimulated
5. **C**	10. **D**	5. **D** appealing—alluring	10. **A** collide with—are in opposition to

LESSON 3

Matching		Multiple-Choice	
1. **C**	6. **B**	1. **D** intolerable—unbearable	6. **D** looks the same as its environment
2. **B**	7. **A**	2. **B** enrich—enhance	7. **B** analysis—examination
3. **D**	8. **D**	3. **A** vital—indispensable	8. **C** annoying—bothersome
4. **A**	9. **C**	4. **A** ongoing—current	9. **A** ancient—old
5. **C**	10. **D**	5. **D** revitalize—restore	10. **D** anticipated—predicted

LESSON 4

Matching		Multiple-Choice	
1. **C**	6. **B**	1. **B** deceptive—misleading	6. **C** insist on reducing them
2. **B**	7. **A**	2. **C** petition—appeal	7. **D** asserted—declared
3. **A**	8. **D**	3. **B** concurred—agreed	8. **B** arbitrary—haphazard
4. **D**	9. **A**	4. **B** become stagnant—stop moving	9. **A** designated—authorized
5. **A**	10. **D**	5. **A** astounding—astonishing	10. **C** astute—perceptive

LESSON 5

Matching		Multiple-Choice	
1. **B**	6. **B**	1. **C** shed—discarded	6. **A** interests a lot of scientists
2. **D**	7. **D**	2. **A** brilliance—radiance	7. **A** cautioned—warned
3. **A**	8. **A**	3. **D** unique—rare	8. **D** work out—develop
4. **B**	9. **B**	4. **A** persuade—convince	9. **A** bears—produces
5. **C**	10. **C**	5. **A** in conjunction with—along with	10. **B** baffle—puzzle

LESSON 6

Matching		Multiple-Choice	
1. **C**	6. **B**	1. **A** immense—massive	6. **B** instantaneous—available without delay
2. **C**	7. **B**	2. **C** conventional—traditional	7. **D** complex—intricate
3. **A**	8. **A**	3. **A** routinely—ordinarily	8. **A** emitted—released
4. **C**	9. **D**	4. **B** curious—peculiar	9. **B** commonplace—standard
5. **A**	10. **A**	5. **B** rigid—stiff	10. **C** coarse—rough

MATCHING | **MULTIPLE-CHOICE TEST QUESTIONS**

LESSON 7

Matching		Multiple-Choice	
1. **B**	6. **A**	1. **B** reveals—discloses	6. **A** is entirely interested only in itself
2. **D**	7. **B**	2. **D** purposefully—deliberately	7. **D** eventually—gradually
3. **A**	8. **B**	3. **C** distort—deform	8. **D** convenient—practical
4. **C**	9. **C**	4. **C** diverse—different	9. **C** confirms—proves
5. **C**	10. **A**	5. **B** prosperous—thriving	10. **A** concealed—hid

LESSON 8

Matching		Multiple-Choice	
1. **C**	6. **B**	1. **B** flaws—defects	6. **D** kept ballooning from becoming more popular
2. **D**	7. **A**	2. **B** reflect—mirror	7. **A** cultivated—grown
3. **D**	8. **C**	3. **D** they reach a compromise	8. **C** crush—grind
4. **A**	9. **A**	4. **A** distinguish—discriminate	9. **D** derived—obtained
5. **B**	10. **D**	5. **D** fragments—particles	10. **B** engendered—produced

LESSON 9

Matching		Multiple-Choice	
1. **C**	6. **D**	1. **B** vibrant—brilliant	6. **C** population is the largest per square kilometer
2. **D**	7. **B**	2. **D** there was an abundance of progress	7. **A** display—exhibit
3. **A**	8. **A**	3. **C** gigantic—enormous	8. **D** dense—thick
4. **B**	9. **A**	4. **A** impressive—imposing	9. **C** accounts for—gives details for
5. **A**	10. **D**	5. **A** installation—establishment	10. **D** currency—money

LESSON 10

Matching		Multiple-Choice	
1. **C**	6. **C**	1. **D** rudimentary—basic	6. **C** the most talented are few in number
2. **B**	7. **A**	2. **D** superficial—shallow	7. **C** dramatic—emotional
3. **D**	8. **C**	3. **A** prime—chief	8. **B** drab—colorless
4. **D**	9. **C**	4. **B** hazardous—dangerous	9. **A** dominant—major
5. **A**	10. **D**	5. **C** phenomenal—exceptional	10. **C** distinct—definite

LESSON 11

Matching		Multiple-Choice	
1. **B**	6. **A**	1. **C** encircles—surrounds	6. **B** are more numerous than compacts
2. **A**	7. **A**	2. **C** eliminated—deleted	7. **B** erratic—inconsistent
3. **B**	8. **D**	3. **D** elementary—primary	8. **D** prevalent—commonplace
4. **B**	9. **C**	4. **B** element—component	9. **D** exaggerates—embellishes
5. **D**	10. **C**	5. **A** precipitated—hastened	10. **A** dispersed—scattered

LESSON 12

Matching		Multiple-Choice	
1. **C**	6. **A**	1. **D** evaporated—disappeared	6. **B** were alleged to exist
2. **C**	7. **D**	2. **D** eroded—deteriorated	7. **D** burgeoning—thriving
3. **D**	8. **B**	3. **C** entirely—completely	8. **C** broaden—enlarged
4. **A**	9. **A**	4. **B** benefit—assistance	9. **A** recovered—retrieved
5. **B**	10. **A**	5. **B** endorsed—supported	10. **D** enormous—tremendous

MATCHING		MULTIPLE-CHOICE TEST QUESTIONS	

LESSON 13

1. **B**	6. **B**	1. **A** suitable—appropriate	6. **B** in front of each other
2. **D**	7. **C**	2. **C** crucial—critical	7. **B** evident—apparent
3. **B**	8. **B**	3. **A** inaccessible—remote	8. **A** exhausted—depleted
4. **A**	9. **D**	4. **D** predicted—anticipated	9. **C** face—confront
5. **C**	10. **A**	5. **B** heroines—idols	10. **A** facets—aspects

LESSON 14

1. **C**	6. **A**	1. **B** ample—abundant	6. **A** basically well designed and built
2. **D**	7. **D**	2. **C** arid—dry	7. **D** functions—roles
3. **A**	8. **D**	3. **C** defying—resisting	8. **B** freshly—recently
4. **B**	9. **D**	4. **D** avert—prevent	9. **A** fertile—rich
5. **A**	10. **A**	5. **B** spacious—expansive	10. **C** feigning—pretending

LESSON 15

1. **B**	6. **C**	1. **B** halt—stop	6. **D** was nearly entirely eliminated
2. **D**	7. **B**	2. **A** substantially—significantly	7. **B** perilous—dangerous
3. **B**	8. **D**	3. **D** mysterious—baffling	8. **D** harmful—unhealthy
4. **D**	9. **A**	4. **A** rejects—refuses	9. **B** handle—manage
5. **A**	10. **C**	5. **C** boosts—promotes	10. **D** adept—talented

LESSON 16

1. **C**	6. **D**	1. **D** systematically—methodically	6. **B** more conscious of the situation
2. **C**	7. **B**	2. **A** recover—retrieve	7. **B** infancy—beginnings
3. **A**	8. **D**	3. **D** meticulous—conscientious	8. **D** inadvertent—unexpected
4. **B**	9. **B**	4. **D** encompass—include	9. **C** emphasizes—highlights
5. **B**	10. **B**	5. **B** unlikely—doubtful	10. **A** heighten—intensify

LESSON 17

1. **A**	6. **B**	1. **A** evoke—produce	6. **B** occurs slowly over time
2. **B**	7. **D**	2. **B** inundated—overwhelmed	7. **A** agitated—disturbed
3. **A**	8. **A**	3. **A** intrinsic—inherent	8. **D** nominal—moderate
4. **A**	9. **A**	4. **D** intentionally—deliberately	9. **C** confidential—secret
5. **D**	10. **B**	5. **C** appallingly—abysmally	10. **A** inordinate—excessive

LESSON 18

1. **B**	6. **B**	1. **C** culminated—resulted	6. **B** information for and against
2. **A**	7. **B**	2. **B** means—method	7. **B** feasible—possible
3. **A**	8. **A**	3. **A** absurd—ridiculous	8. **C** robust—strong
4. **A**	9. **B**	4. **A** limber—flexible	9. **D** swift—fast
5. **D**	10. **C**	5. **C** lack—shortage	10. **C** fallacy—misconception

MATCHING / **MULTIPLE-CHOICE TEST QUESTIONS**

LESSON 19

Matching:
1. **B** 2. **C** 3. **A** 4. **A** 5. **A** 6. **D** 7. **C** 8. **C** 9. **C** 10. **D**

Multiple-Choice:
1. **B** examine—look over
2. **A** novel—original
3. **B** notion—concept
4. **D** triggered—generated
5. **D** normally—typically
6. **D** are against its continuation
7. **A** unbiased—objective
8. **C** emulating—mimicking
9. **A** coherent—logical
10. **B** transformed—altered

LESSON 20

Matching:
1. **B** 2. **D** 3. **B** 4. **C** 5. **A** 6. **C** 7. **A** 8. **D** 9. **A** 10. **B**

Multiple-Choice:
1. **A** embedded—inserted
2. **A** partially—somewhat
3. **B** overcome—conquer
4. **B** outlandish—bizarre
5. **C** omit—neglect
6. **A** play in an offensive way
7. **D** disguise—concealment
8. **A** narrate—relate
9. **D** innovative—inventive
10. **C** accentuate—emphasize

LESSON 21

Matching:
1. **A** 2. **D** 3. **B** 4. **B** 5. **D** 6. **B** 7. **C** 8. **D** 9. **C** 10. **B**

Multiple-Choice:
1. **B** plentiful—abundant
2. **D** sheltered—protected
3. **C** philanthropic—humanitarian
4. **D** phenomena—occurrences
5. **A** decrease—decline
6. **A** combines chemically with the acid
7. **C** placid—calm
8. **A** reactions—responses
9. **D** scenic—picturesque
10. **D** vanish—disappear

LESSON 22

Matching:
1. **B** 2. **D** 3. **C** 4. **B** 5. **A** 6. **D** 7. **B** 8. **A** 9. **C** 10. **D**

Multiple-Choice:
1. **A** predominant—principal
2. **C** disregarded—overlooked
3. **A** practical—functional
4. **D** hasten—accelerate
5. **A** influx—inflow
6. **C** explain what causes them
7. **B** induces—prompts
8. **C** archaic—ancient
9. **A** hue—color
10. **D** alleviate—lessen

LESSON 23

Matching:
1. **D** 2. **C** 3. **C** 4. **B** 5. **B** 6. **D** 7. **A** 8. **A** 9. **C** 10. **C**

Multiple-Choice:
1. **B** reliably—dependably
2. **A** readily—freely
3. **C** proportions—dimensions
4. **C** prophetic—predictive
5. **D** prone—inclined
6. **B** is famous for the violin players
7. **D** analogous—similar
8. **D** periodically—regularly
9. **A** compelled—obliged
10. **D** intruded—imposed

LESSON 24

Matching:
1. **B** 2. **D** 3. **A** 4. **A** 5. **C** 6. **C** 7. **A** 8. **C** 9. **A** 10. **D**

Multiple-Choice:
1. **C** somewhat—slightly
2. **D** reciprocated—responded
3. **B** contaminated—polluted
4. **D** scattered—distributed
5. **C** remarkable—exceptional
6. **A** insufficient—inadequate
7. **C** discern—determine
8. **A** mediocre—average
9. **D** parallel—similar
10. **B** potent—powerful

MATCHING		MULTIPLE-CHOICE	TEST QUESTIONS

LESSON 25

Matching		Multiple-Choice	Test Questions
1. **A**	6. **A**	1. **D** situated—located	6. **B** on a moment's notice and without thinking
2. **A**	7. **B**	2. **B** profoundly—significantly	7. **C** impulsive—capricious
3. **D**	8. **C**	3. **A** sharply—severely	8. **A** isolated—secluded
4. **B**	9. **B**	4. **A** infrequently—rarely	9. **B** brief—fleeting
5. **C**	10. **D**	5. **D** founded—established	10. **C** exhibits—displays

LESSON 26

Matching		Multiple-Choice	Test Questions
1. **C**	6. **B**	1. **A** streams—flows	6. **B** abolished—eliminated
2. **B**	7. **B**	2. **D** striking—remarkable	7. **B** legitimate—authentic
3. **D**	8. **A**	3. **C** spontaneous—instinctive	8. **A** chaotic—disorganized
4. **A**	9. **C**	4. **D** particular—specific	9. **A** exemplifies—symbolize
5. **C**	10. **B**	5. **B** spanning—covering	10. **D** gratifying—satisfying

LESSON 27

Matching		Multiple-Choice	Test Questions
1. **C**	6. **C**	1. **C** automatic—involuntary	6. **C** the ship's name, *Titanic*, was appropriate
2. **D**	7. **A**	2. **D** synthesis—combination	7. **A** odd—strange
3. **D**	8. **D**	3. **B** deviated—differed	8. **B** marvel—wonder
4. **B**	9. **A**	4. **B** sustained—consistent	9. **C** demonstrations—displays
5. **B**	10. **C**	5. **A** supposedly—presumably	10. **D** ingredients—elements

LESSON 28

Matching		Multiple-Choice	Test Questions
1. **A**	6. **A**	1. **D** underestimates—miscalculates	6. **B** combat disease-causing bacteria
2. **C**	7. **C**	2. **A** undeniably—absolutely	7. **C** curative—healing
3. **C**	8. **D**	3. **C** trite—cliche	8. **A** debilitating—weakening
4. **B**	9. **B**	4. **A** tranquility—peacefulness	9. **C** aggravating—irritating
5. **D**	10. **C**	5. **C** toxic—poisonous	10. **C** conceivably—possibly

LESSON 29

Matching		Multiple-Choice	Test Questions
1. **C**	6. **A**	1. **C** acknowledge—concede	6. **D** may be somewhat difficult to find
2. **A**	7. **A**	2. **A** requisite—required	7. **A** disregard—ignore
3. **B**	8. **B**	3. **D** unravel—separate	8. **B** vast—huge
4. **B**	9. **C**	4. **D** vague—unclear	9. **D** assortments—selections
5. **A**	10. **C**	5. **A** precious—fine	10. **A** acquire—obtain

LESSON 30

Matching		Multiple-Choice	Test Questions
1. **C**	6. **B**	1. **B** woo—attract	6. **C** authorities impose a large fine
2. **C**	7. **B**	2. **A** sporadic—occasional	7. **C** witty—humorous
3. **C**	8. **A**	3. **C** widespread—extensive	8. **A** wanton—senseless
4. **A**	9. **B**	4. **A** come across—encounter	9. **C** charisma—appeal
5. **D**	10. **C**	5. **C** forfeit—relinquish	10. **D** endure—persevere

CHAPTER 6

THE iBT PRACTICE TEST

GENERAL DIRECTIONS

Essential Words for the TOEFL provides you with a 39-item TOEFL practice test for the reading section of the iBT. This section tests reading comprehension, including specific vocabulary items and whole phrases or words in combination. The ITP TOEFL contains 40–50 items in the Reading Comprehension section, while the iBT contains 36 to 70 items in this section. This test contains the kinds of passages that are likely to be found on the iBT. Each passage is followed by 13 questions. The iBT version contains the same kinds of items found on the paper-based version, plus some additional item formats. Thus, this test will be helpful to you regardless of which version of the TOEFL you plan to take.

After you have studied the vocabulary lessons in this book, take the test in a single sitting. Using a watch or a clock, time yourself when taking the test. Write down on a piece of paper your start time and the time at which you will stop. Allow yourself 60 minutes to take the test. Use the full 60 minutes. If you finish early, go back and check your work, following the helpful strategies and hints for test takers covered in Chapter 1 and Chapter 2 of this book.

When taking the test, follow the directions for each question. For multiple-choice questions, circle the correct answer in your book. For other types of questions, do as indicated. Although this test is not administered on a computer, every effort has been made to make it like the iBT version of the TOEFL.

After you take the test, score it using the answer key provided on page 338 of this book. For each vocabulary item you answer incorrectly, look up the word tested in this book. Try to understand why you made the mistake so you won't make it again. If necessary, look up the tested word or the options in your English dictionary. This will provide you with additional information on the meaning of the word in different contexts, and perhaps another example sentence demonstrating its usage.

For information on interpreting your performance and converting it to the TOEFL scale, follow the directions in Scoring Your iBT Practice Reading Test at the end of this chapter.

Now, review Chapters 1 and 2; then, write down your starting time, and take the TOEFL Practice Test, Reading Comprehension section.

iBT READING SECTION

In this section of the iBT you will read three passages. Each passage is followed by 13 questions. You should answer all questions on the basis of what is stated or implied in the passage. You will be asked to perform a variety of tasks in this section. Read and follow the directions for each test question carefully before you answer. After you have completed this test, you may refer to the Score Conversion Table to determine your approximate iBT or ITP score for the Reading Comprehension section of the TOEFL.

Questions 1–13

Transportation

1 A key component of any vigorous economic system is its transportation system. The growth of the ability and need to transport large quantities of goods or numbers of people over long distances at high speeds in comfort and safety has been an index of civilization and, in particular, of technological progress. Communication and commerce are facilitated by the smooth and rapid movement of goods and people from one place to another. Such movement requires a well-developed infrastructure. The term "infrastructure" is used to describe all the facilities that an economic system has in place, inclusive of its network of roadways, railroads, and ports, as well as the vehicles and vessels to use them. These facilities must be in place before trade can be handled on a regular basis. Transportation systems are necessary in order for goods to reach markets where they can be sold or exchanged for other merchandise or services, and for consumers to reach those goods.

2 There are many established benefits associated with a well-developed infrastructure. Infrastructure allows each geographic area to produce its goods and then to trade its products with other regions. [A ■] In addition to direct, or back-and-forth trading, it is also possible to use transportation to link a number of different steps in the production process, each occurring at a different geographic site. For example, car parts may be manufactured at various sites, and then shipped to and assembled in

one specific, strategically located site, which is designed to facilitate assembly and distribution of the cars.

Distances are erased by speedy means of transportation. [B ■] For example, air transport allows perishable foods to be distributed to larger market areas. In addition to well-developed systems of roads that allow workers to reach their job sites quickly and efficiently, thus enhancing the opportunities for improvements to worker productivity, a well-developed infrastructure also makes it possible for a producer to reach a larger number of markets over great distances. This means that the quantity of production can be large enough to promote production economies of scale as companies can increase their customer base over a wide geographical area.

The consumer also benefits from the efficient use of a well-developed infrastructure. Transportation networks make markets more competitive. [C ■] A transportation system improves the way goods and services are used because it widens the number of opportunities for suppliers and buyers to trade goods and services. This phenomenon increases availability and promotes pricing competition to the benefit of the consumer.

Transportation projects have proved to be a fertile ground for investors, inventors, innovators, and entrepreneurs. [D ■] Much of the vigorous growth in the economies of the United States and other countries in the twentieth century can be directly attributed to the development of transportation. Take, for example the development of the U.S. rail and road systems.

During the mid-nineteenth century, railways expanded westward, bringing with them development. The presence of the railroad spurred the growth of towns, which were clustered around railroad lines. These towns quickly became cities. Then, as these cities grew, streetcar and bus lines within the cities attracted development. These lines were deemed so valuable that companies were sometimes bribed by land developers to have new lines serve their undeveloped land, thus increasing its value.

Eventually the development of infrastructure made it possible for city dwellers to flee the central city, giving birth to massive residential subdivisions located in areas just outside city limits.

With the advent of automobile and truck transportation, the need arose for a means of swift and safe passage from one city to another. In the 1930s and '40s, a national system of roads emerged, constructed by the federal government. However, this national system of roads was ill equipped to handle increasing volumes of auto traffic and commerce. Consequently, the mammoth U.S. Interstate Highway system was developed in response to strong public pressures in the 1950s for a better road system. The Clay Committee, established by President Dwight

Eisenhower, studied the feasibility of constructing a new federal highway system. It recommended that an interstate highway system be constructed with federal funding. Taking more than 25 years to construct, the interstate highway system reached a total length of more than 45,000 miles, connecting nearly all of the major cities in the United States and carrying more than 20 percent of the nation's traffic on slightly more than 1 percent of the total road and street system.

1. Why does the author give the example of the car manufacturing process in paragraph 2?
   Ⓐ To explain the importance of a good geographical location for a business
   Ⓑ To demonstrate how regional manufacturing strengths can contribute to the manufacturing process
   Ⓒ To point out the benefits of a strategic location for a business
   Ⓓ To define the relationship between the assembly process and distribution of the final product

2. Look at the four squares [■] that show where the following sentence could be inserted into the passage:

   Thanks to well-developed infrastructures, products such as fresh fruits and vegetables from around the world can be found on the shelves of many modern grocery stores.

   Where could the sentence best be added? (A), (B), (C), or (D)

   Click on a [■] to insert the sentence into the passage.

3. The word **spurred** in paragraph 6 is closest in meaning to
   Ⓐ stimulated
   Ⓑ controlled
   Ⓒ hindered
   Ⓓ spread

4. The phrase **This phenomenon** in paragraph 4 refers to
   Ⓐ the use of transportation systems.
   Ⓑ the improvement in the way merchandise and services are delivered.
   Ⓒ the increase in the number of opportunities for trade.
   Ⓓ the pricing competition that results from efficient models of trade.

5. According to the passage, all of the following are mentioned as benefits of a good system of transportation EXCEPT:
   Ⓐ Merchandise arrives faster to the marketplace.
   Ⓑ Increased price competition benefits consumers.
   Ⓒ A greater selection of goods is available to the consumer.
   Ⓓ Good infrastructure may provide employment opportunities.

6. According to the author, what caused the expansion of the United States toward the West?
   Ⓐ The availability of goods and services from the local populations who lived there
   Ⓑ The high value of land around cities
   Ⓒ The expansion of the railroad system
   Ⓓ Movement away from large cities into suburbs

7. The term **on a regular basis** in paragraph 1 is closest in meaning to
   Ⓐ daily
   Ⓑ effectively
   Ⓒ well
   Ⓓ productively

8. Which of the following sentences best expresses the essential information in the sentence below? Incorrect answer choices omit important information or change the meaning of the original sentence in an important way.

   In addition to well-developed systems of roads that allow workers to reach their job sites quickly and efficiently, thus enhancing the opportunities for improvements to worker productivity, a well-developed infrastructure also makes it possible to reach a larger number of markets over great distances.

   Ⓐ A highly developed system of roads not only allows employees to reach their job sites more quickly, but also limits the number of markets a specific industry can serve.

   Ⓑ Along with the possibility of facilitating access to jobsites and enhancing worker productivity, a highly developed infrastructure gives businesses greater access to develop distant markets for their products.

   Ⓒ Worker productivity can be improved when employees have access to good roads and public transportation, which can give businesses improved access to a larger pool of potential employees.

   Ⓓ Improvements to worker productivity depend upon a single system of transportation that gives industry complete access not only to local, but also to distant markets.

9. According to the author, why was a system of interstate highways a necessity?

   Ⓐ Streetcar and bus lines were inadequate.

   Ⓑ Federal funding was available at the time.

   Ⓒ There was an increase in car ownership and interstate commerce.

   Ⓓ The Clay Committee recommended its construction.

10. The word **fertile** in paragraph 5 is closest in meaning to
   Ⓐ risky
   Ⓑ expansive
   Ⓒ exciting
   Ⓓ productive

11. According to the definition of infrastructure in the passage, all of the following are examples of infrastructure EXCEPT:
   Ⓐ restaurants
   Ⓑ bridges
   Ⓒ bicycles
   Ⓓ jets

12. Why does the author mention economies of scale in paragraph 3?
   Ⓐ To explain the importance of business competition
   Ⓑ To demonstrate how small businesses can grow into large companies
   Ⓒ To point out how consumers can benefit from price competition
   Ⓓ To highlight the need for infrastructure improvements and maintenance

13. **Directions:** An introduction for a short summary of the passage appears below. Complete the summary by selecting THREE answer choices that mention the most important points in the passage. Some sentences do not belong in the summary because they express ideas that are not included in the passage or are minor points from the passage.

The growth of a vigorous economic system depends upon the extent to which its transportation system is developed.

•

•

•

Ⓐ The infrastructure must be well organized to support production and access to new markets.

Ⓑ Rail transportation allows goods to be transported over long distances.

Ⓒ Well-developed infrastructure promotes business opportunities for investors, entrepreneurs, and innovators.

Ⓓ Good roads allowed city dwellers to escape from the hectic lifestyle of the city.

Ⓔ Road projects, such as the U.S. interstate highway system, have facilitated quick and efficient transportation across long distances, thus enhancing economic activity.

Ⓕ The consumer benefits from efficient transportation systems because the cost of goods and services is reduced.

Questions 14–26

Nursing

The advancement of the noble profession of nursing has its origins in two sources, one scientific, the other social. From the period of the Renaissance to the eighteenth century, there was little advancement in the field of medical science. However, there was an explosion of discovery during the nineteenth century. At that time, germs were discovered as the leading cause of death. Hence the "germ theory" of disease was developed and methods of preventing and treating infectious diseases were discovered. In addition, anesthesia was discovered. Since the time of these advancements, the sheer volume of medical knowledge has challenged healthcare professionals to keep abreast of the latest developments in the field of medicine. In fact, medical research has produced more medical and health knowledge since the 1950s than in all previous centuries combined. This expanding mass of new information to be applied by health services workers has challenged the educational systems for physicians, nurses, and other healthcare professionals, and applied pressure on the delivery system of services to a public that is better informed about healthcare issues.

This medical renaissance created an immediate need for caregivers who could better meet the everyday needs of the sick and wounded. This need gave birth to modern nursing. Before this explosion of information, nursing was viewed as a profession with low status. This perception was a product of the nature of the duties related to the general hygiene and psychological needs of patients that nurses performed. In general, only less educated women elected to pursue nursing.

However, during the nineteenth century, there was a movement toward the elevation of the status of nursing led by Florence Nightingale. Nightingale was a formidable figure who had a strong background in science, mathematics, and political economics. She researched nursing practices of several countries, formulated ideas about the emergent role of nursing, and wrote extensively on the changes that nursing had to undergo to meet the healthcare challenges of her time.

Her work attracted the attention of British government officials. In 1854, Nightingale was asked to go to countries where the absence of sewers, laundering facilities, nutritional information, organized medical services, and nursing led to death rates of more than 50 percent among the sick and wounded.

The services that she, and the nurses whom she recruited, performed, brought about sufficient improvement to lower the death rates to less than three percent in some of the countries where she set up nursing programs. As a result of her work, Florence Nightingale received several monetary gifts which she used to establish schools of nursing at St. Thomas's Hospital in London.

6 Florence Nightingale believed nursing to be a suitable and worthy career for capable, trained women, and that nursing services had to be administered by professionals with special preparation. She insisted that there was a substantial body of knowledge and range of skills to be learned in nursing and that skilled and knowledgeable professionals had to be prepared for hospital nursing and care of the sick at home, if they were to teach good health practices to patients and families. [A ■] She strongly believed that a team relationship had to be present between physicians and nurses in order for patient needs to be met. She maintained that schools of nursing should be established by nurses and physicians as part of the hospital workforce.

7 Largely because of Nightingale's efforts, by the end of the nineteenth century, the status of the nursing profession had been elevated. [B ■] And the idea that a nurse needed to be educated and trained had spread to most of the Western world. [C ■]

8 Modern nursing education has had to change dramatically to prepare nurses for their expanded roles. [D ■] Traditional hospital-based nursing schools do not provide community nursing experience, nor can they offer the liberal arts curriculum of the university. Moreover, traditional nursing schools have tended to isolate students from the mainstream of higher education. To correct this situation, nursing education is now increasingly found in academic rather than in clinical settings dedicated solely to training nurses. Indeed, in some countries, the training of nurses has moved exclusively into universities.

14. According to the passage, all of the following are true of Nightingale's views on nursing EXCEPT:
    - Ⓐ The roles of nurses had to be expanded.
    - Ⓑ The profession had to attract educated professionals.
    - Ⓒ Nursing had to be taught at universities.
    - Ⓓ Nursing could greatly improve survival rates.

15. The word **emergent** in paragraph 3 is closest in meaning to
    - Ⓐ developing
    - Ⓑ increasing
    - Ⓒ important
    - Ⓓ varied

16. Why does the author mention the "germ theory?"
    Ⓐ To explain how the theory helped to discover anesthesia
    Ⓑ To illustrate an important step in the treatment and identification of diseases
    Ⓒ To identify the origin of germs and ways to eradicate them
    Ⓓ To explain how diagnoses became more reliable

17. Based on the information in the passage, which of the following can be inferred about nursing training before the nineteenth century?
    Ⓐ Nurses were poorly trained, receiving little or no professional preparation.
    Ⓑ Nurses were provided with only a basic liberal arts education.
    Ⓒ Nurses were mainly trained in community health settings.
    Ⓓ Nurses were trained in schools whose educational programs had a narrow focus.

18. The word **sheer** in paragraph 1 is closest in meaning to
    Ⓐ total
    Ⓑ previous
    Ⓒ unique
    Ⓓ surprising

19. Look at the four squares [■] that show where the following sentence could be inserted into the passage:

    In fact, as a result of the advances in nursing, nurses have followed doctors into specialties, including pediatrics, surgery, orthopedics, ophthalmology, psychiatry, and public health.

    Where could the sentence best be added? (A), (B), (C), or (D)

    Click on a [■] to insert the sentence into the passage.

20. Which of the following sentences best expresses the essential information in the sentence below? Incorrect answer choices omit important information or change the meaning of the original sentence in an important way.

    The expanding mass of new medical and health knowledge to be applied by health services workers has compelled educational systems for physicians, nurses, and other healthcare providers to stay up-to-date, and has applied pressure on the delivery system of services to a public that is well informed about healthcare issues.

    Ⓐ Along with the growth of healthcare knowledge, many doctors, nurses, and healthcare educational institutions find it challenging to keep up with the latest advances in medicine.

    Ⓑ As the general public ages and becomes more informed about healthcare issues, medical professionals have felt considerable pressure to expand the capacity of healthcare clinics and hospitals and to provide for better education of healthcare workers.

    Ⓒ The demands placed on healthcare workers and educational institutions by the mass of new healthcare information, has led, in addition to patients who are better informed, to increased pressure on schools, clinics, and hospitals to deliver quality healthcare.

    Ⓓ The extreme volume of medical information available to the public has challenged medical institutions to maintain a high standard of quality healthcare delivered by well-trained medical professionals.

21. Based on the information in the passage, which of the following can be inferred about the results of Nightingale's work in other countries?

    Ⓐ Nursing programs in needy countries were immediately established.

    Ⓑ The need for professional nursing training was acknowledged.

    Ⓒ Other countries set up programs to fight major diseases.

    Ⓓ Clean water was identified as a key element to healthy living.

22. Based on the information in paragraph 1, which of the following best explains the term **to keep abreast of**?
    Ⓐ To understand
    Ⓑ To implement
    Ⓒ To stay up-to-date
    Ⓓ To explain

23. All of the following statements apply to the field of medicine in the eighteenth century EXCEPT:
    Ⓐ Doctors often had insufficient information to make good diagnoses.
    Ⓑ It was difficult to identify the causes of illnesses.
    Ⓒ Medical treatments were not reliable.
    Ⓓ Germs were discovered as the leading cause of death.

24. According to paragraph 8, which of the following is true about modern nursing training?
    Ⓐ Traditional nursing schools remain as the only training ground for nurses.
    Ⓑ Traditional nursing schools are being replaced by colleges and universities in many countries.
    Ⓒ Nursing plans of study are exclusively focused on certain areas of specialization.
    Ⓓ Clinical settings are the most important settings for nursing education programs.

25. The phrase **This perception** in paragraph 2 refers to
    Ⓐ the view that the explosion of health information would benefit patients.
    Ⓑ the notion that nursing was not an important profession.
    Ⓒ the idea that nurses were not well educated.
    Ⓓ the impression that only women would choose to become nurses.

26. **Directions:** An introduction for a short summary of the passage appears below. Complete the summary by selecting THREE answer choices that mention the most important points in the passage. Some sentences do not belong in the summary because they express ideas that are not included in the passage or are minor points from the passage.

Over the years, nursing's status as a profession has been elevated in the western world from one of a menial, female dominated profession, requiring little education, to a highly respected job, requiring specific skills and knowledge.

•

•

•

Ⓐ Despite the emerging importance of the nursing profession, modern programs designed to professionally prepare nurses for the workplace are largely relegated to small, private, hospital-based nursing schools.

Ⓑ Long promoted by Florence Nightingale, the idea that nursing not only involved considerable knowledge of a large body of information, but also specific skills in order to deliver healthcare to patients, finally gained acceptance in the western world.

Ⓒ The "germ theory" generated an explosion of the medical knowledge base which, in turn, created the need for an increase in the number of doctors and skilled healthcare providers.

Ⓓ Due to the efforts of professionals such as Florence Nightingale, the idea that nursing is a demanding profession, requiring specific knowledge and training, has spread across the entire globe.

Ⓔ Nightingale insisted that a patient's needs could only be met if a team relationship was nurtured between nurses and doctors.

Ⓕ Nursing education programs have now expanded from small, hospital-based nursing schools to universities and colleges, giving further recognition to the idea that nursing is a key component of the healthcare system.

Questions 27–39

Skyscrapers

The skyscraper was born in the late nineteenth century, but it wasn't born in that astounding city best known for iconic skyscrapers, New York City, home of the Empire State Building. Rather, it was much farther west, along the western edge of Lake Michigan, that modern urban architecture's most striking innovation first took shape.

Prior to the 1870s, U.S. architects looked to Europe for their models and inspiration. For decades, their styles derived from European history. [A ■] Townhouses, churches, and banks that resembled European temples, cathedrals, and castles were the norm. [B ■] Meanwhile, advances in engineering, and particularly in the use of tough, flexible steel structures called skeletal frames, were opening a radical alternative—namely, the possibility of putting the skeleton up first and *hanging* a building's exterior sheath on the frame like a coat draped on a hanger. [C ■] Once that design breakthrough had been achieved, it was possible to imagine structures that could grow taller because their weight was suspended and distributed across a framework. It made an entirely different cityscape imaginable. [D ■]

Chicago was incorporated as a city in 1837, but it was the railroad that eventually joined the East and West Coasts and put the city on the map economically. The railroad made it possible to transport beef cattle from the remote plains lying to the west via the stockyards in Chicago to the slaughterhouses and kitchens in heavily populated Eastern cities. Despite a fire that gutted the city's downtown in 1871, it soon became a boomtown again, home to big business and international banking, and commercial buildings constructed on a revolutionary principle.

Economic conditions and social attitudes in Chicago favored the birth of a new, assertive architecture. At the city's commercial core, land was at a premium: property values had soared after the downtown was rebuilt and unrelenting westward expansion continued to fuel the city's robust economy. Thus, any plan to build taller, more narrow buildings was bound to attract capital investment. Many refugees fleeing hard times, unrest, and economic uncertainty in Europe and elsewhere had flocked to Chicago to find work, and bigger buildings meant more work and a demand for more workers. Taller buildings also appealed to Chicago's energetic business community. The city had grown up quickly, it had recovered from a fire, it had proven itself to be a tough survivor, and now the time had come to declare its preeminence. It was time for Chicago to claim the heights.

Skeletal framing was first used in the Western Union Telegraph Building in 1873, but it really took off as a structural principle once Louis Sullivan arrived in Chicago in 1875. Louis Henri Sullivan was a Bostonian who had studied architecture at the Massachusetts Institute of Technology (MIT) and in Paris. In the next 40 years, he would design dozens of buildings, primarily in the Midwest—the Auditorium Building (1889), the Wainwright Building (1891), the Carson Pirie Scott Department Store (1904), the National Farmers' Bank (1908). Though many were only a few stories high, Sullivan's design approach clearly showed that taller buildings were now possible. By distributing a building's weight across its steel underpinning, he was able to build a more solid structure that could support greater heights. Later, his famous axiom—"form follows function"—would be adopted by many architects. It means that architects should start with the function of a building in mind, not its decorative potential, and represent that function honestly in the building's design. Instead of smothering buildings in a lot of historical detail, architects after Sullivan would proudly design buildings that revealed how they were constructed and what was going on inside. By the time he died in 1924, he had replaced a nineteenth-century preference for disguised and horizontal buildings with the belief that building height is mainly limited by a lack of imagination. The Sears Tower, erected 100 years after the Western Union Telegraph Building, and for a time the world's tallest building, was part of his legacy.

6 Today, skyscrapers are found all over the world. By the end of the twentieth century, the tallest one was no longer in Chicago, or even the United States. The tallest in the world, at 452 meters, was the Petronas Tower in Malaysia. But the skyscraper had started more modestly a long time before that in a tough, enterprising city on a lake. It sprang from the insight that buildings didn't have to rise slowly, stone by stone, from the bottom up. Instead, they could be hung on powerful steel frames and thereby soar to unimagined heights.

27. What is the main topic of the passage?
    - Ⓐ Chicago was a powerful U.S. business hub in the late 1800s.
    - Ⓑ Skyscrapers are indicators of economic growth and technological innovation.
    - Ⓒ The skyscraper was an outgrowth of European architectural styles.
    - Ⓓ Louis Sullivan was an important architect in the nineteenth century.

28. Which factor led to the construction of taller buildings?
    Ⓐ The revival of traditional construction techniques
    Ⓑ An emphasis on the function of the building to be constructed
    Ⓒ A need for more space in crowded cities
    Ⓓ The development of skeletal framing construction methods

29. The word **striking** in paragraph 1 is closest in meaning to
    Ⓐ interesting
    Ⓑ prominent
    Ⓒ peculiar
    Ⓓ appealing

30. The word **preeminence** in paragraph 4 is closest in meaning to
    Ⓐ honor
    Ⓑ legitimacy
    Ⓒ position
    Ⓓ supremacy

31. All of the following are mentioned in the reading as factors in the emergence of the skyscraper as a building type in the nineteenth century EXCEPT:
    Ⓐ The railroad gave Chicago a big economic boost.
    Ⓑ Skeletal framing was used in building cathedrals.
    Ⓒ Sullivan took advantage of structural innovations.
    Ⓓ Funds were available for real estate investment.

32. Why does the author state that Chicago proved to be a tough survivor?
    Ⓐ Chicago received many refugees looking for better opportunities.
    Ⓑ Chicago thrived due to favorable circumstances.
    Ⓒ Chicago endured difficult situations.
    Ⓓ Chicago lost jobs as the railroad reached completion.

33. The word **core** in paragraph 4 is closest in meaning to
    Ⓐ architecture
    Ⓑ business
    Ⓒ economy
    Ⓓ center

34. The word **expansion** in paragraph 4 is closest in meaning to
   Ⓐ isolation
   Ⓑ distribution
   Ⓒ movement
   Ⓓ growth

35. In stating that **form follows function** in paragraph 5, the author means that the design of a building should
   Ⓐ hide or disguise its true purpose.
   Ⓑ stress purpose over appearance.
   Ⓒ stress appearance over purpose.
   Ⓓ reveal the architect's personality.

36. With which of the following statements would the author of the reading passage most probably agree?
   Ⓐ Innovation always stems from a single cause.
   Ⓑ Engineering can sometimes inspire architects.
   Ⓒ Chance is the primary motivation for change.
   Ⓓ Architects always follow popular preferences.

37. Look at the four squares [■] that show where the following sentence could be inserted into the passage:

   These structures were typically made of stone and built from the ground up, like the pyramids, block by block.

   Where could the sentence best be added? (A), (B), (C), or (D)

   Click on a [■] to insert the sentence into the passage.

38. What can be inferred from the passage about Chicago's economic success?
   Ⓐ Chicago would not have developed much without the presence of the railroad.
   Ⓑ Chicago was destined to become the home of the first skyscraper.
   Ⓒ Chicago's economic power was a result of innovative architecture.
   Ⓓ Chicago's modern architecture closely resembles that of old European styles.

39. **Directions:** An introduction for a short summary of the passage appears below. Complete the summary by selecting THREE answer choices that mention the most important points in the passage. Some sentences do not belong in the summary because they express ideas that are not included in the passage or are minor points from the passage.

The development of the distinct architectural styles of skyscrapers was influenced by traditional preferences, and advances in technology and engineering.

•

•

•

Ⓐ Innovations in engineering permitted buildings to be constructed upon steel frames, which allowed for an even distribution of weight, which consequently made construction of taller buildings possible.

Ⓑ Skeletal framing was first used in Chicago, where the Western Union Telegraph Building was constructed in 1873 and the Farmer's National Bank in 1908.

Ⓒ Modern social and economic attitudes have encouraged the designers of modern day skyscrapers to build even higher edifices.

Ⓓ A pivotal change of thought about building construction was introduced by Louis Sullivan, whose "form follows function" approach was adopted by many architects who desired to construct functional buildings.

Ⓔ In the early stages, architects were limited by antiquated construction methods and traditional building styles found in Europe.

Ⓕ In the modern age, most architects first considered the decorative design of their buildings, rather than their function.

ANSWERS TO iBT PRACTICE TEST

1. **B**	10. **D**	19. **D**	28. **D**	37. **B**
2. **B**	11. **A**	20. **C**	29. **B**	38. **A**
3. **A**	12. **B**	21. **B**	30. **D**	39. **A D E**
4. **C**	13. **A C E**	22. **C**	31. **B**	
5. **D**	14. **B**	23. **D**	32. **C**	
6. **C**	15. **A**	24. **B**	33. **D**	
7. **A**	16. **B**	25. **B**	34. **D**	
8. **B**	17. **A**	26. **B C F**	35. **B**	
9. **C**	18. **A**	27. **C**	36. **B**	

SCORING YOUR iBT PRACTICE TEST

Essential Words for the TOEFL contains a practice test. This test is provided so you may determine what effect the study of this book has had on your knowledge of TOEFL vocabulary and on your ability to answer vocabulary questions in the TOEFL format. The test will also provide you with a fairly accurate estimate of how you would do on Section 3 of the TOEFL.

To score your iBT Practice Reading Test, please follow the procedures described below.

1. Go to the key (list of correct answers) for the test. It is located at the top of this page.
2. Score the test using the key. Place a C next to each correct answer in the book.
3. Count the number of correct answers and write that number in the space called Number Correct below.

Number Correct	iBT Scale Score	ITP TOEFL Scale Score
____________	____________	____________

4. Now, go to the Score Conversion Tables on page 340. Find your Number Correct Score in the left column. Using a ruler or straightedge, draw a line under your score and across to the center column to find the iBT Scale Score that corresponds to your Number Correct Score. Write that number in the space above.

5. Now, in the right column, find the ITP TOEFL Scale Score that corresponds to your Number Correct Score. Write that number in the space above where it says ITP TOEFL Scale Score.

Now let's practice these procedures in order to verify that you are following them correctly. Suppose on the Practice iBT you answered 25 questions correctly. According to the chart on page 340, your iBT Scale Score would be 20. Your reading score is approximately 25 percent of your iBT score.

When you take the TOEFL at an official administration, if your score on the Reading section is different from your Scale Score on the iBT or the ITP TOEFL Reading Practice Test, the difference is probably due to the fact that on any given day and on any given set of items your performance will vary slightly. However, your Scale Score will probably not vary by more than three points from the score you got here. So, you can feel some degree of confidence that the score you obtained here is similar to the score you would obtain on the real TOEFL Reading test, if you took it today, after using this book.

iBT AND ITP READING SECTION SCORE CONVERSION TABLES

Number Correct Score	iBT Scale Score	ITP TOEFL Scale Score
39	30	
38	29	
37	29	
36	28	67
35	27	66
34	27	66
33	26	65
32	25	64
31	24	63
30	23	63
29	23	61
28	22	59
27	22	58
26	21	57
25	20	57
24	20	56
23	19	56
22	19	54
21	18	53
20	18	52
19	17	51
18	16	50
17	16	49
16	15	48
15	15	47
14	14	46
13	13	44
12	12	43
11	11	41
10	10	40
09	09	38
08	08	36
07	07	34
06	06	32
05	05	31
04	04	31
03	03	31
02	02	31
01	01	31
00	00	31

INDEX

This index is a list of all the key TOEFL words introduced and taught in this book. You may use the list to determine which words you have not mastered. Identify the location of each word whose meaning you do not know. Then learn the key word, the words related to it, and the synonym associated with it.